J.K. LASSER PRO™

PREPARING FOR THE RETIREMENT BOOM

The *J.K. Lasser Pro* Series

J.K. Lasser Pro Wealth Building: Investment Strategies for Retirement and Estate Planning
David R. Reiser and Robert L. DiColo with Hugh M. Ryan and Andrea R. Reiser
J.K. Lasser Pro Fee-Only Financial Planning: How To Make it Work for You
John E. Sestina
J.K. Lasser Pro Preparing for the Retirement Boom
Thomas Grady

The *Wiley Financial Advisor* Series

Tax-Deferred Investing: Wealth Building and Wealth Transfer Strategies
Cory Grant and Andrew Westhem
Getting Clients, Keeping Clients
Dan Richards
Managing Family Trusts: Taking Control of Inherited Wealth
Robert A. Rikoon, with Larry Waschka
Advising the 60+ Investor: Tax and Financial Planning Strategies
Darlene Smith, Dale Pulliam, and Holland Tolles
Tax-Smart Investing: Maximizing Your Client's Profits
Andrew D. Westhem and Stewart J. Weissman

J.K. LASSER PRO™

PREPARING FOR THE RETIREMENT BOOM

Thomas Grady

John Wiley & Sons, Inc.
New York • Chichester • Weinheim • Brisbane • Singapore • Toronto

*To my wife Charlotte for her
patience and devotion.
She waited a long time for this.*

Contents

J.K. LASSER PRO™

PREPARING FOR THE RETIREMENT BOOM

Introduction

Remember this tidy proverb: Here today, gone tomorrow?

Today	Tomorrow
We are the experts.	Everyone is an expert.
Everyone needs us.	We're lucky to get the time of day.
We're the only show in town.	Competition is a mouse-click away.
We take care of everyone.	Everyone is self-reliant.
Our clients love us.	What clients?

The financial advisory profession is most assuredly moving from Today to Tomorrow. Though the trip is in its early stages, it's well under way and irreversible. It's not plodding along, either. It's humming like a team of 700-megahertz Pentium processors, adding additional megahertz as it builds momentum.

Our practices are being assaulted on a variety of fronts: consumer markets, technology, the Internet, changing compensation methods, disintegrating self-perceptions, and more.

We face a monstrous but spectacular market group that has bulldozed through the past 55 years and is now amassing on the retirement starting line in front of us: Baby Boomers. It seems everything we read and hear is about Baby Boomers. That's because they're an estimated 78 million strong.

Boomers have detoured the economy down an innovative road, one that has led to enduring methods of doing business and generating profits—the road of quality service. Boomers were bred to expect to be served. Superior service is their Holy Grail. While busying themselves accumulating assets during their careers, they tolerated the exercise of product peddling and the marginal service from the financial services profession. Now that they are on the brink of perpetual tee times, they will be far less tolerant of inferior service.

Unfortunately for us as financial advisors, our practices and procedures—especially those concerning compensation—in their present traditional form cannot accommodate the Boomers' pursuit of their Holy Grail. Our true intentions shine bright when we refer to prospective clients as "buying units." Compensation for selling a product occurs once and up front, and then, quickly, we move on to the next signature or ticket, for we must win this year's free trip. On the other hand, compensation for providing the Holy Grail is a continual, demanding, incessantly painstaking process—otherwise, the money flow ceases. Somehow accountability creeps into this latter scenario.

A common notion among financial services folks is that streaming compensation, as opposed to up-front pay, permanently enfeebles cash flow. That's a myth, and we'll prove it. Those of us who overcome the limitations of these fables and move quickly to realign our operations and compensation methods will be first in line when Boomers jump from the retirement starting block.

Those of us who don't may be summoned by the Internet. And the Internet isn't calling quietly in the night, it is blaring at us every day. Within five years, the Internet's magnitude will rival electricity's for creating leaps of efficiency so great that standards of living will rise without extra effort. The Internet, after only a few years, now surrounds us with all the universe's knowledge, free at our fingertips. It *is* free. It offers total information, just a touch away.

Unless we change, our value to Baby Boomers will wither. They'll yawn at our offers to create their financial plans or to build, monitor, and report on their portfolios. With a stroll across the living room and the touch of a finger, they can do it themselves at a sliver of what we charge them.

Success in the twenty-first century for financial planners and other advisors will require wrenching changes. Our practices will take new shape and become more efficient and less costly for clients. Each of us has instinctive strengths toward which we gravitate and other tasks that we loathe. Forming working alliances with advisors who have offsetting skills is essential. Some advisors possess great people skills, some are analytical comprehensive planners, and some are methodical investment gurus. Having a representative of each, forming a triangle, moves our work from product pushing to service delivery. Although compensation is shared three ways, the capability of the whole not only has the potential to create heftier doses of income relative to operating as a jack-of-all-trades but also can deliver far greater service.

A couple of other professionals are walking onto our stage— CPAs and attorneys. Certified public accountants can share fees, and attorneys are not far behind. Massive amounts of income-generating assets have a tendency to attract attention, and Boomers' retirement funds are just that. If we thought we could conceal this from the rest of the world, we were wrong. These other professionals are here to stay, and forming alliances with them holds more promise for us and our clients than taking up arms against them. This arrangement, in conjunction with the aforementioned internal triangle, only enhances an already streamlined service delivery mechanism.

The primary vehicle for Boomers' participation in the market is mutual funds. They are under siege. Index funds are all the rage. Recently, with the breadth of the stock market thin, most picks by mutual fund managers were stale. The growth curve of the industry itself plateaued and expense ratios became less favorable. Internet trading makes owning individual securities easy and fun for individual investors, and e-brokers are going to spend billions to make certain these attitudes hold up. The thought of mutual funds and their returns induces drowsiness. We must fix that. We must build and maintain mutual funds of our own (in concept and structure) and offer them to clients. Doing so will save Boomers hundreds of millions of dollars.

The old method of randomly grabbing at funds or assembling them based on the shallow precept that somehow the funds themselves perform, rather than the managers, will perish. Structured investment discipline, offering a complete spectrum of risk levels, is the replacement for this method. In other words, we will create and manage mutual funds (portfolios) for Baby Boomers. We'll research them, build them, determine when to buy in or when to wait, and monitor them. Doing all this will dramatically cut costs to the clients. We will work a bit harder, but this will ultimately enhance our compensation.

Allowing us to manage these portfolios is the rapid advancement of technology, including new software and the Internet. These are the very things that seem to threaten our practices. However, by gaining control of them and putting them to use to the degree that Boomers themselves could never do, we remain of value to the Boomers. Adding to some of the old reliable technologies are software packages and Internet sites and services specifically designed to assist us in managing portfolios. Harnessing the Internet instead of defying it is our means of countering the threat it represents.

Our method of compensation, including all the perks, speaks volumes to Boomers. When we are paid on an ongoing basis instead of up front, our service level must be heightened. We'll dispel the notion that we will make less money if we accept compensation that is streaming as opposed to a one-time payment. Furthermore, the practice of piling clients through the door in order to annually replenish our pay is a sure formula for service disaster. Before we know it, our client base will be unwieldy.

Charging an up-front and ongoing fee for managing portfolios is the method best suited for presenting Boomers with their Holy Grail. Flowing all no-commission investment products, including life insurance and annuities, through a managed account and applying the fee accordingly ensures the purest form of compensation—that is, up front, ongoing, and with the freedom to exit at will. It also saves Boomers huge sums of money. Moreover, it significantly reduces the temptation to deceive, which invites regulatory compliance into our lives. Finally, on the compensation front, we'll explore the numerous reasons cited for why we can't transition to noncommission, fee-only work. We will dispel these rationalizations rooted in a tradition that is becoming increasingly creaky.

Because we develop deeply intertwined relationships with our clients, walking away from them for the sake of our retirement is difficult. Those who are employed by large financial institutions have a smooth means of transition in place but exercise little or no control over their clients' destinations. Independents must engage in complex business agreements that, once in place, offer greater flexibility, rewards, and wealth accumulation opportunities. We'll examine a structure based on recurring income, where buyouts are easy.

As we shall conclude, the salesperson is dead.

A final note on terminology paranoia. Unbeknownst to the general public, there is great gnashing of teeth among regulatory bodies in the securities industry about what financial services people can call themselves. And it is a blessing to the profession that such anxiety has thus far been hidden from the public.

Here is a list of designations. Creativity ensures that it's not exhaustive.

Rep

Representative

Broker

Stockbroker

Salesperson

Financial advisor

Financial representative

Financial consultant

Advisor

Consultant

Friend (allowed only once a week)

Registered investment advisor

RIA (this one's blatantly against the law)

Investment advisor

Investment professional

Stock picker

CFP

Portfolio manager

Subaccount consultant

Money manager (unless you really are one)

Market timer

Stock market consultant

In fact, what the financial service profession does is simple: It brings to the investor products and service. The products are securities. The service is advice on owning or not owning the securities, and, if owned, how much they are worth. There are numerous types of securities and there are varying perspectives on how and when an investor should put them to use.

Each person who assumes one of the preceding titles offers securities and advice on them, much of it the same.

The designation used in this series of books is *financial advisor.* It was chosen for two reasons:

1. In the most fundamental way it represents the product (financial) and the service (advisor).

2. Within seven years it will be the most accurate title for all financial services professionals. It will be universal.

Welcome to the world of the Twenty-First Century Financial Advisor.

CHAPTER
1

The Holy Grail

Origins on the USS *Missouri*

Remember the photograph in high school history books of the USS *Missouri* deck at the Japanese surrender in World War II? Seated on one side of a rectangular table were two or three Japanese, and on the other, two or three American naval officers. There were a few swords lying around on the table and a few stacks of paper the sea breeze was catching. The Japanese, burdened with despair, were signing away their will and ability to fight. The American officers waited with noble confidence. Sailors in their white uniforms, standing at quiet attention and dignified authority, lined every edge of the battleship decks. Do you know what was on their minds?

Sex!

It was at this very instant that the Baby Boomer generation began. Little did all those sailors know that this moment marked the culmination of the most potent amassing of passionate anticipation known to mankind. Minds and hearts were frenzied.

People believed at first that the Boomer generation began with the rapidity of conceptions and subsequent births after soldiers arrived home. It is now known that the true moment was when their parents' generation grasped that they had the freedom to

7

conceive, the knowledge that no longer could anything stand in their way—not Hitler, not the Empire of the Rising Sun. They had abstained long enough. It was the first time in recorded history that the very same thing was simultaneously on the minds of 20 million men and women. To the best of anyone's knowledge, this phenomenon has not been duplicated.

Even before birth, Boomers had an impact on the economy. Imagine being in the tuxedo or wedding gown business in 1945. Or home construction. Or rental property ownership. The furniture business. Car dealerships. Encyclopedia sales. The parents of Boomers didn't busy themselves setting up house strictly for the sake of shelter. They knew a great wave was on its way.

Once they arrived, Boomers' economic force increased. For 19 uninterrupted years, a Boomer was born every seven seconds of every day. Seventy-eight million strong, they contributed to the creation of hundreds of industries and advanced existing ones to new levels of growth. The magnitude of this phenomenon spanned almost a generation. As the original Boomer editions of 1945 were buying the new Mustang in 1964, the final editions were trying out Pampers and spitting Gerber Carrots 'n' Spinach across the kitchen.

A quantitative analysis of the comparative economic impact of Boomers is sketchy. There are government records of gross domestic product (gross national product or GNP, back then), but World War II and the Great Depression make trend and systematic analysis relative to the power of the Boomer generation of only partial value.

It is known that for 35 years prior to the start of World War II, GNP grew at 4.9% (without adjusting for inflation) year after year. But the standard deviation of this growth rate was a staggering 12.3%, a demonstration of extreme volatility. The highest level of pre–World War II growth was in 1918, when the economy grew 26.4% over the previous year. The lowest growth rate was a quick three years later, when GNP sank 24% from 1920. (See Figure 1.1.)

The demands of Boomers, as a group, fixed all this. Not only did they apply a brute driving force to the economy after the war, they also stabilized it. From 1945 to 1997, the economy grew 7.5% year

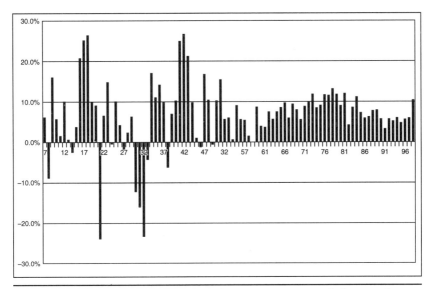

FIGURE 1.1 Gross domestic product: percentage of change from previous year.
(*Source*: U.S. Labor Dept.)

after year (unadjusted for inflation) with a standard deviation of 3.7%. By the power of their sheer size, they increased growth by more than 50% while reducing volatility by 330%.

It's apparent that the economy in general has been hefty under Boomer influence. That could have been predicted as a consequence of the general peacetime and the magnitude of their generation. But what is far more interesting is the way Boomers have shaped the economy.

The Seeds

Kids like one thing: toys. The things they need annoy or bore them—clothes, food, shelter, books, transportation. These merely reduce their precious time with toys. (Although kids do recognize that transportation can sometimes be good because it can take them to huge sources of new toys.)

Boomers were no different, as a representative list of their toys shows:

Erector sets

Tricycles (Some kids flipped the body over, reattached the wheels, and turned their trikes into the first Hot Wheels. Boomers were way ahead of the toy engineers on this one.)

Beds full of stuffed animals

Hula hoops

Barbie and Ken and their annual fashions

Crayons and coloring books (clever devices to prepare Boomers for school)

Lightbulb ovens

Keds and Converse shoes (the only nontoy items that enjoyed the status of toys)

Play-Doh

Garish plastic knights' armor

Tea sets, little tables, and all the accompanying frills

BB guns

While Boomers were engulfed in all their toys, something they could not recognize simmered around them. World War II shoved the United States into a permanently industrialized culture. Once on the run, the country never glanced back at the farm. As a result, a relative cushiness surrounded the children of this postwar era. Boomers can only imagine what a child's life was like on a farm in the early 1900s. Certainly, the nine-year-olds of that era didn't jump out of bed at eight in the morning, yell downstairs that they were up and wanted breakfast (preferably delivered to their rooms), and set about strategically lining up their green plastic toy soldiers to do battle or their dolls for a tea party.

What emerges is the scene of which Boomers' mothers seem to perpetually remind them, with a finger wagging in the face: "I did two hours of chores and then walked four miles to school every day—even in 10 feet of snow." Most children prior to World War II were cherished offspring first and working, productive family units a very close second. What toys?

By contrast, children of the postwar industrial era were not expected to contribute to a household's economic well-being. In fact, certain laws were created along the way that strictly forbade it. Boomers were the first generation of the completely transformed industrial revolution. They grew up believing it was their God-given right to be pampered.

Boomers realized that being pampered was kind of nice. But all this pampering created problems for them as they reached adulthood. By the time these Boomers reached college age, many of their parents had had enough, prophetically suggesting, as their offspring walked out, that in the not-too-distant future the tables would turn.

Boomers were then faced with finding other means of pampering. After lengthy meandering and great soul-searching, they finally found it from the most unlikely source: each other. And what's most important, they discovered that they could actually charge each other money for it. This pampering is called *service!*

Pinnacle service is the Baby Boomers' Holy Grail. They created it. They abide by it. They pass judgment on it. Like no other element of their upbringing, service is deeply ingrained in their souls. It is the natural economic culmination of childhood pampering.

Compromise it and you perish.

Empirical Proof

During Boomers' beginning years (from 1945 to 1963, ages 0 to 18) the average per-year increase in the service sector of the GDP was 0.158% (see Figure 1.2). From the time their parents nudged them out onto the sidewalk until age 35 they became the core consumer element of the economy. During this period the per-year increase nearly doubled to 0.331%. This is a clear indication that their pampering during childhood was economically transparent. They didn't pay their parents for it; nothing was recorded. Once their parents quit doing it, Boomers had to pay each other for the service, which was recorded and had a very significant economic impact.

As Boomers began assuming control of the levers of commerce, it dawned on them: This pampering stuff is good business. Pampering moved from being a nebulous fetish to a hardened business strategy. Many Boomers built companies around it; many of them

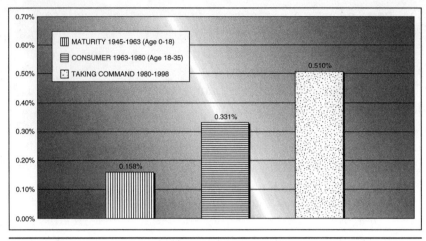

FIGURE 1.2 Average per-year increase in service sector.
(*Source*: U.S. Labor Dept.)

became wealthy from it. From 1980 until 1998, while Boomers exercised command, the per-year increase in the service sector was 0.510%, a 54% increase over the precommand period and a 223% increase over the maturity period.

Each phase of Boomers' existence witnessed an increase in year-over-year service growth:

Maturity	0.158%
Consumer	0.331%
Command	0.510%
Total era	0.343%

Excluding agriculture, government, forestry and fishing, and mining, the service sector has grown from 62% of GDP in 1945 to almost 80% of GDP in 1998 (see Figure 1.3).

Hamburger or Prime Rib?

There is hamburger and there is prime rib.

Very little equals the way a mother pampers her children. So for 20 years Boomers dined on prime rib. They will tolerate hamburger only when they are on the very brink of starvation.

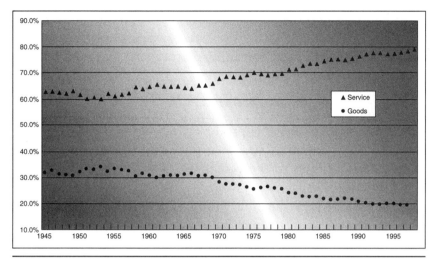

FIGURE 1.3 Percent of GDP, excluding government, agriculture, fishing and forestry, and mining.
(*Source*: U.S. Labor Dept.)

It took Boomers a while to cultivate this stance. Once out their parents' front door, they stood on the sidewalk unsure of where to seek the pampering to which they'd become accustomed. They had tasted the good life, all right, but they could not duplicate it—at first. Nevertheless, they struggled and prevailed.

It's clear when the final stage of their transformation took place, when they punched through the barrier of business mediocrity and took their Holy Grail to commercial preeminence. This mastery occurred when female Boomers themselves became mothers. Unlike their own mothers, staying at home wasn't their style, and they infiltrated the workforce. In 1970 only 14% of the gainfully employed were female. Currently, the figure is more than twice that. Female Boomers brought their intuitive prime rib to work and began serving it up. A natural assimilation quickly occurred and the mark of service excellence became so important that no one dared serve hamburger ever again.

This petrified male business Boomers at first. The cost of prime rib was far higher than that of hamburger. But, realizing that profit margins were fatter from delivering high-quality service and after witnessing an increase in sales, male Boomers joined in with the kind of zeal usually reserved for a Super Bowl party.

Today the Boomers' Holy Grail has matured into an integrity steeped in wisdom that is so absolute it provides a basis for illustrious national awards of business supremacy.

False Holy Grails

The antithesis of service is product. Purveyors in the economic marketplace recognize that, as a group, Boomers are monstrous, even when it comes to the consumption of products. Boomers don't dislike products; after all, they still enjoy their toys—DVD players, cell phones, jogging shoes, tennis rackets, computers, cars, camcorders, and so on. What they don't like is being offered a product that should be a service or a service that is really a product. When this happens, it confuses and upsets them. They must be able to clearly discern whether someone wants to pamper them or sell them a toy. If they can't decide, they conclude that deception is probably in progress.

There are those Boomers who manufacture or broker products and who also recognize that service is the Boomers' Holy Grail. Many of them realize the benefit of presenting these products under the guise of service. Such profit seekers know this will at least grip Boomers' initial attention, during which time it is hoped they will engage in binding decisions. Usually the subterfuge lifts quickly or Boomers identify the ploy and don't sign on the dotted line. Occasionally, however, they discover that they have been cleverly trapped by a ploy aimed at their incessant need for excellent service. Confusion ensues. Bitterness simmers.

Generally, Boomers have disdain for the financial services industry. They first observed its effects as children. In their cotton pajamas printed with dancing alphabet blocks, Boomers sat on the living room floor and watched the glossy insurance salesmen (à la Bill Murray's buddy in the movie *Groundhog Day*) preach from cash-value ledgers spread out all over the coffee table. The razzle-dazzle started with the sparkling white smile. Talk of needs and benefits was bandied about. Objections were overcome. Their parents squirmed. Fears of desolation were heightened and intensified. A few trial closes were floated. Then, finally, the application and the pen appeared from nowhere along with the slam-dunk close. Curious young Boomers watched a weary confusion pale their parents' faces as they signed here and signed there.

The modern financial services industry metamorphosed from this environment. However, the basics of the sales process employed by these life insurance agents remain intact. Most of today's financial advisors have refined and adjusted the process to fit the approach of Boomers. Monday morning pom-pom meetings are proof of this. If Boomers could sit in on one of these sessions, they'd come away in tears. Thrown around are terms and concepts such as these:

Buying unit. This is one, single potential application signature. It's used as a measure of the success of a planned event, such as a seminar. "I had 56 buying units last night at our seminar. If I can get half to sign up, I'll win the sales contest." A family of four represents four buying units: husband, wife, and two children (perhaps a couple of nice variable life policies or two college custodial accounts holding a little IBM and AT&T).

Sales contest hoopla. Who's ahead of whom in the contest to win the free golf trip to that plush seaside locale? The contest is based on the number of applications turned in prior to the end of the month. Standings are handed out. A few egos are acclaimed; most are bruised. Special tutoring on conniving ways to maneuver Boomers are reviewed. This might include the nifty use of trial closes.

Trial closes. This involves asking Boomers specially designed probing questions to determine the probability of a yes response when the almighty signature question is posed. "Do you feel pretty good about this mutual fund?" "Does this life insurance policy accomplish your goals?" "Do you want explosive growth from your stock investments?" When we get yes answers to these trial balloons, we produce the application and the pen and the slam dunk gets under way. If we get *no* for an answer or uncertainty, the way is still clear to press on with contrived persuasion, maneuvering the Boomers into a corner until they either walk away or succumb to future trial closes.

Role-playing. These are childlike sessions where one salesperson plays the client and another salesperson plays the salesperson. Peers watch their cohorts spend three or four minutes making fools of themselves as the fake salesperson tries to corner the fake Boomer into producing a fake signature or agreeing to a subsequent fake meeting. Sometimes the hilarity intensifies when they turn their backs to each other and hold their fists to their ears as if this engagement were taking place over the telephone.

The word *service* in the appellation "financial services" is by shrewd design. It invites Boomers' warm memories of childhood pampering. But soon the practice of reps, driven by the prospect of compensation, free trips, and sales contests, reveals itself as a façade for the product. Unfortunately for many Boomers, after the ploy disintegrates and they realize that quality service—their Holy Grail—is nowhere to be found, it is often too late. Their ability to change their minds after they've signed is blocked by the up-front compensation structure of the rep or agent. This agitates Boomers to their roots and incites their deepest suspicions.

From the Brink of Starvation with a Vengeance

So this is the baggage the financial services industry carries into the last two minutes of the Baby Boomers' ball game. During the 35 years in which they've commanded the economy, Boomers have been so preoccupied with creating personal wealth that they had no choice but to endure this decrepit nonsense from us. We served hamburger and they were forced to stomach it. Once they stop pressing the buttons of commerce and start to gather in the vast tunnel of retirement, their demands will become more and more acute and they will become less and less merciful. They simply will become intolerant of the silly, blathering, self-serving sales pitches of the past.

As with all industries, professions, and businesses in general that have put themselves (or, luckily, found themselves) in the path of this behemoth of a demographic group, the financial services profession will discover that Baby Boomers will get their prime rib and will no longer accept the hamburger we've fed them.

Those of us who do not deliver prime rib prepared exactly the way they want it, will expire. Because disgruntled retired Boomers will have the time, the smarts, and the means (the Internet) to get their choice cut all by themselves.

CHAPTER 2

Point and Click

The Internet is a commercial leap like no other to date. There will undoubtedly be progressions of similar magnitude in the future. Perhaps the next technological leap will be the ability to instantaneously move from one spot to another like Captain Kirk and Mr. Spock. But the powers behind technological progress can't expect us to absorb two Internet-like disruptions in one lifetime.

A few developments emerged in the past that boosted progress to some varying and previously unequaled degree: railroads, the telephone, the internal combustion engine, electricity, radio and TV, jet travel, plastics, and transistors.

But the Internet is different. All those other breakthroughs were products or services, from which their owners and issuers expected profit. The Internet is neither. It is a means of presenting products and services. It is owned by no one. Because it is not forever contriving ways to get into our wallets, we instinctively warm to it. It does not require production factories, a labyrinth of new networks, warehouses, armies of personnel, inventory, or layers of management.

Like the Internet, previous developments mentioned were disruptive technologies. And like those in the past, the Internet has barged onto the world's economic stage, swirling and rico-cheting around, disrupting our tidy, long-playing feature. Corporate executives assign traditional business plans for revision, only to ultimately toss them in the dumpster in frustration. The first blank page of the new blueprint is on the monitor, as strategists scratch their heads.

Their concern is deep because the Internet is many things:

- A portal into a global shopping mall, open 24 hours a day, 365 days a year

- The world's largest library

- An instantaneous and perpetual communication link with someone on the other side of the planet—or down the hall

- A ceaseless global gossip house

- A means of conducting all commerce from home or office

- A research lab

- A worldwide document delivery system that is 86,400 times faster than FedEx Overnight and 259,200 times faster than the U.S. postal system

- The greatest and cheapest auction hall ever

- A monstrous example of advertising's least expensive and most enduring method: word of mouth

At this moment and within the next five years, as the Internet burrows itself as deeply into our lives as electricity, its impact can be summarized in three words: ubiquity, knowledge, and efficiency. It provides more information to more people, more quickly, at lower cost and higher quality than any other advancement or discovery in history.

Financial services? Get ready.

Ubiquity

Ubiquity is when something is everywhere. For example, automobiles are all around us, as are televisions, telephones (and now cell phones), and computers. These are objects that make our lives easier. We can put them to use within moments. After these sorts of items are introduced and assimilated into commercial use and consumers' lives, standards of living increase through heightened efficiency and an enhanced flow of knowledge.

Ubiquity is perhaps the most significant feature of the Internet. It's sitting in living rooms and offices throughout the country, and will soon permeate the world. Getting to it requires a mere walk across the room. For something to become ubiquitous it must continually add users until its destruction would diminish the standard of living and be a severe blow to the economy. Imagine if every automobile and every telephone suddenly disappeared from the planet. We'd be in a bit of a mess.

Soon nearly 150 million folks will regularly be plugged in throughout North America—slightly less than 50% of that half-hemisphere's population. The United States looks over its shoulder at other regions of the world and notices them catching up fast. It is estimated that roughly 30% of the population of Europe is wired. And that's expected to increase to 60% in two years.

It is estimated that by 2003, 60 million computers a year will be pitched out just in the United States. Think about that for a minute. In two years, more than one-fifth of the American population will throw their computers away, to be replaced by faster and more technologically advanced units, all equipped to latch onto the Internet with little user effort.

The more quickly users are added, the more quickly ubiquity is accomplished. In 1995, the general public began wiring into the Internet. A mere three years later, more than 3 billion business e-mail messages were sent daily, pushing the Internet past the omnipresent telephone as the premier means of commercial communication. Since 1995, Internet sales, including software and support equipment, have reached nearly $450 billion, a few billion more than sales for the entire auto industry. This figure is predicted to reach $1.5 trillion by 2003. A swelling growth rate like this can only spell trouble for many industries and professions.

The Internet is moving swiftly and deeply into every form of commerce on the planet, especially the financial services profession.

Knowledge

Sir Francis Bacon advised us long ago that knowledge is power.

With the exception of emotional outbursts, action without knowledge is not possible. As we add more knowledge to our intellectual database, our actions become quicker, more refined, and more often proper. This increases the likelihood that others' reactions to our actions will be correspondingly faster, clearer, and more appropriate. The more and the faster knowledge is added to this unending cycle, the more behavior becomes precise, accurate, and efficient, thereby squeezing out most, if not all, unsuitable actions and decisions. What's most vibrant about the Internet is that it does not simply increase the amount of knowledge made available for actions. It makes available literally all knowledge for all actions (unfortunately, bad actions as well as good ones).

Consumers need information in order to make decisions before they buy anything. Most important, before making a purchase, they need to see what they are buying, acquiring at least visual knowledge. Traditionally, information about products or services has come to consumers through television, radio, and print. But time always separated the attainment of that knowledge from the ability to buy. Even if a consumer decided to act immediately upon information, the barriers (snow, rain, traffic, distance, crowds) were very often annoying enough to abort the process. The Internet eliminates the time disconnection and all obstructions. Point, click, shop. Point, click, buy.

Combine this newfound ease with the fact that the Internet provides consumers worldwide with unlimited data on any product or service in the global marketplace. If they're not pleased with the information about one company's product or service, alternatives are a mere click away.

The amount of knowledge flowing to consumers about financial services until recently was limited compared with the volume of available broad and general information. Only a handful of monthly investment magazines catering to the general public existed prior to the Internet. There was a significant time lag between each edition. Moreover, such publications were consumed in the home during leisure time, so there was a further delay between digestion of the information and the ability to act on it. This inefficiency favored inaction.

Ultimately, most investors grew weary of trying to do it themselves. They threw up their hands and called a financial advisor to do it for them. After all, advisors have those vast sources of privileged analysis and research at their fingertips to make appropriate and immediate decisions. These were resources the consumer did not have.

That was then.

This is now. Here they are. Across the room. A click away. Free.

Resource	Number of Web sites
Mutual funds	449
Investment magazines	69
Market information and research	616
General financial planning	59
Retirement planning	107
Estate planning	9
Newsletters	210
Investment software	261
Investment calculators	21
Investment news and media	346
Internet trading brokerages	89
References and guides	148
	2,384

The prospect that investors will flock into the arms of financial advisors because of information overload is unlikely. Sure, all the world's data is now available in consumers' homes and offices, and wading through it seems a daunting task—perhaps even more so than plowing to the mall. But Internet portal companies like Yahoo! and Excite generate millions in revenue by devising ways to make journeys through cyberspace pleasant and effortless. As well, they allow consumers to build, isolate, and save their own personal Internet universes that can be opened up and played with at a mere touch of the mouse.

Inside that universe there might be a favorite cybermall, bookstore, flower shop, investment center, road map, and so on. In the investment center, after reviewing many of these other sites, the consumer might choose one investment magazine, one newsletter, a financial planning site, a few calculators, portfolio tracking software, a couple of research sites, and, finally, an online brokerage.

Free knowledge is now organized and easily accessible. For example, the consumer reviews all the calculators and decides on three. One is from the Securities and Exchange Commission (SEC), which, believe it or not, is one of the simplest to use. The SEC's calculator provides investors with the means to quickly and easily discover how much mutual fund loads affect future balances. It walks the investor through information tasks by asking the following 11 questions:

- How many years are in the fund?
- How much is invested?
- What type of investment is it—bonds, money market, or equities?
- What is the expected rate of return?
- What title should be used on the printout?
- Is there an up-front sale charge?
- If so, what is the percentage?
- Is there a deferred sales charge?
- If so, what is the percentage?
- Do the shares convert later?
- What is the total operating expense as a percentage?

The calculator then displays the 10-year cost of using a fund with those conditions, as well as the ending value of the fund. So when investors enter identical data in front-load and no-load scenarios and discover that with $1 million over 10 years they relinquish $205,000 in ending value, they quickly and effortlessly become educated.

Before the existence of the Internet, when investors engaged a financial advisor after losing patience with their own inability to act, that advisor certainly wasn't going to usher compensation out the door by presenting the preceding quantitative analysis. Such knowledge was, at best, ignored; at worst, guarded. The investor had no exact knowledge of the impact of loads.

Times have changed. Investors are and will continue to be educated. There can be no more restraint of knowledge. The Internet has taken information from being a commodity that had a cost associated with it to being a universal and free consumer tool—and investors are using it plenty.

Economic potential is now directly related to the accessibility and management of all knowledge.

Efficiency

It is human instinct to steadily reach for a better standard of living. This is the most significant gift we hope to bestow upon our children. Standards of living are improved by accomplishing today's daily tasks more quickly, better, and more cheaply than yesterday's.

Time, quality, and cost are the elements of efficiency. If one of these moves in a favorable direction, efficiency increases. If two of the three move in the right direction, then we become even more efficient. And if all three move properly we have streamlined the engine and are really humming.

Even if we had the time and money, there is an array of tasks that the vast number of us can't accomplish ourselves for our own consumption: manufacturing a car, refining oil into gasoline, blowing glass, building a computer, raising and butchering livestock, growing and gathering fruits and vegetables, flying, building furniture, producing movies for our own entertainment, and so on. We could try to get these done in our basements or backyards, but the quality of the work would be so laughable that it would render the product or service useless and probably hazardous to our health—not to mention being pretty annoying to our neighbors.

So we pay companies to do them for us. And their accomplished efficiencies steadily lower what we pay. Competition sees to that. Sources that manufacture and deliver similar products and services incessantly explore means of increasing their efficiencies by decreasing costs and the amount of time needed to create or deliver the product or service while maintaining or increasing the quality. They then pass along to us reduced prices and higher quality. If one company is more successful than another, its sales, margin, and shareholder value advance more quickly.

Then there are those chores that many of us have the ability to do but for which we lack the time necessary to maintain the integrity level of the outcome: changing the oil in our cars, hanging drapes, managing investments and financial affairs, doing tax returns, steam-cleaning carpets, spraying for bugs, giving haircuts (to dogs, too). It is more efficient for us to hand these jobs over to experts. It would cost us more in time to sufficiently master the task to maintain the quality than to pay someone who is practiced at it.

When we exchange money for a product or service, we believe that what we're getting in return expands our standard of living by increasing our efficiency. We're willing to draw down our monetary resources to save time and improve the quality of our lives. The value of the product or service to us is equal to or greater than what we pay for it. At worst, it's a simple trade-off.

But what happens when we are handed a once-in-a-lifetime opportunity to streamline our efficiency engine by improving our quality of life, decreasing our costs, and saving even more time for a broad spectrum of tasks? The answer is always the same: We put it to use, we engage it, we embrace it. By instinct, we always pursue a higher standard of living.

The Internet is such a once-in-a-lifetime opportunity. Its impact will be rapid and significant, enhancing consumer efficiencies like never before. When we shopped yesterday, we climbed into our car (perhaps with a pack of snarling kids), consumed fuel to get to the mall, barely beat some kid with multiple facial piercings to the closest available parking spot, trudged into the mall, found the store, found the department, corrected the kids for the umpteenth time, found the product, waited in line, paid $42, reversed course to the car, and drove home. Time: 45 minutes. Nerve damage: factor of eight. Cost: $42 plus fuel and 45 minutes.

Today we click to the Internet, go to "Favorites," click on our preferred cyberspace mall, click to the appropriate department, browse around for the product, put it in the shopping cart, check it out for $36 plus $3 shipping, and go find out why the kids are so quiet. Time: 10 minutes. Nerve damage: none. Cost: $39 plus 10 minutes.

Or consider this: I was not entirely certain it was Sir Francis Bacon who had contributed the aforementioned aphorism. So I hopped on the Internet and in less than three minutes verified it. Three years ago I would have had to drive to the library, muck through a card catalog, and so on—a one-hour task.

The result is a savings of time, quality, and cost. Streamlined efficiency, indeed.

Middlemen

The Internet allows buyers and sellers worldwide to communicate instantaneously. Evidence of the popularity and coziness of this direct relationship is the flourishing of Internet auction sites. Another example is Toyota, which allows buyers to configure a vehicle over the Internet and take delivery in a week. And a few years ago, computer manufacturers such as Dell and Gateway quickly popped onto the Internet to sell computers. This struck a blow to CompUSA, a middleman sidewalk retailer whose primary revenue source was the sale of hardware.

People or procedures wedged into the flow of products and services from the maker to the consumer are quantifiable costs. When these costs become unnecessary, they disrupt and slow the process, decaying efficiency and standard of living. These people and procedures are commonly referred to as *middlemen.* As a result of advancements like the Internet, market forces eventually realign the middleman's value or abolish the excessive layer altogether.

If the middleman represents an inefficiency in the distribution of a product from the maker to the buyer, the Internet will be ruthless. Few middlemen will survive. Their value, their necessity will wither to nothing.

If the middleman is a service and is deemed worthwhile by the market, the energy of the Internet will reconfigure its value in one of two ways:

- *A reduction in cost.*   The cost of the service will drop in accordance with what the market now believes the service is worth. What's more harrowing to middlemen is that revenues will drop accordingly. This will require an equal decrease in the cost of doing business if middlemen want to maintain the status quo in their standard of living.

- *An increase in service.*   If middlemen find the threat to their status quo unthinkable, the only alternative is to increase the number of services or the quality of service to justify the same cost. The market will continue to pay the identical costs if it believes it is receiving an equal portion of the standard-of-living increase.

Irrespective of what middlemen are in the middle of, their choices are being squeezed by the Internet.

Financial Services in the Middle

Like many other business entities, financial advisors will seek cover from e-commerce and not find it. Of the three abstract effects, efficiency will supply the greatest jolt to our profession. The traditional way of conducting business places us squarely between the manufacturer and the consumer. We are a wedge in the commercial flow. The consumer will take mouse in hand and stalk our inefficiencies.

In compliance with the Boomers' insistence upon their Holy Grail, the Internet will cast off product pushers, demanding that they convert to being efficient service providers or perish. The Internet will also insist that current service providers (fee-based and fee-only advisors) rebalance cost and service.

As an example, let's take a look at the two methods investors employ to buy mutual funds: working alone and working with a financial advisor. We'll examine yesterday's courses of action, as well as today's.

Bruce Warner's Diversification: Yesterday and Alone

Bruce Warner realizes he has far too much exposure to a single investment—his nuclear power plant. So he decides to diversify by investing $2 million. Bruce borders on obsessive greed and refuses to seek outside help. But he has little time or energy to research the thousands of individual stocks on all the markets. Besides, those stockbrokers are a perpetual nuisance and are grossly overpaid. Moreover, he's not at all inclined to share personal information with anyone.

Tom Wax advises his boss that mutual funds would be ideal for him because each one has a person who does all the research, as well as watches the companies closely for faltering health. Bruce grills Wax on how this person gets paid. Convinced that a single dollar will not come directly from his wallet and he will not have to divulge any personal data in order to participate, Bruce decides that mutual funds will be his vehicles. He orders Wax to gather the *Wall Street Journal,* all the popular personal investment magazines, and current Morningstar reports.

He and Wax pore over the statistics. Based on various criteria, including past 10 years' performance and expense ratio, Bruce chooses 10 no-load funds (see Table 2.1): the top four domestic growth, the top two domestic growth and income, the top domestic aggressive growth, the top foreign, the top emerging markets (five-year performance), and the number one bond fund.

He calls the mutual fund families and orders applications. When the packets arrive, Bruce peruses the prospectuses to ensure there are no surprises. Satisfied, he completes the applications and sends each back, along with a $200,000 check.

Bruce spent 14 hours at an initial cost of $360 to invest $2 million in a diversified portfolio with a 10-year historical return of 17.15% and a composite Morningstar rating of 4½ stars. In addition, he paid $948,866 over 10 years to have his funds professionally managed.

Bob North's Emporium: Yesterday with Help

On the same day Bruce decides to diversify, Bob North suddenly realizes he has allowed the profits from his business, The Emporium, to accumulate to $2 million. For weeks he considers what to do with such a large sum. He doesn't subscribe to any of the personal finance magazines or the *Wall Street Journal.* If someone suggested he review Morningstar, he would be up just before dawn looking skyward. And he knows that in order to properly research the mutual fund choices, he would have to drive to the

TABLE 2.1 Bruce Warner

TIME	Minutes	
Fetching all the research material	120	*
Analysis	360	
Calling the fund families	50	
Examining prospectuses	240	
Filling out the applications	60	
Writing checks	10	Hours
TOTAL	**840**	14

QUALITY	10-Year Return	10-Year Rating	Expense Ratio
Spectra	25.8%	5.0	2.12%
Janus Twenty	25.8%	5.0	0.91%
American Century 20th Century Ultra	24.0%	5.0	0.80%
Fidelity Blue Chip Growth	23.2%	5.0	0.70%
Dreyfus Disciplined Stock	19.9%	5.0	0.90%
Safeco Equity No-Load	19.8%	5.0	0.73%
Kaufmann	20.9%	4.0	1.88%
Glenmede International	11.8%	4.0	0.14%
J.P. Morgan Emerging Markets	-10.4%	2.0	1.65%
Vanguard Long-Term Corporate Bonds	10.8%	5.0	0.32%
WEIGHTED AVERAGE	**17.15%**	**4.5**	**1.02%**

COST	*Initial*	
One year subscription to Morningstar		$360
		$360
After 10 years		
Value *(before management fee)*	$9,737,622	
Value *(after management fee)*	$8,788,756	
Management Fee	$948,866	**$948,866**
TOTAL		**$949,226**

SUMMARY		
PORTFOLIO VALUE	$8,788,756	
TIME (hours)	14	
QUALITY	4.5	17.15%
INITIAL COST	$360	
TOTAL COST	$949,226	

*Even though Wax retrieved the research material for Bruce,
we must attribute the two hours to Bruce. Most people don't have
a Tom Wax and have to actually go get all the stuff themselves.

library and grind through all the publications, a burden that would only serve to intensify his anxiety and paralysis. Besides, The Emporium consumes nearly all of Bob's time.

For weeks he frets, until he recalls that Lewis Tyler, in addition to being an attorney and real estate broker, is also a financial planner. When Bob calls, Tyler instructs him to come see him first thing Monday morning at his office in downtown Springville, 20 miles from Bob's home.

That morning Tyler explains the incredible advantages of the mutual fund families that he uses exclusively. He has spent years researching all the available fund families in the market, and his are clearly without peer. As well, he has spent months investigating each fund inside each family to ensure that he has further gleaned the very finest-performing, lowest-cost funds for his clients.

Bob begins to feel warm inside.

Tyler illustrates with spectacular colored graphs how each of the funds he has chosen for Bob has whipped the pants off each benchmark since the beginning of time and is very likely to continue to do so (huh-oh, Tyler, compliance?).

Bob North now feels cozy by the fire. After all, what's a paltry 3.625% load when he'll beat the general markets every year? Where does he sign? (See Table 2.2.)

Bob spent three hours at an initial cost of $72,600 to invest the net amount of $1,927,400 in a diversified portfolio with a 10-year historical return of 13.76% and a composite Morningstar rating of 3¾ stars. In addition, after 10 years, Bob paid $732,593 for the management of the his $1,927,400. As well, Bob will spend an additional 20 future hours in annual reviews.

Bill Randall's New Business: Today with Help

Bill Randall inherits $2 million from a relative he didn't know existed. The check shows up in the mail one day. So, flinging aside diversification, he invests in the one industry from which he garners the most pleasure. He buys Brian's Tavern. Brian Stone had always claimed he would never sell. But this is an offer he can't refuse. At $2 million, the price is just right.

A few years prior to selling, Brian's suppliers encouraged him to participate in the twenty-first century and install a computer so he could order his liquor and food over the Internet. So Brian is quite proficient and comfortable buzzing around inside all the portals. He opens an E*Trade account and quickly finds plenty of investment sites. He goes to work on choosing the very best mutual funds.

But his impatience finally corners him. He can't make up his mind what's most important: return, risk, expense ratio, diversification. And those Greek letters have him stumped. Also, just

TABLE 2.2 Bob North

TIME	Minutes			
Drive to Tyler's office	30			
Review recommended mutual fund portfolio	75			
Review, complete, and sign applications, prospectuses, delivery forms, suitability forms, etc.	45			
Drive home	30	Hours		
TOTAL	**180**	3		

QUALITY	10-Year Return	10-Year Rating	Adjusted Load	Expense Ratio
AIM Value	21.43%	5	3.75%	1.04%
Putnam Investors	20.16%	4	3.50%	0.95%
AIM Weingarten	18.78%	4	3.75%	1.07%
Putnam Vista	18.35%	4	3.50%	0.98%
AIM Charter	18.79%	4	3.75%	1.09%
Washington Mutual Investors	17.76%	4	3.50%	0.62%
Putnam Voyager	20.31%	4	3.50%	0.96%
AIM International Growth	7.32%	3	3.75%	1.47%
AIM Emerging Markets	-14.52%	2	3.75%	2.10%
Bond Fund of America	9.19%	4	3.50%	0.68%
WEIGHTED AVERAGE	**13.76%**	**3.80**	**3.63%**	**1.10%**

COST		
Initial		
Loads *(adjusted for breakpoints)*		$72,500
		$72,500
After 10 years		
Value *(before management fee)*	$6,996,288	
Value *(after management fee)*	$6,263,695	
Management Fee	$732,593	$732,593
TOTAL		**$805,093**

SUMMARY		
PORTFOLIO VALUE	$6,263,695	
TIME (hours)	3	
QUALITY	3.80	13.76%
INITIAL COST	$72,500	
TOTAL COST	$805,093	

what in the hell is this Sharpe Ratio thing? Frustrated, he seeks help. Through research and graphing on various Internet sites and participation in chat room sessions, Brian is well aware of the effect mutual fund loads have on an ending value of a portfolio. As well, he cringes at the thought of those mounds of commission stockbrokers shovel in for buying and selling stock.

So Brian calls Lewis Tyler and explains that he will pay Tyler an hourly fee ($125) to research and recommend an appropriate portfolio. Brian makes it clear he has no interest in loaded funds and no interest in having Tyler manage the account. All he requires is a broadly diversified portfolio at the lowest possible cost. Tyler should e-mail the recommendations to him and he will make the purchases in the E*Trade account he has already opened. Tyler obliges by choosing the best-performing index mutual funds in five markets: Standard & Poor's 500, mid-cap, bonds, international, and emerging markets. (Take a look at Table 2.3.)

Brian spent three hours and an initial cost of $250 to invest $2 million in a diversified portfolio with a 10-year historical return of 14.23%. In addition, after 10 years, Brian paid $245,983 for the management of his $2 million.

Ellen Smith's Lucky Find: Today and Alone

On the curb right outside Brian's Tavern, 13-year-old Ellen Smith finds a lottery ticket on her way home from school one

TABLE 2.3 Brian Stone

TIME	Minutes	
Complete on-line application	15	
Aborted analysis	120	
Discussion with Tyler	30	
Purchase recommended funds	15	Hours
TOTAL	**180**	**3**

QUALITY	10-Year Return	10-Year Rating	10-Year Ratio
Vanguard S & P 500 Index	16.95%	5	0.18%
Dreyfus Midcap Index	18.24%	3	0.50%
Vanguard Long-Term Bond Index	8.68%	2	0.20%
STI Classic International Equity Index	11.88%	4	1.06%
Vanguard Emerging Stock Index	1.75%	2	0.61%
WEIGHTED AVERAGE	**14.23%**	**4.1**	**0.33%**

COST		
Initial		
Tyler's 2 hrs of research @ $125/hour		$250
		$250
After 10 years		
Value *(before management fee)*	$7,565,398	
Value *(after management fee)*	$7,319,415	
Management Fee	$245,983	$245,983
TOTAL		**$246,233**

SUMMARY		
PORTFOLIO VALUE	$7,319,415	
TIME (Hours)	3	
QUALITY	4.10	14.23%
INITIAL COST	$250	
TOTAL COST	$246,233	

spring day. Inside the tavern she hears Brian and Bill Randall negotiating the price of something. In principle, the lottery constitutes gambling to Ellen and therefore is fraught with inappropriate and uncontrollable risk. But since she wagered nothing on the ticket she decides to keep it.

Good decision. She wins $2 million. Despite her father's frantic pleadings to buy Brian's Tavern before Bill can, she invests the money.

In school, Ellen won a statewide investment contest sponsored by Ameritrade. She grew $100,000 to $153,547 in nine months, a sturdy 71% return. She accomplished this by diligent research on the Internet, where the students also maintained and monitored their portfolios in artificial Ameritrade accounts.

So, using those same painstaking habits, Ellen decides to invest and manage the proceeds herself. She opens an Ameritrade account and, through meticulous groundwork, builds her own personal mutual fund of 20 individual stocks (two from each Standard & Poor's sector), Mid-Cap S & P Depository Receipts (SPDRs), three no-load mutual funds, and 10 bonds of two corporate issues. (See Table 2.4.)

Ellen spent nine hours at an initial cost of $284 to invest $2 million in a portfolio of stocks diversified across all 11 S & P sectors with a 10-year historical return of 19.19% and a composite Morningstar rating of almost four stars. In addition, she paid $356,764 over 10 years to have 30% of her funds professionally managed.

Notable Quantitative Facts

Referring to Table 2.5 will provide a snapshot of how our investors did. Ellen Smith got the most for her money and time.

1. Ellen's portfolio value was highest after 10 years.

	10-year Value
Ellen	$11,313,223
Bruce	$ 8,788,756
Brian	$ 7,319,415
Bob	$ 6,263,695

TABLE 2.4 Ellen Smith

TIME	Minutes	
Internet Analysis	480	
Purchase Securities	60	Hours
TOTAL	**540**	**9**

QUALITY	10-Year Return	10-Year Rating	Expense Ratio
Ameren / UE	12.06%	4	0.00%
Aetna	8.65%	4	0.00%
Applied Materials	43.82%	4	0.00%
Atlantic Richfield	7.25%	4	0.00%
Anheuser-Busch	19.57%	4	0.00%
Citigroup	33.87%	3	0.00%
Enron	25.21%	4	0.00%
Federal Express	14.14%	4	0.00%
GE	27.52%	4	0.00%
GM	11.60%	3	0.00%
GTE	16.72%	3	0.00%
Intel	43.84%	5	0.00%
J.P. Morgan	16.74%	3	0.00%
Minnesota Mining (3M)	12.52%	4	0.00%
Phelps Dodge	12.50%	3	0.00%
Pfizer	37.30%	5	0.00%
Procter & Gamble	25.86%	4	0.00%
Ryder Systems	6.37%	3	0.00%
AT&T	19.16%	4	0.00%
Union Carbide	30.48%	4	0.00%
Wal-Mart	27.57%	5	0.00%
Exxon	16.46%	4	0.00%
Mid-Cap SPDR	19.31%	4	0.32%
General Motors Bonds	6.75%	5	0.00%
Lehman Brothers Bonds	7.25%	5	0.00%
Hotchkis and Wiley International	12.47%	4	0.89%
SSgA Emerging Markets	4.86%	2	1.25%
Janus Venture	17.40%	4	0.94%
WEIGHTED AVERAGE	**19.19%**	**3.9**	**0.31%**

COST

Initial		
Stock Trades @ $8 each		$184
Mutual Fund Trades @ $0 each		$0
Bond Trades @ $5 each		$100
		$284
After 10 years		
Value *(before management fee)*	$11,669,987	
Value *(after management fee)*	$11,313,223	
Management Fee	$356,764	$356,764
TOTAL		**$357,048**

SUMMARY

PORTFOLIO VALUE	$11,313,223	
TIME (hours)	9	
QUALITY	3.89	19.19%
INITIAL COST	$284	
TOTAL COST	$357,048	

TABLE 2.5 Comparison

	Bob	Bruce	Brian	Ellen
Portfolio Value	$6,263,695	$8,788,756	$7,319,415	$11,313,223
TIME (hours)	3	14	3	9
Quality	3.80	4.50	4.10	3.89
10-Year Return	13.76%	17.15%	14.23%	19.19%
Initial Cost	$72,500	$360	$250	$284
Management Fee	1.10%	1.02%	0.33%	0.31%
10-Year Cost	$732,593	$948,866	$245,983	$356,764
Total Cost	$805,093	$949,226	$246,233	$357,048
Forfeited	$5,049,528	$2,524,467	$3,993,808	$0
Return per $1 of Cost	$7.78	$9.26	$29.73	$31.69
Hours in 10 Years	87,600	87,600	87,600	87,600
Cost per Hour	$9.19	$10.84	$2.81	$4.08
Return per $1 of Hourly Cost	$681,536	$811,077	$2,603,959	$2,775,645

2. Each investor contributed a specific amount to the profitability of various mutual fund companies.

Contribution

Bruce	$948,866
Bob	$732,593
Ellen	$356,754
Brian	$245,983

3. However, there is a return on each contribution. The investors showed the following dollars coming back to them for each dollar of management fees they spent over the 10 years.

Returned

Bob	$ 7.78
Bruce	$ 9.26
Brian	$29.73
Ellen	$31.69

4. Each investor forfeited, for some specific reason, the opportunity to make more money by not following Ellen's method, the best performing.

	Forfeited	*Every Hour for 10 Years*	*Reason*
Bob	$5,049,528	$57.64	Limited access to knowledge
Bruce	$2,524,467	$28.81	Unwilling to research broader choices
Brian	$3,993,808	$45.59	Unwilling to take time to educate himself

5. In Bob's case, Tyler's compensation was roughly $45,000. Tyler spent two hours preparing for his meeting with Bob and two hours with him personally. And over the next 10 years Tyler will probably spend, with spontaneous phone calls and a few planned meetings, a total of 20 hours with Bob. In Brian's case, Tyler spent two hours researching and compiling recommendations.

	Tyler's Compensation	*Hours Worked*	*Per-Hour Rate*	*Per-Minute Rate*
Bob	$45,000	24	$1,875	$31.25
Brian	$250	2	$ 125	$ 2.08

Pulling all these efficiency factors together:

	10-Year Value	*10-Year Cost to Attain It*	*Dollars Returned for Every Cost Dollar Spent*	*Per-Hour Cost of Advice*	*Dollars/ Hour Forfeited for 87,600 Hours*
Ellen	$11,313,223	$356,754	$31.69	0	0
Brian	$ 7,319,415	$245,983	$29.73	$ 125	$45.59
Bruce	$ 8,788,756	$948,866	$ 9.26	0	$28.81
Bob	$ 6,263,695	$732,593	$ 7.78	$1,875	$57.64

Ellen Smith brought in $31.69 for every dollar she spent in mutual fund portfolio fees. Though Brian Stone's performance was close, he forfeited $45.59 per hour for 10 years. Neither

Bob's ($7.78) nor Bruce's ($9.26) dollar returns were close to Ellen's or Brian's ($29.73) due to their hefty donations to the revenue streams of various mutual fund companies.

Notable Qualitative Facts

For different personality reasons, two of these characters chose to invest on their own. The other two sought assistance.

Alone Yesterday.   Bruce was confined to delivery of information by the print media, and his only two routes to the market were through mutual funds or a stockbroker. Since he was greedy and winced at the thought of paying someone directly, he used mutual funds. He held great confidence in the quality of his own research. Though he chose the highest-performing funds, their meaty composite expense ratio of 1.02%, or $948,866 over 10 years, suppressed the final return. Dollars returned for each spent: $9.26. Personality characteristics that produced this return: greed and demand for privacy.

Alone Today.   With access to the Internet, Ellen's research was not restricted by the availability of information. Her choice of Ameritrade as her broker was not driven by greed. It was simply less expensive, and, because heaps of information were seconds away, she did not need the opinion of a financial advisor. Achieving diversification by spreading her stock choices over all 10 S & P sectors minimized her need for mutual funds and their accompanying expenses. Dollars returned for each spent: $31.69. Personality characteristics that produced this return: intelligence and diligence.

With Help Yesterday.   Bob's frustration and apprehension concerning knowledge of investing pushed him to seek Lewis Tyler's expensive help. All the material available to Montgomery Burns was also available to Bob, but his fretting personality prevented him from employing it. Claiming little time, he seized up and ran into the arms of Tyler. This short-term maneuver cost him dearly, due not only to management expenses but to a hefty front load. Dollars returned for each spent: $7.78. Personality characteristics that produced this return: fear and perceived lack of time.

With Help Today.   Like Ellen, Brian possessed the tool (the Internet) and the skills to use it. The tool informed him of the impact high loads and commissions have on investment results and also provided him with the ability to buy and track the securities. But unlike Ellen, he did not have the patience to educate himself about what securities were best for him. So Brian, with clear instructions, commissioned Tyler to perform the research for him. The expense ratio of 0.33% and Tyler's compensation were reasonable, but the mundane performance of index funds dulled the outcome. Dollars returned for each spent: $29.76. Personality characteristics that produced this return: impatience and thrift.

Alone:

Bruce Warner—greedy and private

Ellen Smith—intelligent and diligent

With help:

Bob North—fearful and too busy

Brian Stone—impatient and thrifty

Whether driven by greed, the need for privacy, intelligence, or diligence, those folks who planned and executed their own financial destinies yesterday will not be perched at our office door today because of the upheaval occurring. In fact, all the changes only equip these investors further to master their own fate. Type A personalities constitute 25% of the U.S. population and the chances of them seeking our help will now all but vanish.

The rest, by nature, search quietly and patiently everywhere for efficiencies and the chance to upgrade their standard of living. This group will not ruthlessly eliminate the financial services middlemen. They will do it politely and obscurely, creeping away without fuss to the Internet sites those meddling Type As show them. Nevertheless, they will do it. Their transition will not be a noticeable event, a prominent moment we can point to as the peak before the slide. It will, rather, be a gradual, seemingly immeasurable trend.

Because of efficiencies created by the Internet, fees, charges, and commissions spent by investors are moving from financial services' pockets of yesterday back into the investors' pockets of today and tomorrow. And the flow will only get stronger with time.

Out There in Cyberspace

The preceding examples are at once generic and specific. They expose four general approaches to investing, while dissecting with precision the methods and consequences of each.

We are no different from them. How often has it dawned on us as we relax at home that we have an interest in buying this or that product? At first we mentally survey the local brick-and-mortar storefronts to see if there isn't an outlet close by that carries the desired item. Failing to coax our weekend memories to work, we start wondering where the Yellow Pages are. Then it hits us: the Internet. We scurry across the room and in 10 minutes we find what we're looking for, order it, and expect to receive it in three days.

Stalking savings on the Internet has become a consumer obsession, a sport. On accommodating Web sites, consumers plug in the names of products they're pursuing and then click on a search engine to find the lowest possible price in the universe for that item.

A client or prospect, during halftime on *Monday Night Football,* noses through the business section of the paper and comes across an advertisement for a seminar on annuities. "Hmmmm," he muses, "I've thought about those." He drags himself off the couch and clicks into Yahoo!'s Investment and Finance section, where he types the names of annuities into the search sleeve. Up pop hyperlink addresses. A few indicate that they offer direct and low-load annuities, as well as heaps of information—what's good and bad about them, who they're for and not for—and an offer to answer any e-mail questions. He has a few questions, so he sends them to one of the addresses. They're answered satisfactorily within 24 hours. Three days later he buys.

Without uttering a word to a financial advisor (assuming he deals with one of us), he has purchased an annuity. We don't know it because he didn't consult us, and we won't know it until the next time we review his balance sheet. So, from our perspective, we were never affected by the Internet. The Internet's not bothering us. What Internet?

An irony of this particular incident, which will happen far more often than we think, is that we paid a $2,400 newspaper advertising bill that triggered a sale we not only did not make but did not know about.

A Microscopic Sampling

Across the room. Free. Easy.

Annuities and Life Insurance

Paragon Life (www.paragonlife.com) and Ameritas Life (www .veritas.com) are two prominent locations on the Internet where the general public can purchase annuities and life insurance, variable or otherwise, at no load or low load, meaning no commission for us or anybody else.

Consumers can click Ameritas into their living rooms and compare their ledgers with the ones you sent home with them. Here's the question they ponder: Why should I pay a financial advisor more than $3,400 over 10 years for something I make a decision on once and then live with?

RightQuote (www.rightquote.com) offers low-cost term insurance.

Trading

Then there's on-line trading. In 1999, more than 3 million new on-line brokerage accounts were opened, which accounted for 45% of retail trades. Investors, computer mouse in hand, have increased such activity by 23% every six months since the second half of 1998. If that keeps up, all retail trades will occur over the Internet by the end of 2002. E*Trade (www.etrade.com), Ameritrade (www .ameritrade.com), and dozens just like them offer participation in individual securities at a cost 90% less than that charged by traditional full-service stockbrokers and 50% less than that charged by discount brokers. The knowledge advantage of full-service brokers is diminished considerably by the dozens of research hyperlinks at these on-line trading sites. Some grant access to initial public offerings (IPOs). E*Trade even has a bevy of its own mutual funds, based on indices. And if investors want more flavor from their mutual funds, on-line Discover Brokerage (discoverbrokerage), owned by Morgan Stanley Dean Witter, has almost 100 no-load, no-transaction-fee fund families. That means it costs consumers no money whatsoever to invest. Pretty cost effective, no?

Research

Investors eager for more on-line brokerage research can visit EDGAR (Electronic Data Gathering, Analysis and Retrieval). EDGAR (www.edgar.com) is a service offered by the SEC. "Its primary purpose is to increase the efficiency and fairness of the securities market for the benefit of investors, corporations, and the economy by accelerating the receipt, acceptance, dissemination, and analysis of time-sensitive corporate information filed with the agency," declares its Web site. Cost to investors: 0. See a trend?

Advice

It used to be that when investors wanted advice on a particular stock or on what you, as financial consultant, thought was the finest investment of the time, you handed out your recommendations for free and recovered your cost of doing business by commission on the transaction. So for $500, investors received full brokerage guidance and a transaction. Now investors find a few newsletters, such as the *Bull & Bear Report* (www.thebullandbear .com) or the *Stock Advisor* (www.thestockadvisor.com), with which they feel comfortable. These dispense investment suggestions and supporting rationale. They even track their own recommendations to prove or disprove their acumen. (The subscription price of the *Bull & Bear Report* is $30 per year; the *Stock Advisor* is free.) And if relentless tenacity is the investment goal, DRIP Investor (www.dripinvestor.com) is the location. (DRIP is the Dividend Reinvestment Program.) The advice is free. Now, instead of paying $500 for a string of investment actions, it cost the investor no more than $30. Most people would drive a few hours to save $475 on any purchase. Now it's right across the . . . well, you know where it is.

Financial Planning

If you use financial planning as a means of exposing free cash flow or idle assets to assist in forcing more efficiency from them, the Internet has not overlooked you. (If you do comprehensive financial planning for a fee and for the sole sake of planning, the Internet *has* overlooked you—and probably will continue to overlook you for some time, if not forever. Superquality, directly compensated, detailed relationship work will probably never be found on the Internet.) There are plenty of accessible financial planning sites. For example, consumers can go to Save Wealth (www.savewealth.com), where sophisticated advice is dispensed on retirement, estate, and tax planning. Or investors can go to Deloitte & Touche's retirement site (www.dtonline.com/ prptoc/prptoc/htm) and learn how to create their own personal blueprint for the future. Even the Social Security Administration (www.ssa.gov) has a location on its Web site that offers rudimentary retirement planning.

And if investors want humor injected into their planning, they can visit ReliaStar Financial's Web site (www.ihatefinancialplanning.com). The general mood of the site is one of fun and levity and it even includes a panic button that, when clicked, gives off a hair-pulling scream of frustration.

Reporting

If you stake your claim to quality service by generating quarterly performance reports, unfortunately the Internet is not only going to affect you, it's going to best you. For instance, there's a piece of software called Fund Manager (biely.com/fundman/ index.html), which is downloadable from the Internet. It generates more than a dozen reports and 30 charts. Prices can be retrieved in daily downloads. The cost: $40. Despite the name, it reports on individual securities as well.

Tracking

Daily portfolio tracking is something most of us weren't even doing for clients a year ago. They were able to see how well (or poorly) they were performing only 12 times a year. How efficient is that? Now most of us offer Internet access so clients can view their accounts anytime. But Yahoo! and hundreds of other investment sites offer elements presented directly as line items, which most of ours do not, including to-date return, annualized return, earnings per share, price to earning (P/E) ratios, and historic yield. In addition, investors' positions are updated with only a 15-minute delay (real-time, if they really want to get fancy).

Yeah, Yeah, but We Have a Relationship

We're all aware of Wal-Mart's original strategy. They move to a location outside a small or medium-size town and, as reported in some locations, they covertly gather prices from the local businesses that line the town square. Then undercut them until the little shops' lives are squeezed out.

In hundreds of quiet, cozy towns throughout America, thousands of small retail business owners shuttered their windows. To get a lower price, their neighbors were slipping off to Wal-Mart. These business owners were residents of the towns, churchgoers and little league baseball coaches.

But none of that mattered to the folks down the street and across town. After all, lower prices are lower prices. Abandoned and suffering good citizens are a source of sorrow, but, by golly, when you can get the same pair of shoes for $19.99 instead of $24.99, you do it. You can put that five bucks toward your daughter's college tuition instead of into the pocket of your neighbor. Besides, he goes on those two-week golf jaunts to Palm Springs every year. How does he pay for those? Maybe he should lower his prices. (He's tried that, and Wal-Mart responds in kind.)

Money coldly and calmly redefines relationships.

Beware: The foundation of financial service is relationship.

Yeah, Yeah, but My Business Is Booming

Here's a probable reaction to the threat coming from cyberspace: "That all sounds logical to me but my business is booming. The Internet doesn't affect me." As you read this, it may not. But five years from now, you will remember with anguish your claim of immunity. The Internet is a Model T that will become a Formula II in 10 years.

This ubiquitous cost reduction and convenience will cause investors to question our value and our place as financial advisors in the near future. We better be ready to respond.

The Bottom Line

There is no shelter from the Internet. This 100% knowledge accessibility increases the pace of consumers' lives, improves their standard of living, and lowers their cost of living. The Internet is a godsend to some industries and professions, while it dooms others. It is difficult to predict with absolute certainty which are golden and which are worthless because the Internet itself has not stopped evolving. As it continues to unfold through time, it will create new industries, devour others, and callously root out decayed layers of middlemen.

In the old days, we, the financial advisors, were the experts. We held and guarded the refined knowledge necessary to assist the client in making the appropriate decisions. Today we are privy to nothing. Our knowledge is escorted onto the world stage by the Internet, and admission is free.

It's easy to become incensed with this Internet presence. But the fact is that seeking the least expensive distribution of products is every single company's directive. It lowers costs and increases shareholder value, public or private. Financial advisors are just potential casualties of this situation.

Maybe.

Town Squares

A ll the buzz about increased productivity as a result of technology is really buzz about increased productivity as a result of computers, in terms of both hardware and software. Improved productivity in commerce means employees create more units per hour of work, decreasing the cost of production and lowering the cost consumers pay for the unit. This ultimately results in higher living standards.

Over a span of 20 years, companies have progressively put more computers to work. But only recently have computers accelerated their impact on the economy and the financial services profession. There are four reasons for this delayed action:

1. *Speed.* When computer chips broke through the 133-megahertz barrier in 1996, they became fast enough even for the most impatient of employees. Processing speed developed at such a rapid pace, enhancing the effectiveness of the computer to an equal degree, that equipment became obsolete nearly every 18 months. Upgrade after upgrade forced the computer deeper and deeper into our lives until it is today as necessary as the telephone. Now approaching 1,000-megahertz speeds, computers switch from program to program almost as fast as scenes change

on television. And soon televisions and computers will be one and the same.

2. *Price.*   The cost of a basic computer broke below the $1,000 level in 1999. Efficiencies at manufacturing microchips, the most costly element of a computer, forced prices down and made them more affordable, broadening the potential consumer base significantly.

3. *Home use.*   Greater speed and lower prices moved the computer from being a tool at the office to a tool and a toy for the home.

4. *The Internet.*   The arrival of the Internet matured the computer from adolescence to adulthood—from being a toy, a spreadsheet producer, a word processor to an instrument as significant as the automobile, embedded in our daily routine and serving as a means to a better life.

Computers are the fundamental reason changes are occurring in worldwide commerce. In the financial services profession, computers are altering securities transactions—the core of the industry.

Purging the Market Makers

Your neighbor wants to sell her 100 shares of Yahoo!, and she knows you like this Web company. She can't just mosey over and start dickering price until you both agree, then give you the shares while you give her the cash. This seems reasonable as an isolated transaction, but with millions of securities trades a day all over the world, sauntering up to the back fence limits the market as well as invites criminal activity.

Investors take their trades to a central market, much like the old days when buyers met sellers at the town square to exchange bread, pottery, meat, eggs, and other commodities. Yesterday, tightly ringing the parameter of the town square were financial advisors. They intercepted investors coming to market and, for a fee, would take their shares to the square and execute the trades for them. We have already reviewed how, today and tomorrow, investors won't even encounter financial advisors on the way to the market.

The New York Stock Exchange (NYSE) is one such town square. Its first trade occurred in 1792 under a buttonwood tree on Wall Street when shares of the Bank of New York were exchanged. Now more than 200 years later, in the pits of the NYSE, market makers scurry about in a frenzy, scream at each other, flash bizarre hand signals, and collapse when the market closes. A second town square is the Nasdaq, which was established in 1971 when the SEC decided that over-the-counter stock trading tempted moral breaches by being obscure and random. The Nasdaq has no pit and no people behaving strangely. There are still market makers in the Nasdaq system, but they trade through 500,000 worldwide computers.

Market makers are folks or companies that make a living off trades. They hold inventory of stock in various companies, and when trades are executed in these companies, they keep the spread—the difference between the bid price and the ask price. It is obvious that, within ethical limits, it is in their best interest to keep this spread as wide as possible. In 1994, the SEC caught a number of Nasdaq market makers operating way outside the ethical box. They were price-fixing. So to help eliminate this naughty behavior, the SEC imposed a few new rules. One of these rules included the injection of competition into the trading mix by approving the use of a third town square: Electronic Communications Networks (ECNs).

Market makers are middlemen. The Internet is eyeing them for a possible purging.

Archipelago, Island, Instanet, Attain, the BRASS Utility, and Strike Technologies are all ECNs. They're private computer-driven trading units separate from the NYSE and the Nasdaq. The SEC pressed competition further by announcing in the spring of 1999 that ECNs could apply to become stock exchanges. Since there are no market-maker middlemen in ECNs, orders are matched automatically and the potential for unethical behavior disappears.

Even now many on-line (and some traditional) brokerages send trade orders to ECNs because there is no human intervention and they are executed at a fraction of the cost. As a result of this efficiency (in cost and speed) over the established market maker arrangement, ECNs will gain momentum as the primary means of trading. Proof is in the mushrooming of asset-based fee accounts available to investors at brokerage firms. Since once-hefty trade commissions have become dangerously anorexic, revenues are rejiggered into steady fees based on assets in the account and charged directly. This is a good turn of events. (More about this later.)

If computers are seizing the functions at the very core of the financial services industry, it is unequivocal that both computers and the Internet are inevitabilities. Surely, nestled in their future are further developments and improvements just waiting to rupture the status quo and dramatically increase efficiency for investors.

This, joined with the fact that the ring of financial advisors around the town square has vanished for good, means that investors now have an efficient, inexpensive straight shot at trading.

Money Is Blood

*If the retail brokerage industry were being created today
from the ground up, a majority of the Committee that
developed this report would not design a compensation
system based only on commissions paid for completed
transactions. The prevailing commission-based
compensation system inevitably leads to conflicts of interest
among the parties involved.*

> The Committee on Compensation
> Practices, created in 1995 by the
> SEC, Executive Summary, page 3.

Coursing through the lives of every business and human entity
in the world is money. Unlike blood, money is not self-
generating. It comes and it goes. Therefore, every entity,
whether solitary or conglomerate, must continually generate
revenue, forever move money from some other account into
theirs. Without this revenue stream, the entity faces death.

This places money quite high on the priority list of all entities
on this planet. Even Mother Teresa had to stoop so low as to
raise funds for her marvelous work.

In the current world of financial services, three entities

embrace to exchange money for products and services: investors, financial advisors, and financial services companies. When investors agree that financial advisors add value to their futures, they turn over all or part of their assets to them. The assets are then sent to the financial services companies. This triggers the commencement of fees and charges. What products or services advisors and investors agree are best for investors will determine how the fees and charges are collected and how much is collected. Once the siphoning begins, the financial services companies route a portion of the fees and charges back to financial advisors. The cycle is then complete.

In the financial services world, there are hundreds of fees and charges that run the gamut of products and services. This chapter examines the most common and most prominent of these that are encountered by the average investor, and therefore are the most frequent means of compensation for financial advisors.

Investors

To investors, the entire field of financial services revenue flow is nebulous. Indeed, it can often be nebulous to us as financial advisors. What investors do know is that our pay ultimately springs from their pockets. From their perspective, how that happens is as important as how much is taken. There are four factors regarding payment of fees and charges that are significant:

- Whether the compensation is direct or indirect
- Whether it is one-time and up-front or a continuous stream
- Whether it traps investors or preserves their freedom
- Whether it is associated with a service or a product

Investors probably don't analytically ponder these issues. More likely, investors mull the factors randomly until one or two are resolved and the others are accepted or ignored.

In the Light or in the Dark

Fees and charges are direct when investors immediately witness the movement of money from their wallets or accounts to the accounts of the financial services companies or the financial advisor. They are indirect when buried in the operations of the companies and in six-pound, thousand-page prospectuses printed in a six-point font. In reality, most investors are blind to the indirect charges, despite the fact that they are told (or should be told) about them.

Direct payments include:

- Ticket charges on securities trades
- Commissions on securities trades
- Front loads on Class A mutual fund shares
- Back loads on Class B mutual fund shares for early withdrawal
- Trust account fees
- Asset-based management fees
- Net-worth-based management fees
- Consulting fees
- Fee-only comprehensive financial planning
- Surrender charges on annuities for early termination
- Surrender charges on life insurance contracts for early termination

Indirect payments include:

- C-share 12b-1s
- A- and B-share 12b-1s
- Management and administrative fees within C-share mutual funds
- Management and administrative fees within A- and B-share mutual funds
- Mortality and expense charges in annuity contracts
- Mortality and expense charges in life insurance contracts
- Subaccount management fees in annuity contracts
- Subaccount management fees in life insurance contracts
- Extra expense on Class B mutual fund shares until conversion

The Stones and the Streams

Some fees and charges are stones (one time only and blunt), while others are streams (continuous). The stones are events investors acknowledge and to which they agree. But, like having a rock dropped on a bare foot, they are the most painful and sometimes the hardest for consumers to accept. A few fee streams are indirect, and—though investors are informed of their existence, both verbally and as referenced in those monstrous prospectuses—they hastily fall out of sight and out of mind.

The direct streams are those that investors pay constantly. In comparable investment cases, these direct fee streams are quantitatively smaller than the direct stones. After all, they must be smaller, for they are perpetual until the contract ends or the financial advisor is relieved of duty.

The stones include:

- Ticket charges on securities trades (direct)
- Commissions on securities trades (direct)
- Front loads on Class A mutual fund shares (direct)
- Back loads on Class B mutual fund shares for early withdrawal (direct)
- Consulting fees (direct)
- Fee-only comprehensive financial planning (direct)
- Surrender charges on annuities for early termination (direct)
- Surrender charges on life insurance contracts for early termination (direct)

The streams include:

- Mortality and expense charges in annuity contracts (indirect)
- Mortality and expense charges in life insurance contracts (indirect)
- Subaccount management fees in annuity contracts (indirect)
- Subaccount management fees in life insurance contracts (indirect)

- Extra expense on Class B mutual fund shares until conversion (indirect)
- Trust account fees (direct)
- Asset-based management fees (direct)
- Net-worth-based management fees (direct)
- C-share 12b-1s (indirect)
- A- and B-share 12b-1s (indirect)
- Management and administrative fees within C-share mutual funds (indirect)
- Management and administrative fees within A- and B-share mutual funds (indirect)

The Free and the Trapped

"Free" and "trapped" represent the degree of independence investors have after engaging advisors in relationships and paying initial charges. When free, investors can disengage from the relationship without incurring further costs. When trapped, investors cannot depart, at least for some protracted amount of time.

Free relationships involve:

- Ticket charges on securities trades (direct, stone)
- Commissions on securities trades (direct, stone)
- Consulting fees (direct, stream)
- Trust account fees (direct, stream)
- Asset-based management fees (direct, stream)
- Net-worth-based management fees (direct, stream)
- C-share 12b-1s (indirect, stream)
- Fee-only comprehensive financial planning (direct, stone)
- Management and administrative fees within C-share mutual funds (indirect, stream)

Trapped relationships involve:

- Management and administrative fees within A- and B-share mutual funds (indirect, stream)
- Surrender charges on annuities for early termination (direct, stream)
- Surrender charges on life insurance contracts for early termination (direct, stone)
- Front loads on Class A mutual fund shares (direct, stone)
- Back loads on Class B mutual fund shares for early withdrawal (direct, stone)
- Mortality and expense charges in annuity contracts (indirect, stream)
- Mortality and expense charges in life insurance contracts (indirect, stream)
- Subaccount management fees in annuity contracts (indirect, stream)
- Subaccount management fees in life insurance contracts (indirect, stream)
- Extra expense on Class B mutual fund shares until conversion (indirect, stream)
- A- and B-share 12b-1s (indirect, stream)

The Holy Grail and the Toys

Each fee or charge can be linked with its corresponding means of delivery—product or service. The Baby Boomers' Holy Grail is premier service. It annoys them when a product is presented as a service. Each of these fees and charges is the result of service (the Holy Grail) or a product (a toy).

The Holy Grails include:

- Consulting fees (direct, stream, free)
- Trust account fees (direct, stream, free)
- Asset-based management fees (direct, stream, free)
- Net-worth-based management fees (direct, stream, free)
- Fee-only comprehensive financial planning (direct, stone, free)

- Management and administrative fees within C-share mutual funds (indirect, stream, free)

- C-share 12b-1s (indirect, stream, free)

  The toys include:

- A- and B-share 12b-1s (indirect, stream, trapped)

- Ticket charges on securities trades (direct, stone, free)

- Commissions on securities trades (direct, stone, free)

- Surrender charges on annuities for early termination (direct, stream, trapped)

- Surrender charges on life insurance contracts for early termination (direct, stone, trapped)

- Front loads on Class A mutual fund shares (direct, stone, trapped)

- Back loads on Class B mutual fund shares for early withdrawal (direct, stone, trapped)

- Management and administrative fees within A- and B-share mutual funds (indirect, stream, trapped)

- Mortality and expense charges in annuity contracts (indirect, stream, trapped)

- Mortality and expense charges in life insurance contracts (indirect, stream, trapped)

- Subaccount management fees in annuity contracts (indirect, stream, trapped)

- Subaccount management fees in life insurance contracts (indirect, stream, trapped)

- Extra expense on Class B mutual fund shares until conversion (indirect, stream, trapped)

Summary

Given Baby Boomers' craving for superior service and our national insistence on independence, it is assumed that, of the four conditions, service and freedom are the most cherished. Take a look at Table 4.1. Only 35% of all fees and charges are

$$\textbf{TABLE 4.1}\ \text{Holy Grail Compensation Emotions}$$

Product or Service	Key	Product / Service	Free / Trapped	Direct / Indirect	Once / Continuous
Fee-Based Asset or Net Worth Management	1	Service	Free	Direct	Continuous
Fee-Only Comprehensive Financial Planning	5	Service	Free	Direct	Once
Trust Fees	8	Service	Free	Direct	Continuous
Mutual Funds (C shares)	2	Service	Free	Indirect	Continuous
Individual Securities	4	Product	Free	Direct	Once
Mutual Funds (A & B shares)	3	Product	Trapped	Indirect	Continuous
Life Insurance	6	Product	Trapped	Indirect	Continuous
Annuities	7	Product	Trapped	Indirect	Continuous

attached to a service, and only 45% leave investors with their freedom. The complete table can be found in Appendix B.

It's no coincidence that the same seven fees or charges attached to service also offer freedom. These are:

- Asset-based management fees

- Net-worth-based management fees

- Consulting fees

- Fee-only comprehensive planning

- Trust account fees

- C-share 12b-1s

- Management and administrative fees within C shares

The third most important element is whether a fee or charge is direct or indirect. Investors who are charged fees directly identify them as such each time they occur. Nothing can be disguised or remain undisclosed about the fact that the fees exist and are being removed from the client's account. If the Holy Grail is the added value, Boomers readily accept the direct method.

Though C shares admirably pass through the first two filters, they can't slip through the direct payment filter and are eliminated from the preceding list. Financial services companies require that, with fee-based work, clients be mailed a letter every time (usually quarterly) their accounts are assessed a fee. This way clients are reminded regularly that a fee is charged directly. If the financial services industry would do the same for C shares, perhaps boldly indicating on monthly statements adjacent to each fund that approximately $XXX is being charged (forfeited) based on the fund's balance, then C shares would fly through the direct payment filter along with the rest. Yet they don't. And as we shall see in Chapter 7, Class C shares are excessively costly to clients and grossly lucrative to financial advisors.

Compressing the remaining fees and charges into specific delivery-of-service tasks helps further clarify their application:

- Fee-based asset or net worth management

- Trust account fees

- Fee-only comprehensive financial planning

In each of these instances, investors' payments for services rendered are direct and up front every time they occur, and they leave clients their freedom. Thus, if investors catch the slightest notion that the quality of attention is deteriorating, they can walk away without incurring further cost.

At the other end of the spectrum, mutual funds (A and B shares), life insurance, and annuities all share the same attributes. They are products with indirect charges that entrap investors for various time periods. Yet, remarkably, these products, relative to the three services that made it through the first screens, dominate the market, along with trading individual securities.

There's a reason for this: financial advisors and their compensation.

Financial Advisors

Money doesn't motivate. Rather, the absence of money in the face of a desire to live better motivates. If we're pleased with eating bonbons and watching television all day, then all we need is enough money to buy the bonbons and pay for the TV. If, however, we want annual international vacations, a Mercedes-Benz or two, a few golf trips a year, Dartmouth for the kids, and a significant nest egg, we'll need a bit more money than the bonbon eater. If we don't currently possess the money for these stark necessities, we become motivated. We will rely on our talents to earn the money—hopefully, within the law.

A Peculiar Breed

Money pays the bills (present and future); it squares our relationship with the world of commerce, whether that relationship is meager or extravagant. If we fail to settle up, the law comes after us and our reputations are soiled.

Most of the employed world is on a fixed-compensation program that increases only at the hands of a benevolent supervisor or boss. The planet's sales force, however, gets paid only when an incident occurs—the engagement of a client or customer in the transaction of a product or service.

The traditional dread on the sales front is that cash flow is unpredictable. This fluctuation normally depends on how many new engagements occur. A car salesperson knows roughly how much income is generated from selling one car. So it can be determined that getting 50 vehicles out the door equals, say, $50,000 of income. The person who sells private jets knows that one unit produces, say, $25,000 of commission. Selling four means living twice as well as the car salesperson.

But financial advisors are a special breed. We offer such an array of products that it contorts our compensation flow, rendering useless the simple per-unit math. We engage in cases that throw off clumps of income, sometimes massive, sometimes miniature. For example, a financial advisor wraps up a case involving a $500,000 annuity, which generates $32,500 of income—enough to buy one of those James Bond–style BMW roadsters. The next day a client's son comes into the office and starts a $2,000 IRA using B shares. This might pay for a pretty good cigar and the next golf game (including cart). A week later, this advisor buys 2,500 shares of IBM for a client—enough to pay for a short cruise in the Caribbean.

If we happen to sell ten of those annuities in a year, we're fairly rich. On the other hand, if all we sell are ten of the little start-up IRAs, we'll be scrounging for things much more fundamental than cigars and golf games. For many in our profession, this potentially sporadic income is a serious danger. Optimism, though the essential ingredient of progress, can distort reality and result in excessive behavior. If we think we're going to sell ten $500,000 annuities and no puny IRAs, our lifestyle tends be more lavish. But when we, in fact, sell only three $150,000 annuities, we become desperate. We even start scrambling to find a few of those start-up IRAs. Anything would help because the necessity of squaring our accounts with the world of extravagant commerce is just over our left shoulder and closing in rapidly. After all, the credit card statement came in the mail yesterday.

Managing the uncertainty requires acute measures of discipline. To some personalities (conservative, cautious, greedy) such control is second nature. For others, in varying degrees, judicious monetary behavior can be tedious and frustrating. The $32,500 commission check that lands on the financial advisor's desk is matched by gleeful and irresponsible thoughts of quickly purchasing something of equal value. Generating the willpower to suppress these urges and behave responsibly is the difficulty of this profession.

The Allure of Immediate Pleasure

Some of us are stockbrokers. Some toil for life insurance companies. Others work for banks. And a few of us brave independence, operating outside the corporate umbrella.

But we all work the same trenches. It is our duty to persuade investors to part with their money by involving themselves in various investment vehicles for various reasons. We dance with them around the benefits they will receive for all the fees and charges we want to transfer from their accounts to our companies' accounts and eventually back to us.

Once investors place their trust in us, we send their assets to our financial services companies with the paperwork to set in place specific investment programs. Fees and charges are activated. We receive some percentage of this infusion. For those who are employees of a financial services company, this percentage can range from 40% to 80%. For those who are independent, the range is from 85% to 100%. And in most cases, different investment products and services carry different payouts. Where each of us falls within these spreads depends upon the volume of new investor money we drain off throughout the year and to what degree we are independent.

Of the different common fees and charges we discussed previously to which investors are exposed, only 11 result in money being funneled back to us. The other 9 are charges leveled by financial services companies, all of which stay in-house and help support their bottom lines. The money that returns to us comes from:

- Consulting fees
- Trust account fees
- Asset-based management fees
- Net-worth-based management fees
- Comprehensive financial plan fees
- B-share mutual funds commission

- A-share mutual funds commission
- C-share mutual funds commission
- Securities trades commission
- Annuities commission
- Life insurance commission

Examining the compensation results of a $1 million case using these 11 methods demonstrates a variety of results. First, here are the ground rules:

1. There is an 85% brokerage payout on mutual fund, annuity, and life insurance business.

2. There is a 70% brokerage payout on individual securities business.

3. There is a 100% brokerage payout on managed asset fees.

4. There is a $150 per hour consulting fee.

5. The investor's net worth is $3 million.

6. A-share mutual fund breakpoints are 3.625% at $100,000; 2.625% at $250,000; 2.125% at $500,000; 0% at $1 million.

7. There is a 4.75% B-share payout.

8. There is a 0.75% mutual fund family haircut.

9. There is an annuity product payout of 6.5%.

10. The life insurance product payout is 100% of target and 0.5% trails.

Consulting

The client wants the consultant to research and recommend a diversified portfolio relative to the client's risk. The client will then take up the positions in the portfolio on the Internet.

Type: Service

Time: 10 hours

Direct fee: $1,500

Continuous fees: 0

Freedom: 100%

Trust Account

The client decides on a trust account at a bank, where the money will be managed with no commissions.

Type: Service

Direct fee: 0

Continuous fee: 1% annually on asset balance

Freedom: 100%

Asset-Based Management

The client works with a personal asset manager who uses only individual securities in accounts that charge no commission.

Type: Service

Direct fee: 0

Continuous fee: 1% annually on asset balance

Freedom: 100%

Net-Worth-Based Management

The client works with a personal net worth manager who uses only individual securities in accounts that charge no commission.

Type: Service

Direct fee: 0

Continuous fee: 0.5% annually on net worth

Freedom: 100%

Comprehensive Financial Plan

The client wants a very thorough picture of his or her financial present and future, including a portfolio recommendation relative to risk tolerance.

Type: Service

Time: 25 hours

Direct fee: $3,750

Continuous fee: 0

Freedom: 100%

C-Share Mutual Funds

The client feels comfortable with the diversification mutual funds offer and works with a financial advisor to create a portfolio of five C-share funds.

Type: Service

Direct fee: 0

Continuous fee: 1% annually (12b-1s)

Freedom: 100% (usually after the first year)

B-Share Mutual Funds

The client absolutely refuses to pay front loads, so the advisor recommends five B-share funds.

Type: Product

Direct commission: $34,000

Continuous fee: 0.2125% annually (12b-1s)

Trapped: 7 years, on average

A-Share Mutual Funds

The client feels uneasy about front loads, but is convinced that, of all share types, A shares produce the highest end balance, and invests in five funds.

Type: Product

Direct commission: $30,812.50

Continuous fee: 0.2125% annually (12b-1s)

Trapped: 7 years, on average

Commission on Securities Trades

The client doesn't like mutual funds and, through a stockbroker, buys 10 stocks in the new portfolio.

Type: Product

Direct commission: $7,500

Continuous fee: 0

Freedom: 100%

Annuity Contract

The client wants to pay no taxes on the investments and doesn't need the money until after retirement.

Type: Product

Direct commission: $55,250

Continuous fee: 0

Trapped: Up to 9 years

Life Insurance

The client will never need the $1 million and wants tax deferral, but doesn't want heirs to be stabbed with a massive tax bill when they inherit the money. A $5,750,000 single premium variable universal life insurance policy is purchased and funded immediately with the $1 million, making it a modified endowment contract.

Type: Product

Direct commission: $55,000

Continuous fee: 0

Trapped: At least 12 years

Given the powerful drug of instantaneous gratification, it's no coincidence that Class A and B mutual funds, annuities, stock trades, and life insurance are the four ruling products on the market. We push them and we push them hard. Refer to Table 4.2.

The advisor providing the annuity made over $55,000, more than 36 times the income of the consultant who merely recommended a portfolio and roughly 5 times the income of those who managed the assets for a fee. Compared to relationships built with these products as a foundation, those assembled on a service footing throw off minuscule numbers.

Remember our parents' instructions the few times we caught one of them in a moment of hypocrisy? "Don't do as I do, do as I say." By succumbing to the force of up-front, lump-sum compensation, we are not practicing what we preach to our clients: Think and plan long term. Take a close look at Table 4.3.

Financial advisors do these quantitative studies for a living so

TABLE 4.2 Fee or Commission

Fee or Commission	Direct Compensation	Continuous Compensation	Product / Service
Annuity Commission	$55,250	$0	Product
Life Insurance Commission	$55,000	$400	Product
B-Share Commission	$34,000	$1,250	Product
A-Share Commission	$25,500	$1,250	Product
Commission on Securities Trades	$7,500	$0	Product
Comprehensive Financial Plan Fee	$3,750	$0	Service
Consulting Fee	$1,500	$0	Service
Net-Worth-Based Management Fee	$0	$15,000	Service
Asset-Based Management Fee	$0	$10,000	Service
C-Share Fee	$0	$10,000	Service
Trust Account Fee	$0	$10,000	Service

this little table is not hard to figure out. It compares the annual balances of the annuity salesperson's chunk of money, fully invested and untouched and growing at 12%, with the annual balances of the asset manager as the client continually adds yearly fees, which also grow at 12%. Because the analysis is of the raw power of compensation methods, taxes weren't factored in. Breakeven is somewhere in the first quarter of the seventh year. And after 10 years, the asset manager has a 64% greater balance.

So if we're paid and regulated to do all that is in the best interest of investors, and long-term performance and planning are among them, why do the vast majority of us do just the opposite with our personal lives?

TABLE 4.3 Annuity Salesperson versus Asset Manager

Yr	Beginning	Growth	Ending	Beginning	Annual Additions	Growth	Ending
1	$55,250	$6,630	$61,880	$10,000	$0	$1,200	$11,200
2	$61,880	$7,426	$69,306	$11,200	$11,200	$1,344	$23,744
3	$69,306	$8,317	$77,622	$23,744	$12,544	$2,849	$39,137
4	$77,622	$9,315	$86,937	$39,137	$14,049	$4,696	$57,883
5	$86,937	$10,432	$97,369	$57,883	$15,735	$6,946	$80,564
6	$97,369	$11,684	$109,054	$80,564	$17,623	$9,668	$107,855
7	$109,054	$13,086	$122,140	$107,855	$19,738	$12,943	$140,536
8	$122,140	$14,657	$136,797	$140,536	$22,107	$16,864	$179,507
9	$136,797	$16,416	$153,213	$179,507	$24,760	$21,541	$225,808
10	$153,213	$18,386	$171,598	$225,808	$27,731	$27,097	$280,636
11	$171,598	$20,592	$192,190	$280,636	$31,058	$33,676	$345,370
12	$192,190	$23,063	$215,253	$345,370	$34,785	$41,444	$421,600
13	$215,253	$25,830	$241,083	$421,600	$38,960	$50,592	$511,152
14	$241,083	$28,930	$270,013	$511,152	$43,635	$61,338	$616,125
15	$270,013	$32,402	$302,415	$616,125	$48,871	$73,935	$738,931

Moreover, the practice of receiving pay up front forces us to continually seek new investors in order to grow. It is five times more costly and time consuming to add new investors than it is to keep the ones we have. Spending this disproportionate amount of resources on seeking fresh compensation must deteriorate the quality of service delivered to existing clients.

At some point, it becomes mathematically impossible to deliver flawless service. If we spend five years hoarding 100 clients a year, we have 500 clients, all of whom were promised during initial meetings that our service was the finest in the land. So if we spend 80% of our time in the sixth year rounding up another 100 new clients and 20% on the existing 500, we will spend a whopping 48 minutes a year on each one.

Finally, direct fee payment by investors drastically reduces, if not outright eliminates, the possibility of unethical behavior by financial advisors. In a lump-sum commission case, the temptation to somehow forget to mention certain contractual charges is great when the compensation is $55,250 and the charges are buried deep inside prospectuses. When the only payment is direct, it is on the table for all to see and choose to agree or disagree. Direct payment by investors would be financially healthy for financial services companies as well, because they could purge 75% of their compliance staff.

Motivations and Their Collective Danger: Sharing the Blame

In the financial services industry there are, in addition to raw money, two other types of motivation: candy and mental fizz.

Candy refers to luxurious items or events orchestrated for our pleasure for which we do not pay. Such items include lavish annual trips for those of us who have accomplished illustrious levels of investor siphoning. They are the black-tie dinners, the magnificent golf outings, the TVs and DVDS for winning contests. They are the rent-free corner offices with heavy, polished mahogany furniture. They are the administrative assistants hired to respond exclusively to our personal beck and call. These tangible rewards drive us because it is never a good practice to refuse something free and plush.

These pieces of candy are dangled in front of us by the financial services companies we represent. They are used specifically to boost the distribution of their products. Given this goal, it is no wonder that winning is based not on service or quality of advice but on volume: Get as many new clients as we can within a given time period and we are rewarded with some candy.

Even vendors—specifically, mutual fund families—recognize the payback of the sweet stuff. They are often the financial pockets for the golf outings. The fund families disguise them with the noble phrase "due diligence." These events, in fact, consist of a couple of generic speeches about the market and the glories of the family's own funds and then, if you're in New York, you're off to a dinner gala and a Broadway show, and if you're on the West Coast, you're treated to a vast luncheon buffet just before tee time.

Here's what due diligence really is: the meticulous and thorough gathering of information on an explicit issue in order to make a sound personal decision or deliver unbiased advice to a third party. The immediacy and pervasiveness of the Internet, e-mail, faxes, overnight mail, and the telephone make the "due diligence trip" what it really is: a piece of candy.

All financial services companies need the metaphorical infusion of millions of gallons of blood to survive. They know that the greater the volume of new customers, the greater the replenishment, so they motivate their financial advisors by offering them fine sweets. But strangely enough, this practice is not considered a reward for giving sound advice or impeccable service.

How would we feel if we discovered that our doctors won free trips based on the number of prescriptions they wrote for us? Or if our CPAs won trips based on the number of tax forms they completed? Or if attorneys were rewarded for the number of hours they billed us? The candy keeps financial service advisors in the substratum of professionalism.

Mental fizz includes the "head" fuels: ego, humiliation, victory, intimidation, competition, fear of failure. Each of these resides to some degree within us all. And each is used in some fashion to make the candy programs work at heightened effectiveness.

For example, ongoing contest standings are often posted on bulletin boards over the copying machines. This identifies, to everyone in the office, who sits on the golden throne and who sits on the porcelain one. The obvious intent is to heap enough humiliation into the souls of the degraded people at the bottom of the list so they respond by clawing their way upward.

Or how about the black-tie dinners? The top performers are called up on stage, introduced with accolades, handed plaques, and then receive lukewarm applause from all those who did not make the stage. This inflates the egos that produced the most signatures on the bottom line. Advisors aren't being applauded for delivering excellent advice and service; they're there because of their volume production.

A compensation structure based on persuasion and volume leaves the door wide open for immoral and illegal behavior. Incremental increases in compensation based on the number of additional persons we have convinced to do something present openings for lying or contorting the truth until it's something else. Under these circumstances, when a financial advisor meets with a prospect, he or she might be thinking . . .

What can be hyped about a particular Internet stock to win the current ticket contest?

What charts can be used in a demonstration to make this sale that will secure the free trip?

What rates of return can be put in a letter to avoid being evicted from the corner office?

What tricks can this life insurance policy be made to pull off in order to secure the golf junket?

What charge on this annuity won't be mentioned in order to climb to the next payout level?

Combine this environment with consumers' historically limited investment knowledge (although this is changing rapidly) and the opportunities to deviate from the truth increase significantly. Witness the number of criminal actions exposed in recent years, more from the life insurance arm of the financial profession than from banks or brokerages. The individuals and supervisors responsible for these indiscretions are certainly waywards at best, culprits at worst.

But the financial services companies themselves also share a healthy portion of blame and will continue to do so for any future violations. It is insupportable to employ a compensation system of commissions derived from indirect charges and fees to investors and then enhance it with contests, awards, and free trips based on volume production. Such a structure lays the groundwork for misbehavior and is most assuredly the mother of compliance regulation. It smacks of a midcentury technique used to reward nuts-and-bolts salespeople.

Our market is not hardware stores and this is the twenty-first century. Sooner rather than later, excellent service and sound advice will overcome volume production as the premier measure for rewarding quality work.

"But goodness, the current compensation system has been with us since the days beneath the buttonwood tree and must be regarded as hallowed tradition," you might say. Nonsense.

This system is calcified and will expire—although not at our hands. We don't have the power to make it do so. But we better have the fortitude to withstand the change.

Realignments

Corporate dictum will not bring balance to service and compensation. The market will.

Remember Bob North, the investor presenting the worst and most expensive performance? He sought professional advice the traditional way. If you recall, Lewis Tyler's commission on Bob's case was $45,000—this for working 4 current hours and probably 20 future hours. Is Lewis Tyler worth $1,875 per hour? Is anybody worth $1,875 per hour?

Even in the traditional setting that's disappearing behind us, this level of compensation merits raised eyebrows. In the Internet setting, Tyler is a product-pushing middleman with a bloated cost. He will be purged. Even if Tyler brazenly claims that his work for Bob was a service because he engaged in discussions and met with him over time, the cost of such service is stratospheric and will be savagely realigned by the market.

As financial advisors, we operate in an arena of grave importance to other folks: that of their financial well-being. All aspects of that arena should be designed and coordinated to eliminate any temptation to position our best interest before theirs, resulting in unethical decisions. Today, with the full consent and encouragement of the financial services industry, there are four misalignments that can foster inappropriate choices.

- The first is rooted in the industry's self-perception.

  Current alignment: *We are salespeople selling products.*

  Realignment: *We should be advisors providing the service of advice.*

- The second is a by-product of the first.

  Current alignment: *Compensation occurs once and up front.*

  Realignment: *All of it should be continuous.*

- The third is rooted in the industry's history.

  Current alignment: *The vast majority of our compensation is indirect.*

  Realignment: *All of it should be direct.*

- The fourth is rooted in superfluous motivational techniques.

  Current alignment: *All are based on volume production.*

  Realignment: *All should be based on quality service.*

These four problem areas are the reason the financial services industry has acquired one of the largest, most pervasive, and highest-paid police forces in commercial history: compliance departments. It is their sole job to oversee activity in this arena to ensure that the human instinct of placing oneself first is not nudged over the edge by the very misalignments the industry espouses.

Each of these misalignments by itself is a problem. Functioning in unison, these problems become a potent force tugging at the willpower of advisors to interpret all aspects of an investor's case in the investor's best interest.

> *Current combined alignment:*   We are salespeople moving from person to person, selling as many products as possible, getting paid in full immediately with money the client rarely sees or realizes, trying to amass hoards of bottom-line signatures in order to win free trips and prizes.

> *Realignment:*   We are advisors dispensing counsel to those who want and need it, getting paid continuously with money the clients always see and acknowledge, trying to win free trips by smothering them with tremendous service.

Let's visit two offices: the first an office today, the second an office of tomorrow. If you've been in the profession for more than a few years, you know the scene in today's office is not fiction. The scene in tomorrow's office is also nonfiction, but is currently a less frequent scenario.

Today's Office

A few minutes after clients leave Lenny's office, Carl comes in and plops down at the conference table. "Well, how did it go with Mrs. Ryan last night?" Lenny inquires as he shuffles papers from the table to his desk.

"I don't know for sure," Carl replies. "She's close. She's not too keen on the annuity, and that's the one I need to get me over. How did you do in here?"

"Done deal," Lenny announces. "I'm in. Going to Pebble Beach. Rolled his $350,000 401(k) into an annuity and they're going to TAMRA a $2 million second-to-die over five years. I'll make over $26,000 on the case, and it'll put me over in production."

"What is this, your fifth year?" Carl inquires.

"Yeah, I think. This year I made it earlier than any other year. It's only September," Lenny proclaims, pulling up a chair at the round table across from Carl. "Listen, did you push the tax advantages of the annuity with Ryan? It'll be a long, cold day in hell before we get to play together at Pebble Beach for free."

"Yeah, but she doesn't like the fact that it doesn't step up, and she keeps wondering about how 'her Robert' will survive after the taxes."

"I take it that's her son."

"Yeah."

"You said she was 60. That could be 25 years of tax savings. Tell her that could be big for him. If she puts it in mutual funds, the taxes she pays over the years could be more than what he loses after inheritance. It wouldn't be right playing the Beach without you. You're a crack salesman. Kick it in gear."

"Don't worry, you won't tee off without me. I got a few young families I'm working on. They're split between using variable life or mutual funds for college. If I have to, I'll steer them toward the insurance. With home office's triple credit for insurance lives in the last quarter, that'll get me 18 lives. I'll make it with that. Though it'll be a hell of a lot more work. All those aps and getting medicals and underwriting . . ."

Tomorrow's Office

A few minutes after clients leave Lenny's office, Carl comes in and plops down at the conference table. "Well, how did it go with Mrs. Ryan last night?" Lenny inquires as he shuffles papers from the table to his desk.

"Fine. It bothers her that the annuity doesn't step up when she dies. She keeps wondering how 'her Robert' will survive after the taxes. On the other hand, the no-load account doesn't have the guaranteed annual floor like the annuity. I ran the numbers, and since it's a large enough amount, we put 40% in the annuity and 60% in the managed account," Carl explains. "How did you do in here?"

"Done deal," Lenny announces. "They loved the plan I did for them. We rolled his 401(k) into a managed account and started a no-commission second-to-die. What did Mrs. Ryan say about the fees?"

"Oh, those don't bother her," Carl says. "She knows there's 1% every year on the no-load managed account. I made sure she knew about the internal fees in the annuity and that I get paid 1% annually on it, too." He stands and stretches. "She knows she can walk away from either one whenever she wants," he says and starts for the door. "Let's go to lunch."

Conclusions

In a nutshell, here's what Baby Boomers are just now starting to demand. Their pressure will become increasingly unbearable.

Stop	*Start*
Selling them products	Giving them advice
Getting paid large up-front chunks	Getting paid small steady pieces
Charging them covertly	Charging them overtly
Basing awards on volume	Basing awards on serving them

There are three reasons why traditionalists are howling their disapproval at these proclamations:

1. Less compensation

2. Harder work and more of it

3. Fewer tee times

We think we'll make less money, work harder, and have less time if we accommodate the Boomers' demands. These are all myths. We'll make more money, work the same amount of time or less, and have more tee times that are more fun. (We'll prove it in Chapter 11, "Mythologies.")

CHAPTER

6

Dinosaurs and Milkmen

We can surmise that what killed the dinosaurs was a dim and cruddy atmosphere after a visit from a comet. We're pretty sure that what killed the blacksmith was the very nerve of Henry Ford. We're almost positive that what killed the milkman was pasteurization.

We will be absolutely certain that what kills the salesperson will be the Internet. The Internet has *become* the salesperson.

A quick look at the history of salespeople tells us that their day is just about up. The salesperson's job was to physically take the product to potential consumers, show how it worked and how it would increase their standards of living, and then convince them to purchase. When consumers exchanged cash for product, the salesperson received a percentage of the cash, referred to as *commission* (or "commish" in seamier offices). The salesperson was the sole conduit between the manufacturer and the consumer.

Gradually, however, the process of selling products moved closer to consumers until today every conceivable item potentially sits in their living rooms. It's doubtful that they'll allow salespeople to sleep on the couch in order to jump up and intercept them before they get to their computers to place an order.

Out of Sight, but in Mind

When roads were dirt, manufacturers could not easily see consumers in person. But they could envision them. They knew millions were out there, distributed across the land. They had no way to get their products and the subsequent benefits of those products to them without employing traveling salespeople. But relinquishing 20% to 30% of the profits, in addition to expense reimbursement, was an annoying drain on the bottom line.

Meeting Halfway

Soon roads were paved and travel was pervasive. Population centers multiplied and became denser. Sellers met buyers halfway, as retail shops flourished, large and small. The old response to the question of what it takes to be successful in retail (location, location, location) was true. As well, the postal system brought catalogs and their graphic product depictions to consumers. Getting the wares closer to buyers without the high cost of a sales staff saved manufacturers money, much of which they passed on to the consumer.

Eyeball to Eyeball

The only roads that matter now are the ones in cyberspace. And there's no more meeting halfway. Sellers have set up permanent camp in our living rooms (talk about location!), shooting past the sales staff, who, like those who can't swim, flail about, trying to get involved in the transaction. In deference to their long-term and illustrious place in the history of commerce, the Internet will allow salespeople to exist for an additional 15 to 20 minutes. Then it's the ax. After all, efficiencies are efficiencies.

While it could be argued that the element of persuasion is alive and well in the sales process, you would be shorting the intellect of the American consumer—specifically, that of the Baby Boomer. Inducement has always been nothing more than controlled, filtered information, the most cherished tool of the salesperson. With knowledge going public over the Internet and the education levels of consumers rising, persuasion plays less of a role in the sales process.

The financial services profession isn't spared this evolution. But with proper preparation, the salesperson can be transformed into an integral member of a triangular team formation that is paid well to serve clients. This triumvirate of varying and complementary skills will operate like a machine, making each person's job easier and delivering the Holy Grail to Boomer clients in a way not possible before.

CHAPTER

7

Triangles

ach of us has a few dominant strengths and a few dominant
weaknesses, as well as a few qualities at which we shrug our
shoulders. Those of us who are bubbly around complete
strangers are able to pied-piper them through the door. At the
other end of the spectrum, there are those of us who are more
analytical and would prefer to be left in isolation, preferably with
a computer. And there are a few who demonstrate healthy doses
of each personality type and are susceptible to mood swings or
burrowing inescapably into one rut or the other.

The gregarious one who promised her new clients a first-rate
comprehensive plan and then a thoroughly diverse portfolio is
pulling her hair out trying to keep her word by swimming
through all those nasty numbers, those brokerage statements,
those trust documents, those life insurance policies. Moreover,
satisfying the asset allocation model is so tiring, and she has yet
to figure out how she can watch the investments like a hawk as
she promised when she really wants to go out and about and be
bubbly.

Meanwhile down the hall, the fellow who sports a facial suntan
from his computer monitor has added a whopping three clients
in the last 12 months. He's got one in the pipeline if he can ever
get himself to make the call. The ones he's already added were

substantial enough to supply a meager income. The thought of bothering people with a cold call and then trying to produce meaningless chitchat paralyzes him. He can just see those on the other end of the line rolling their eyes when he greets them with mock excitement: "Hi, Mrs. Wilson, this is John Doe from Dean, Dean, and Dean brokerage. How are you this evening?" It's so much easier to leave the office at 4:30 and go home, without being a nuisance to any other human being. The same feeling overcomes him when he entertains the idea of attending a social function where potential clients are all about him. He'd rather find something to analyze.

If these two diametrically opposed creatures joined forces, both could wallow blissfully in their strengths and succeed at retaining and servicing clients. The Bubbler, with her warmth and sincerity, could bring clients to the conference table, while the Analyzer, who just can't figure out how the Bubbler does it, could burrow into the clients' financial lives and their piles of documents, searching for the proper strategies to accomplish their goals. Together they would stand before the client as two diverse but equally qualified forces, creating a whole that is far more useful and thorough than each entity operating alone.

But such linkage is rare in the financial services profession. Why? Because we sell products, and we spend so much time calling, meeting, persuading, and wrenching ourselves through the parts we inherently despise that we loathe the idea of relinquishing 50% of the compensation. And, since we often grossly overvalue our own strengths, we conversely undervalue the counterpart's strengths, which encourages the lingering suspicion that our partner in the coalition isn't really worth 50%. Moreover, since the Bubbler seems to never be in the office and appears to be in perpetual bliss when she is, the Analyzer harbors the feeling that she isn't really working. And since the Analyzer never has to forfeit evenings and weekends to root out new clients and pacify the often erratic and curt sides of existing ones, the Bubbler wonders whether the Analyzer is shouldering enough of the burden.

However, once Boomers force us to migrate from product peddling to offering and maintaining excellent service, the single-person assault will fade. Suspicions discarded, unions of personalities will ultimately form in order to deliver the Holy Grail.

Internal Triangles

There are four distinct elements to the financial services process:

1. Retaining a client
2. Compiling a comprehensive financial plan
3. Creating an investment policy statement and monitoring it
4. Remaining by the client's side, becoming irreplaceable

Three separate advisors (Bubbler, Planner, and Investment Advisor), dispensing unique talents, can deliver the first three steps in the process, and together they maintain the fourth.

Gathering Clients

This is the skill that Bubblers bring to the table. This is what they love the most. Bringing clients to the initial interview (II) is their primary job. They instinctively scour the cold prospect market, targeting potential clients and cozying up to them. After a few contacts, their comfort levels buoyed, they invite clients to the initial interview.

Once the clients are at the conference table, all three members of the internal triangle (Bubbler, Planner, and Investment Advisor) conduct the initial interview. Their roles and how these roles complement each other are explained, in a concerted effort to provide unquestionable service. After the initial interview, the Bubbler is back out the door in pursuit of more bubble. Now part of the triangle, the Bubbler no longer has to grind through the process of gathering facts and agonize over all those details of a financial plan or an investment policy. And the Bubbler's dread is the other partners' delight. The Financial Planner and Investment Advisor are ecstatic that a client has been delivered to their door without their having to endure the pain of face-to-face contact with 20 strangers.

Writing the Comprehensive Plan

First up is the Planner, who can't wait to plunge into the fact-finding session and ferret out the details of the client's financial position. Where has the client been? Where is the client now? Where does the client want to be? The Planner records all important qualitative as well as quantitative information in this massive investigation. The Planner craves answers. Fact-finding process complete, the Planner sinks into the facts, devising the strategies that will take the clients where they want to go.

Meanwhile, at the very moment the Planner is doing what he or she does best, the Bubbler is yukking it up in the office of an executive vice president on the thirty-fifth floor, overlooking the magnificent city park.

Managing the Investments

When the blueprint financial plan for the client is complete, the Planner and the Investment Advisor meet to discuss what's needed to accomplish the goals, considering rates of return, risk tolerance, risk needed, time frame. Of the three points in the internal triangle, the Investment Advisor's part is the most routine. Driven less by the event of an incoming client and more by plodding methodology, the Investment Advisor is the primary caretaker of existing clients, managing their assets inside five portfolios: income, conservative, moderate, dynamic, and aggressive. We'll dissect these in Chapter 8. Most of the Investment Advisor's labor involves research, leading to the development of these portfolios. Yet a significant amount of ongoing time is devoted to maintaining them.

Meanwhile, as the Planner and Investment Advisor wind up their meeting, the Bubbler calls to make sure they're available for an initial interview with the high-profile executive she's been courting.

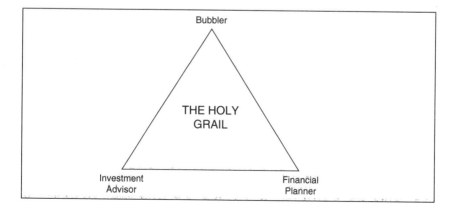

Delivering the Holy Grail

After the clients have moved through the triangle, they join all three advisors for an implementation meeting. The financial plan and investment policy are thoroughly reviewed and explained. At this moment, the pursuit of the Holy Grail is launched, consisting in unending coordination and teamwork among all three parties. With three qualified advisors tending to the financial affairs of their retirement, Boomer clients feel reassured.

From the perspective of financial advisors, this is the way it was versus the way it will be:

	Was	*Will be*
Compensation split	Mine, mine, all mine	Three-way
Client efficiency	Dragging in two a month	Adding six a month
Satisfaction	Fragmented and frustrated	Focused on strength only

The Dreaded Scenario

Springville school superintendent Chambers picks up on the rumors about Principal Ryan's storage room flings with Mrs. Kramer, so he has a surveillance camera installed. A year later, Robert Ryan is a moderately successful financial planner at Lewis Tyler's financial planning agency, affiliated with a national financial services company.

A particularly tough stretch of time plagues Robert. Weeks of fruitless cold-calling have numbed his soul with rejection until, from nowhere, a referral agrees to meet. He sets an appointment with her for early in the morning at a small café near her office. Five cups of coffee later and having finished reading *USA Today*, Robert finally realizes she is a no-show. Back at the office, he calls her and gets, "Oh, darn, I forgot." So they set another appointment. This time she is a mere 20 minutes late. Robert tries to chitchat as she eyes her watch. He explains how he does business. The first step is to write a financial plan to determine goals. If she likes what she sees, the next step is to implement the plan with various investment products she will buy from him.

She agrees to the first step, and they set a fact-finding date. Three days before the meeting, as a precaution, Robert calls her office to confirm. Her voice mail explains that she will be out of town on business for the next 10 days. The wind drains from a couple of Robert's sails. Two weeks later, he calls her. She apologizes sincerely, admitting it was very rude of her but she has been so busy. If they reschedule, however, it will have to be on a Saturday, preferably early morning, and she promises to be there.

She keeps her promise, and Robert is heartened. During the fact-finder she is friendly and proclaims that she and her husband (who isn't at the meeting) need guidance and a disciplined means of saving for their two children's college educations.

She leaves behind a pile of documents and explains that the next meeting will have to be either early in the morning of the upcoming Tuesday or some day six weeks later, when they get back from their trip to Europe. It is late October and Robert needs her case to win this year's trip to Palm Springs. Though pressed for time to complete the analysis, he agrees to meet with her Tuesday anyway.

All day Sunday, he shovels data into the computer. He despises this task, because, for some reason, all software seems to rebel against him. Normally, Robert uses the more comprehensive program, but because the schedule is tight, this time he uses the basic financial planning software. Besides, the tables and graphs are easier to use and he believes, since she is in marketing, that simplicity and clarity are of the utmost importance.

What annoys him further is that he can never seem to find or distinguish important details he jotted down during the fact-finding session, no matter how organized he tried to be. In addition, though Robert has a specific questionnaire to follow, he invariably forgets to ask a pertinent question or two. So on occasion he has to deduce the answers.

Then there are all those brokerage statements, life insurance policies, trust documents—they are scattered across his office floor (as usual). By late Sunday, after yawning his way through the trust

documents, the data starts to merge and meld. Exhausted and fragmented, Robert goes home.

By late Monday he is finished. The financial plan is bound in
emerald green and ready. Both the husband and wife need life
insurance. The husband has three separate brokerage IRAs rolled
over from previous employers' 401(k)s, totaling $725,000. They
have two joint brokerage accounts totaling $68,000. But his pri-
mary target is her $1,750,000 variable annuity, money she inherited
eight years ago from her father. She promised him she would lock
it up for her retirement, forget it, and go on with her life.

Robert has calculated his commissions:

$ 5,500	two variable life policies
1,800	joint brokerage account transfer (B shares)
17,400	his brokerage account IRA transfers (B shares)
96,250	her variable annuity (1035 exchange)
$120,950	Total commission

It took him two years to make that amount as principal of
Springville Elementary; now he's going to do it in two months. He
can barely contain the exhilaration as he reviews the financial plan
to make certain there are no mistakes. When he arrives at the
office Tuesday morning, he finds a voice-mail message from her.
His prospect tells him that her husband wants to wait until after
they have returned from Europe to meet, and they will call when
they get back to set another appointment. There goes Palm Springs.
This time, the wind drains from quite a few of his sails.

He parks the plan on the bookshelf and waits. When she has not
called by mid-December, Robert calls her. She doesn't want to
meet until the holidays are over, so they choose a date in early January. When they finally meet, she and her husband are pleasant and
attentive as they evaluate the financial plan, which demonstrates
the need for variable life insurance to manage risk as well as save
for college. Retirement, 15 years down the path, is well accounted
for, due primarily to her annuity's projected balance of slightly
over $14 million. Yet Robert expresses some reservations that the
subaccounts are not performing as well as they could, and he is con-
cerned about appropriate diversification.

This prompts the demonstration of a portfolio of subaccounts inside the annuity into which he is recommending they transfer. Large dollar signs fluttering around in his gut, Robert explains that after they move the proceeds from their current annuity into his, they can elevate their total return by 1.75% and increase the 15-year balance by $1 million and he thinks th—

They stop him cold. The annuity is part of the trust and can't be changed or moved.

Robert worries that the color draining from his face is too conspicuous. While attempting to manage that problem, he does not notice their visible annoyance that he did not read the trust documents. The integrity of the financial plan and remaining counsel are evaporating fast. Robert's sails are shredding and scattering across the deck.

Robert attempts to salvage the damaged presentation, but to no avail. Upon its conclusion, they politely request time for contemplation. They will call him if they have an interest in implementing any of his recommendations. His sails go down with the boat.

Robert slumps back to his office. Compensation? Mine, mine, all mine. All of *what?*

We Become the Prey

As financial services salespeople, our approach to the market is almost as exquisite as the charge of a rhinoceros. Signs abound as we enter the sales scene, moving immediately toward our prey, smile sparkling, suit buttoned properly, hand held out. Remember Bill Murray's life insurance buddy in the movie *Groundhog Day?* The quarry sees us coming and presses the "glazed-over" button in order to block out everything we say.

Our sales mentality transforms us into game hunters—of either lions or rabbits, depending upon the vigor and age of our practice. We are always stalking and we show it. Dangling on the ends of most of the products we push are big lumps of commission waiting to be plucked. But first we have to wrestle down someone's interest.

If we operate within an internally triangular configuration, we're no longer hawking products. No matter which point in the triangle happens onto the sales scene, each represents a process and the combination of three distinct talents working in unison. Instead of products, systems and procedures are emphasized. Because these are the foundations for the Holy Grail, Baby Boomers' interest will be sharp. They are far more likely to engage a sound methodical progression of services delivered by experts that extend through time than to buy a product from someone whose goal the very next moment is to find another signature in order to win a free "due diligence" trip.

Boomers will not only take notice, they will seek us out. We will become the prey. Client bases will expand by referral. Selectivity will be our privilege. Marketing expenses will drop to near zero. No more costly seminars, mass mailings, telemarketing.

The success of this process will especially hold true for those of us who acknowledge the rationale behind it and immediately redesign our practices or firms around the concept. The first few to the cherry tree will garner the ripest and most coveted pieces of fruit.

Triangles at Work

Bubblers now explain to the prospective Baby Boomer clients that they are but one member of a three-part team designed, constructed, and maintained for the exclusive purpose of taking care of their entire financial retirement trip. "No, I have nothing to sell you," they can say.

Having helped the Boomer clients recover their faculties after the shock of not being sold something, the Bubbler delivers them, all warm and fuzzy, to the initial interview. Making people feel warm and fuzzy is the Bubbler's penchant.

Initial Interview

All three members of the team are present at the initial interview. There are several purposes for the II:

1. To explain in detail how the team operates, the steps it follows, and the clients' role in them

2. To determine whether there is a good personality fit between the team and the clients

3. To determine whether goals are reasonable and can be accomplished within the framework of how the team manages clients

4. To gather pertinent asset information to decide if the clients' total position falls within the minimum parameters the team has set

5. To discuss a time frame for implementing the plan

Because selectivity flows in both directions under the triangular system, the II is concluded with both parties agreeing to consider for a few days whether a long-term relationship is in the best interests of all. If there are two yeses, the next step is the fact finder (FF).

Fact Finder

The Financial Planner is the only team member who attends this meeting. The name of the session precisely describes what it accomplishes. These meetings encompass the Planner's dream moments. When the FF is finished, the Planner has probed every corner of the clients' minds, moved emotions out of the way to get at the realities they hide and then moved them back into place to gauge the impact of the realities, shifted their minds and hearts forward and backward in time, discussed death. In short, the Planner has gathered all the information the Investment Advisor will need to determine investment policy statements.

At the conclusion of the FF, the Boomers are exhausted, but the Planner is revving and already mentally etching the basic blueprints, ready to sit down at the computer and start crunching numbers.

Plan/Investment Policy Integration

This is an internal activity in which the Financial Planner and Investment Advisor work together to fold the results of the financial plan into the investment policy so goals are accomplished at the appropriate risk tolerance level.

Presentation and Implementation

The culmination of all the work occurs at this meeting. The Bubbler is brought back for this meeting, but this is where the Planner and Investment Advisor present their portions, reviewing the detail with the Boomer clients. Applications are completed and the relationship commences. The team makes it clear to the Boomers that any member of the team can be contacted with questions or concerns.

Quarterly Reviews

Clients are received by the Bubbler and handed over to the Investment Advisor, who reviews the performance of the investment portfolio.

Annual Reviews

Again, the clients are received by the Bubbler, who is joined by the other two team members. The financial plan is examined for changes. If there are any, discussion surrounds the decision about whether the Investment Advisor should modify the investment policy statement to accomplish the revisions.

Structural Influences

Banks already use such triangles, although, in general, the financial planning point is the weakest and in most cases it is not even employed. Employees at the points in the triangle used by banks are paid a salary with a tiny bonus attached, which is a recipe for poor personal service. After all, if the bank loses a client, the wallet of each point employee isn't impacted.

Independent firms are better equipped to construct triangles. Because of the freedom inherent in such firms, members of these small companies have greater latitude to design internal arrangements. Since they're not entangled in corporate structures, they can launch a triangle strategy more quickly and efficiently. As well, because the payout to independents is significantly higher than that to "captive" employees, the portion doled out to each point person of the triangle is meatier, making it more worthwhile to engage in the three-way relationship. One-third of 90% (30%) is far more attractive than one-third of 50% (16.7%). This higher payout also increases the likelihood that all three points can operate using the fee-based assets under management model, which we'll review in detail in Chapter 8.

Because of the life insurance industry's history of face-to-face—even door-to-door—relationships, agencies are fairly well positioned to institute the triangle configuration. Normally, they employ numerous agents, which increases the likelihood that there will be plenty of Bubblers and Analyzers to fill the appropriate positions in the triangle. The only downside is the payout level at life insurance agencies, which creates the kind of compensation dilemma outlined previously. Minimal net payouts can go a long way toward straining the fabric of the triangle and could well cause it to tear apart, either by dispute or due to cash flow problems for any or all of the point employees.

The structure of brokerage houses is most restrictive to the functioning of triangles. Historically, brokers and clients consummated business over the telephone and more recently by e-mail, which constituted transactions, the sole retail monetary lubrication. Thus, even the thought of converting these fundamental procedures into something as elaborate as the triangle configuration would be enough to cause paralysis. Besides, brokers face the same problem of skimpy payout as do life insurance agents. Moreover, brokers are not known as sources for deep comprehensive plans, an integral part of the triangle strategy.

External Triangles

A few years ago, certified public accountants (CPAs) officially tapped into the colossal revenue stream of the financial services business. They allowed themselves to become registered representatives and collect compensation for financial services. It is likely that very soon, by conferring upon themselves the right to exercise fee reciprocation with other professionals, attorneys will also be doing the same. The issue is on the docket and will probably appear in the five large states (California, New York, Texas, Illinois, and Michigan) first, prior to filtering down to the smaller ones within a few years of passage. Large accounting firms are encouraging the move in order to staff themselves with attorneys.

Many of us already entrenched in the financial services profession resent the new "experts" entering our domain. The situation is competitive enough without having accountants and attorneys touting their expertise in financial planning and investment advice. In fact, it might not be as easy for them to benefit from their entry into our territory as they think.

A few of these pros will offer financial planning or attempt to sell life insurance, annuities, or mutual funds from their base practice, attaching them as potential profit centers. This seems logical because they already have a captive and fairly steady stream of existing clients, so cold-marketing specifically for financial services is unnecessary. But, perhaps rudely, they will discover what we already know. Without very careful preparation and presentation, a reputation can be soiled swiftly and often irreversibly. In addition, maintaining a complete understanding of the intricacies of all investment vehicles is a responsibility that involves ongoing study. A few incidents of shoddy preparation and ignorance of product will cause clients to call into question the whole practice. The pros who can't envision these potential problems, which are driven by greed, will attempt such practice on their own—for a while. After experiencing client flight a few times, they will seek out partnership with an existing investment advisor.

The vast majority of the lawyers and CPAs who choose to participate will anticipate the difficulties of going it alone and instead will search for partners and team up with current and established financial services organizations. These pros recognize that the option of learning the investment advisory profession to an expert level is not a thrilling one, especially when they must maintain their original practice in order to pay the bills. So farming out the tasks to experts and receiving a smaller percentage of the compensation is more appropriate than attempting it alone and losing the client's business completely. Having 50% of something is more enjoyable than having 100% of nothing.

The construction of triangular arrangements involving CPA firms and law firms should be greeted with enthusiasm by the financial services profession. External triangles succeed for the very same reasons that internal triangles succeed. Refining any process that more readily leads to clients is a priority. Prior to this arrangement, potential clients had to fend for themselves when dealing with CPA firms and law firms. External triangles diminish, if not eliminate, our reliance on those old, painful, often expensive, and always inefficient marketing techniques— cold-calling, direct mail, seminars, audio business cards, attending civic gatherings where herds of other salespeople are grazing, and the like.

Compensation flow becomes an issue, both between individual triangles and among members of the triangles. From the CPA and law firms' perspectives there are two ways to structure the compensation pathway from the financial services firm back to them:

1. All partners of the two adjacent firms register with the National Association of Securities Dealers (NASD) as reps of the financial services firm's broker. Then as each partner sends clients to the financial services firm for planning and investment advice, the sending partner shares the case compensation with the financial services firm at some predetermined split.

2. Only one partner of the other firms registers with the financial services firm's broker dealer as a rep. As partners send clients to the financial services firm, the lone registered partner receives all the shared compensation in his or her name, redirecting it to a revenue account. The firm then handles the internal redistribution of this account as it sees fit.

Similar arrangements are established in the other direction. When the financial services rep sends a client to the other firms, a split is agreed upon and applied. However, it must be recognized that per-case compensation of the two firms can be drastically different and splits should be arranged accordingly.

From a legal perspective, the first method is clean and would receive the NASD's nod. The second may not. Since these shared compensation methods in a highly regulated industry such as securities are relatively new, it may be wise to seek more definitive judgments from the NASD on any redeployment procedures by the initial receiving registered partner. Obviously all points of the triangle must disclose to the client the compensation arrangement among them.

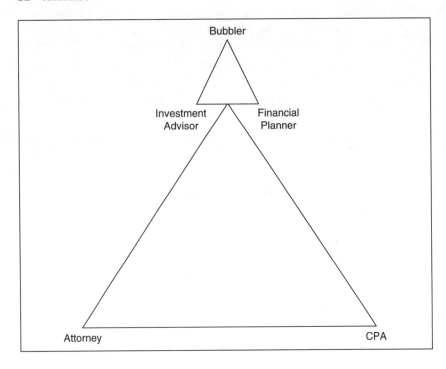

The channel for compensation circulation, from the financial services perspective, is quite different. There are numerous structural intricacies among different financial services organizations that make a clean and fluid sharing of compensation with outside sources difficult if not impossible, or at least simply not worth it.

First, banks already house the components of this triangle and don't need or seek outside points. That leaves brokerage houses, life insurance agencies, and independent financial planning firms as candidates for a triangular arrangement with the other two professional firms. Brokerage houses and life insurance agencies offer such low payouts, ranging from 40% to 60%, that asking their sales staffs to share half with any other source is like requesting that they take a sniff of spoiled food. The sales reps turn away in disgust.

The remaining entity, the independent firm, unassociated with a home office from whence policy is dictated, is the most likely candidate for linkage. Not only are payout levels, ranging from 80% to 95%, more palatable and remunerative for all sides, but the freedom of relationship design that the independents retain is more conducive to objectivity. Objectivity, of course, is the moral cornerstone of the other two professions and the main ingredient for success.

One very distinct design freedom is method of compensation. The atmosphere inside independent financial services firms is more flexible, including varied choices of fee-based work. This is vital for CPAs and law firms, as they are customarily paid a fee, straight up from the client. The inclination of CPAs and attorneys to work amid a product-pushing environment is not strong. And the thought of referring their clients to the persuasive grip of such a tourniquet-like arrangement causes them to cringe. Sure, there will be the few, including those attempting to incorporate financial services sales into their base practice, who will react warmly to the superficial luster of commission. But a prominent majority who are used to the inherent value of being paid for advice will demand fee-based routines.

Here's a common and simple review of the commission impact on all parties if a client purchased a $100,000 annuity. It quantifies the conclusion that working with independent financial services firms is more lucrative.

Brokerage House

Rep payout level	40%
Annuity payout @ 6%	$6,000
Net payout	$2,400
CPA firm @ 50%	$1,200
Financial advisor @ 50%	$1,200

Life Insurance Agency

Rep payout level	50%
Annuity payout @ 6%	$6,000
Net payout	$3,000
CPA firm @ 50%	$1,500
Financial advisor @ 50%	$1,500

Independent Firm

Partner's payout level	90%
Annuity payout @ 6%	$6,000
Net payout	$5,400

CPA firm @ 50%	$2,700
Financial advisor @ 50%	$2,700

Aside from compensation matters, the logistics of handling the clients are done in three basic ways:

- *Scheduled visitations.* A financial advisor takes up residence at the partnered firm on certain days of the week. Clients of the firms who are interested in financial advice visit on those days. From that point, all subsequent meetings can continue on premises or at the financial services offices. Because there is no client reciprocity required with this arrangement, financial services organizations can populate the CPA and law firm market with reps. This system is more useful for life insurance agencies that are always partially staffed with novices who would be more than happy to sit in a CPA firm or a law firm and wait for a jump start to their practices. They probably won't mind the paltry percentage left over after the associated firms get their portion. However, the quality of advice dispensed might be of concern to the adjacent firm.

- *Referral reciprocity.* A financial services organization arranges with a single CPA firm and a single law firm to move clients back and forth for each other's service. Since reciprocity is the key ingredient here, exclusivity is mandatory. In other words, there can be no other referral agreements with any other corresponding firms. It's a closed loop. This is more appropriate for the independent firm or for an advisor at a life insurance agency whose practice is flush with experience. (In Chapter 14 we'll review compensation-sharing methods inside independent firms, as well as buyout structures.)

- *Mergers.* An independent financial firm and one or both of the others merge their businesses and function under a single roof. This is obviously a much more elaborate and lasting union that requires a great amount of due diligence before engagement.

Law firms and CPA firms entertaining a relationship with a brokerage house should consider that brokerages do very little financial planning—their powers lie in stock analysis and trading. Life insurance agencies perform basic financial plans designed and delivered primarily to prove the need for life insurance and seek out excess cash flow or assets in order to make a sale. These plans are only remotely equivalent to the comprehensive planning performed by fee-only folks for thousands of dollars. There can't be too much value in the life insurance financial plan if it's free.

Thus, the CPA and law firms are far more likely to find comprehensive planning inside independent financial services firms.

Summary

The salesperson is dead.

Form triangles inside your operations. Doing so adds strength to combat inherent weaknesses and is essential for delivering the Holy Grail of service. Systematizing procedures within triangles ensures thorough, quality work for Baby Boomer clients. They comprehend and appreciate that a process is in place and is staffed to specifically tend to their retirement needs. Not all members of the financial services industry can employ triangles; some are better suited than others.

The march of other professionals invading our field is inevitable. We can either engage them in battle, to no one's benefit, or we can coordinate, reciprocate, share the wealth, and maintain the pursuit of the Holy Grail.

Forming triangles moves the relationship from being product based to being service based. It cultivates an atmosphere of ease during contact with Baby Boomers, who will surely respond more favorably to a string of coordinated services put into place on their behalf than to the purchase of a product. This relieves the stress, the clutter, and the cost involved in the process of adding clients.

Taking Matters into Your Own Hands

Thus far, by using the triangle strategy to replace product with service, we've added comfort to the process Baby Boomers will experience with the twenty-first-century financial advisor.

At some point in this process, Boomers relinquish their assets to us for management. This is the trigger, unless you are a fee-only financial advisor who is paid on the basis of net worth rather than assets under management (AUM). The process begins to unfold at this moment. All the elements of compensation, performance, and service start to interact. A relationship begins to brew.

The comprehensive financial plan is complete, bringing us to the impact task of investing the assets. How do we manage the money to realize the goals?

(Given the isolated usage of variable life insurance and variable annuities, they will not be covered here. Since these are vehicles designed to alleviate specific problems, the variable sub-accounts are merely policy enhancements inconsequential to active investment strategies. Most clients entering these contracts maintain buy-and-hold philosophies. As general financial instrument choices, they will be dealt with later.)

Picking Willy-Nilly

The three main investment categories are still out there, although they are plagued with issues and annoying nuances:

- Mutual funds
- Individual stocks and bonds
- To a less frequent degree, third-party money managers

Mutual Funds

Expense ratios are creeping up, the mutual fund industry's growth curve has settled into its plateau, and with the market's recent thin advance, managers' ability to spot the narrow band of leaders is questionable. Many funds are underperforming even their own histories. And the Internet makes it simple for investors to pick their own favorite positions.

Most of the time the means by which financial advisors choose funds are influenced by the old sales process itself. This time, we're the targets. Our selections are often made as a result of last week's visit by a wholesaler. "Yeah, but the guy did buy us lunch," we rationalize. Occasionally we behave like a consumer and choose last year's best performers as reported in that personal finance magazine we glanced through while waiting for a dentist appointment. We go back to the office and do the homework to make sure it's a load fund, that it has generated decent 5-year and 10-year returns, and that there are solid 12b-1s.

Sometimes we dutifully research all the available loaded mutual funds and settle on a preferred group or a few whole families, irrespective of what some other wholesaler mumbles while we eat his free pizza. The primary basis for our choices is rate of return over a period we believe is reasonable. But fund performance is not fund performance at all, it is management performance. Some advisors have been heard to pronounce, "I use ABC Growth Fund because it has averaged 18% per year for 10 years." When in fact what they should say is, "I use ABC Growth Fund because its manager, Sarah Jones, has produced 18% per year for 10 years" (if she's been at the steering wheel that long).

As devotees, many of us have no idea when a manager leaves

one of our favorites funds. So, unless our favorite fund choices move around with all the Sarah Joneses we selected long ago, our real faith ultimately lies blindly and only with a fund name and its prospectus objective.

That sounds eerily like something investors can do all by themselves.

Stocks and Bonds

Stocks and bonds trade on the Internet faster and more cheaply than through us. Transactions no longer require a series of cumbersome phone calls to order, execute, and finalize.

Stock selection isn't immune to the ravages of old sales methods, either. When brokerage houses suddenly find themselves awash in an inventory stock that's turning soft on the market, they encourage their brokers to move the stuff off the shelves and onto the backs of individual investors. It's a similar situation when the brokers bust out from their morning meetings and scramble to the phones and e-mail with hot tips from their analysts.

Eventually, as a result of these random suggestions, as well as unsolicited picks, a hodgepodge of positions gathers in most investors' portfolios. Throw in a few mutual funds and it gets even messier.

Third Parties

Third-party management merely adds another layer of fees and transforms us from advisors to foot soldiers for the outfits. Besides, we've already noted that the Internet is pursuing middlemen.

Conclusion

Fragmented investment choices made as a result of these various exposures are not good for clients. Such an approach hardly embodies the sage advice that Ray Kroc, the founder of McDonald's, left with us long ago: "When you have a problem, make it into a process and it will go away."

Heeding Ray Kroc

Process. Method. Practice. Routine.

There are a two technical practices we currently utilize to help make investment selections: suitability and asset allocation. Yet their contribution to methodical strategic investing is questionable.

Suitability involves a simple, one-time analysis (a question, actually) and is insignificant to choosing an investment. In fact, it's useless. It only defines prudent boundaries relative to age and risk tolerance.

Asset allocation is intermittent and far too general. Its role in the investment selection process is suited more for individual equities than for mutual funds. When purchasing shares of companies, we know their market cap and the businesses in which they engage. Business purpose is fixed. When market cap rises to the next level, changing a client's portfolio is simple and quick.

However, with the purchase of a bevy of mutual funds, there are no real guarantees. Besides dealing with broad categories that seem to shift in definition now and then, "drift" must be considered a real detriment to the accuracy and reliability of asset allocation with mutual funds. Drift is the result of a mutual fund manager's pushing away from the fund's recorded objective. Drift commonly occurs when a bonus is on the line and the manager needs a bit more spice in his or her returns to grab it. So if we've accumulated a group of funds as our favorites and then gone off to play golf and ignored potential drift, we have kicked asset allocation out the door. Each fund could have drifted so extensively from its stated objective that the collective objective has taken the asset allocation model that is appropriate for a 50-year-old couple to one that is suitable for a 32-year-old widow. We must remain alert to this possibility for drift.

As we've discussed, with the advent and flourishing of the Internet, our clients can themselves duplicate this selection process. Why should they pay us to be sporadic? We tell them there is rhyme to our reason, but sooner or later they will discover that there is not, and they will point and click on their own for far less money.

We must pay homage to Mr. Kroc's philosophy and build a methodical procedure for meeting that impact task: investing Baby Boomers' assets. Adding this dose of value to the triangular process we have already set in place will elevate our stature as the sole bearers of the Holy Grail.

No one else will come close.

Above and Beyond

If we are to keep Boomers off the Internet and by our sides, we must go above and beyond merely selling them mutual funds, stocks, and bonds. We must take matters—their money—into our own hands and embed our service so deeply into their lives that they cannot do without us.

To do this, we'll either have to put our golf clubs away for a while or wait for a bout of cabin fever, because what we're going to suggest here is work, hard intellectual work—work that is equivalent not to lounging through a compliance meeting but to intense, focused research. If this frightens us, causes our brains to ache, or induces sleepiness, then we're finished reading this book. We can sit back and wait for the Internet to drain our market.

With the triangular process, we devote ourselves to an orderly system. That's what Boomers now expect from us. We have added value to their lives, and they will ultimately question any movement toward haphazard decisions. The process that follows is explained to clients during the initial interview so they are aware that a well-researched and -contemplated method exists for the management of their assets.

We will build and maintain five mutual funds of our own. In the strict sense of the meaning (and law), they are not mutual funds—rather, they are portfolios with varying risk levels. But structurally they mimic mutual funds. They are conglomerates of individual equities, bonds, and, yes, even a few mutual funds, chosen and monitored after systematic research.

When clients climb aboard our practice they also board one of these portfolios, based on their risk tolerance and time frame. When we execute activity in one portfolio, all clients within that portfolio receive the same execution. The portfolio titles are as follows:

Aggressive

Dynamic

Moderate

Conservative

Income

These are not meant to be overly creative, only clear.

Before sinking too thoroughly into a discussion of these portfolios, let's cover a certain opposing opinion: the notion that every client's portfolio must be specially tailored to his or her risk profile. In almost all cases, this is folly. As one moves down from the pinnacle of risk to the cooler chambers of safety, the difference in uncertainty is measured by the amount of exposure to stocks, especially those of the volatile sort, relative to bonds and cash. Five points from which to choose on the risk spectrum, representing gradual shifts down the scale from stock ownership relative to bond ownership, are sufficient for the majority of Boomers.

We will first occupy our portfolios with securities and then we will outline investment management, which includes:

Strategic investing (buy, hold, monitor)

Tactical investing (buy low, sell high)

Entering the market (technical analysis)

Profit protection (buying puts)

Reasonable short-term speculation (buying calls)

During portfolio management, the second, fourth, and fifth items in this list can be switched off if the client desires.

Populating the Portfolio

There are two types of stock positions: core and volatile. The aggressive, dynamic, and moderate portfolios contain both types. The conservative and income portfolios hold only the core stocks. Satisfying the mid-cap class, we use American Stock Exchange Mid-Cap S & P Depository Receipts (SPDRs), whose management fees are minuscule. Four mutual funds are employed, covering the small-cap class, emerging markets class, general international class, and high-yield bond class. Individual corporate and government bonds are purchased. To round out the portfolios, a small cash position is maintained, mostly for the payment of fees.

Core Stocks

The process of choosing the core positions to make available to our five portfolios should be based on a distinct method.

Just as one lays concrete as a foundation for a house, we must also lay a strong base of core investments as a foundation for a profitable portfolio. Thank goodness Standard & Poor's (S & P) has already performed much of the grunt research for us. In fact, very recently they restructured their entire category system and were kind enough to make all their work public. They have placed nearly every stock traded publicly into one of 10 sectors.

Sectors	*Codes*
Energy	10
Materials	15
Industrials	20
Consumer Discretionary	25
Consumer Staples	30
Health Care	35
Financials	40
Information Technology	45
Telecommunication Services	50
Utilities	55

From nine of these sectors, three companies will be chosen and four from the remaining sector. But which ones and how do we decide? Each sector is broken down further into industry groups, industries, and subindustries.

For sectors with three or more industry groups (Industrials, Consumer Discretionary, Consumer Staples, Financials), we will halt our screening at that level and choose one company from three particular industry groups. For those with fewer than three industry groups (Materials, Health Care, Information Technology, and Utilities), we will drop to the next floor, industries, and pick one company from a chosen industry. For those industry groups showing fewer than three industries (Energy and Telecommunications Services), we will go to the basement, the subindustries level, to make our choices.

The domestic stock market is like a huge dinner plate covered with a rubber membrane stretched tight. Under that sheet are many marbles. They represent invested money. These marbles roll around under the membrane, moving from industry to industry in varying quantities depending on the condition of the economy, interest rate altitude, and general investor sentiment and momentum. Only in dicey conditions do some marbles pop from under the membrane and scurry into the bond market. Most stay on the plate, never escaping. Indeed, more and more marbles slip under the rubber membrane over time.

Representing 31 different S & P industries to some degree ensures that we will always be covered by most of the marbles—in other words, we will be very well diversified.

Now that we've systematically outlined the picking field, we decide on which of the numerous fundamental criteria to use for selection: earnings per share (EPS), market capitalization, dividend yield, price to earning ratio (P/E), growth potential, longevity, and so on. The decision on which to use belongs to the investment advisor constructing the portfolios. Each of us has preferences, and this discussion is not intended to defend or promote one or another.

One measure, however, must be strong, at least in a few of the choices: dividend yield. In the moderate, conservative, and income portfolios, dividend income becomes increasingly important. Companies that have growth potential (though perhaps only modestly) and sturdy dividend history are necessary holdings for these portfolios. Their growth allows us to whip inflation while providing fairly predictable income streams.

In order to avoid getting mired in the bog of deep quantitative analysis, the criteria used here, other than dividend yield, will be simple: visibility and longevity. In other words, this means the companies that are well-known and have been around since the start of time (most of them). Because Information Technology is the most robust and categorically rich sector, we will choose four core positions from it—one in software and three in hardware. Keep in mind that not all of these stocks will be present in each of the five portfolios. Refer to Appendix B for a complete list of the S & P breakdown and where each of our choices falls.

Sector	*Company*	*Yield*
Energy	Schlumberger (SLB)	1.25%
	Exxon (XON)	2.41%
	Ashland Oil (ASH)	3.27%*
Materials	Union Carbide (UK)	1.45%
	Phelps Dodge (PD)	3.60%
	International Paper (IP)	1.88%*
Industrials	General Electric (GE)	1.06%
	ADP (AUD)	0.65%
	Southwest Airlines (LUV)	0.13%
Consumer Discretionary	General Motors (GM)	2.89%
	Wal-Mart (WMT)	0.36%
	Times Mirror (TMC)	1.14%*
Consumer Staples	Anheuser-Busch (BUD)	1.66%
	Procter & Gamble (PG)	1.22%
	Sysco (SYY)	1.25%*
Health Care	Pfizer (PFE)	0.86%
	Mallinckrodt (MKG)	1.91%
	Amgen (AMGN)	0.00%*
Financials	J.P. Morgan (JPM)	3.01%
	AIG (AIG)	0.20%
	Charles Schwab (SCH)	0.13%*
Information Technology	Microsoft (MSFT)	0.00%
	Cisco (CSCO)	0.00%
	Intel (INTL)	0.22%
	Dell (DELL)	0.00%*
Telecom Services	Global Crossing (GBLX)	0.00%

	Sprint PCS (PCS)	0.00%
	WorldCom (WCOM)	0.00%*
Utilities	Ameren (AEE)	6.80%
	Enron (ENE)	1.30%
	Peoples Energy (PGL)	5.08%*
S & P Mid-Cap	SPDR (MDY)	0.00%

The last company in each sector (*) is notated as a supplemental position. These companies are used only when the total invested exceeds a specified amount, when 21 domestic positions do not accomplish diversification. This threshold amount is eventually at the discretion of the advisor building the portfolios. However, the $1 million ceiling seems to be the point at which adding 10 more positions keeps the shares purchased, on average, over 100 per company—a tidy number.

Note also that in each of the less volatile sectors of Energy, Materials, Financials, and Utilities, there is at least one choice with a bulky dividend payout. These (as well as General Motors) are available to supply the income and inflation-beating growth in the income and, to a lesser extent, in the conservative portfolios. These are, in fact, the only equity positions held in the income portfolio.

Volatile Stocks

Taking riskier positions beyond the core enhances potential return. Seven volatile positions are used to charge up the aggressive, dynamic, and moderate portfolios. To choose six of them, we return to the vigorous Information Technology sector and fill in a few of the holes left during the core selection. These stocks throw off very little, if any, yield.

Internet software and services—America Online (AOL)

IT consulting and services—Unisys (UIS)

Software/application—PeopleSoft (PSFT)

Software/systems—Oracle (ORCL)[†]

[†]Although we already have Microsoft in the fold as systems software, Oracle was added because its market is business, whereas Microsoft's is more individual.

Telecom equipment—QUALCOMM (QCOM)

Semiconductor equipment—Applied Materials (AMAT)

And for our final volatile position, we guarantee exposure to the strong broadcasting and cable TV subindustry by choosing Comcast Class A Special (CMCSK) from the Media industry group within the Consumer Discretionary sector.

This is nothing more than a systematic method of managing Baby Boomers' retirement funds. As we've pointed out, Boomers will buy into a set of procedures long before they'll buy a product.

Disruptive Stocks

"Disruptive technology" is a catchy economic term that refers to esoteric knowledge percolating into hardware and software that exists nowhere else on earth and threatens established technological routines. Companies that create this technology, it is assumed, will eventually displace companies that deliver current technology, thus threatening their existence and diminishing their value and stock price.

These are also more risky positions than our core stocks constitute. As with the volatile stocks, we offer these only in the aggressive, dynamic, and moderate portfolios:

Telecom equipment—JDS Uniphase (JDSU)

Internet software and services—Nextlink (NXLK)

Internet software and services—Broadcom (BRCM)

Telecom wireless—Level 3 (LVLT)

Semiconductor equipment—Cree Research (CREE)

Electronics/semiconductors—Texas Instruments (TXN)

Communications equipment—C-Cube (CUBE)

Again, the rationale for selecting all stock positions lies with those who are constructing the portfolio. There is no intent to advocate any of our choices here. We took these positions only for the sake of demonstration.

Mutual Funds

If an advisor engineering a portfolio has the time and skill to research the thousands of individual small-cap stocks in a fashion similar to what's unfolding here, he or she deserves congratulations. Most of us, however, lack one or both of those ingredients. The same applies to overseas equities.

So three equity mutual funds are used to finish out the diversification. They are chosen purely on rate-of-return performance after expenses.

Small-cap blend	Lord Abbott Developing Growth
Emerging markets	SSgA
International	Hotchkis and Wiley

Fixed Income

One mutual fund is used in the bond category to satisfy high-yield coverage: Northeast Investors. Specific corporate and government bonds can't be identified until the day of purchase. Corporate bonds are kept in the 10-year, A-grade echelon. Government bonds extend no more than 10 years into the future, as well. A money market position is maintained in order to pay the management fees.

Rebalancing

We examine portfolios annually to determine whether risk has changed significantly enough to warrant rebalancing (taking into account clients' wishes and income tax brackets) and whether the clients are withdrawing, and how much.

Tactical Approach

Tactical strategy necessitates a spicier taste for risk than normal, so it is available only in the aggressive and dynamic portfolios. Even within these, it can be curtailed by the client after a discussion of tax implications. A tactical strategy involves buying equities when they are oversold for no apparent reason and selling them later when they reach fair value. Here's the quandary with this strategy: There are no dictums cut into marble somewhere revealing how to accomplish this task on a regular and dependable basis. It does require meticulous research and patience.

An excellent place to start such work is Standard & Poor's AdvisorInsight, a Web page available only to investment advisors, which we'll cover in Chapter 10. Depending upon the sort of package subscribed to, the cost can range from $100 to $200 per month. One of the marvelous features of this Internet location is that it evaluates thousands of stocks to establish value based on balance sheet fundamentals.

Standard & Poor's determines what a company should trade at by running a few numbers through a proprietary computer model: corporate earnings, growth potential, price to book value, return on equity, and current yield relative to the S & P 500. What spits out is the stock's *fair value,* or the price at which it should trade. If the market in general has the price pegged higher, then the stock is overvalued. If it's lower, then it is undervalued. Remember, however, that this fair value is based on numbers and ratios. What won't be reported on the balance sheet is whether the market hauled the stock price down because, for example, the visionary CEO of the company died of a stroke a month before. Practical analysis also must be done or we could get on board a train that can't get up hills. Furthermore, the company might be part of an industry that a week ago commenced a group slide southward. We won't want to participate.

Once we assume a tactical position, exit discipline should be in place and exercised. We intend to be successful when taking a tactical position. But in order to keep greed from seizing us, we should apply a 40% price increase maximum as the trigger to liquidate (or at least to bring the security under serious review to determine whether there are any news, bright and enhanced fundamentals, or market trends that would prevent us from unloading it). Grudgingly, we must establish a loss floor, as well, because we will be beaten on occasion. A bottom that is one-half the gain's high mark is judicious. So if we watch our mistake in disgust as its price endlessly withers to a 20% loss, it's time to cut it loose and fish through the drawer for the Alka-Seltzer.

When working in the tactical arena, be very careful about taking positions just prior to or during quarterly earnings season. This three-week period four times a year is a lunatic's minefield. How often has a company reported better-than-expected earnings but slightly diminished sales revenues and been chased and stoned down Wall Street? How often have we seen missed earnings estimates accompanied by visionary pronouncements about the glory of the unfolding future and then heard popping corks and fizz from the exchange floor?

Tread lightly during these unpredictable times.

The Entrance Trick

So the hard-working, middle-class Boomers are retiring. They bring to us their $1,500,000 that's been quietly amassing in their 401(k) for 20 years. Enthralled with the way we manage clients' lives, they want to be a part of the process. We write a nice retirement distribution plan for them and take possession of their assets. Do we dump-truck the money into our stocks?

No. We enter after some logical, systematic analysis.

Step One: Fair Value, Stars, and Consensus

Fair Value, as used in the tactical portion of the investment strategy, should also be employed to help determine when to purchase our positions. If any of our stock's Fair Value is high relative to market value, waiting for it to trend back to Fair Value might be wise—and vice versa.

There are two potential sources of consensus: S & P Advisor-Insight and Wall Street analysts in general. Both are available at the S & P Web page. The S & P folks have devised a quantitative (and, again, quite proprietary) STAR (Stock Appreciation Ranking) method to recommend involvement in stocks. In general, a five-star rating is a buy and a one-star rating is a sell. For more detail, jump to the Web site, where subscription info is available. (No, I don't work for Standard & Poor's.)

A general Wall Street analysts' consensus is provided at different levels: buy, buy/hold, hold, weak hold, and sell. The percentage of gurus maintaining each opinion is also offered.

Step Two: Assessing the Curves

We can't all become chartists, but there are four primary charting indicators that can assist in making short-term decisions about when to enter a given stock. When read together, verifying each other, they are remarkably accurate in enlightening us about price trends of a stock. There won't be a convoluted mathematical exposé of these indicators, only a brief explanation of what they are and what they tell us. Refer to Figure 8.1. For a thorough discussion of these and other charting indicators, jump onto the Internet at IQC.com.

Stochastics

This indicator is based on the premise that while the market is pushing upward, prices tend to close near their highs, and, conversely, when the market is heading down, prices tend to close near their lows. Stochastics is plotted as two lines: %K and %D. These wave along between, above, and below two fixed lines on the chart, 20 and 80.

What to watch for: When the stock is overbought (price peaking), the two lines will cross each other above the 80 line, and when the stock is oversold (price bottoming out), the two lines cross each other below the 20 line.

Moving Average Convergence/Divergence (MACD)

This indicator works well with stochastics. This is the difference between two moving averages: slow exponential and fast exponential. These two constantly converge toward and diverge away from each other. The chart shows the difference between the two as cylinders that rise above or fall below a zero baseline. Overlaying these is the moving average of the MACD line itself, which serves as a signal line.

What to watch for: When the cylinders have stretched below the zero baseline and pull away from the trigger line; in other words, air can be seen between the tip of the cylinder and the trigger line. This is an indication that the price of the stock has bottomed and is turning up. The opposite is the case when all the factors occur above the zero baseline.

A final use of this indicator is that when it is marking new highs or new lows and the stock's price is not doing the same, a trend reversal might be just around the corner.

Stochastics and MACD can verify each other. If both are sending the same signal, it improves the chance that a reversal is coming.

Relative Strength Index (RSI)

The RSI compares the price of a stock to itself. It's based on the difference between the average closing price on up days versus

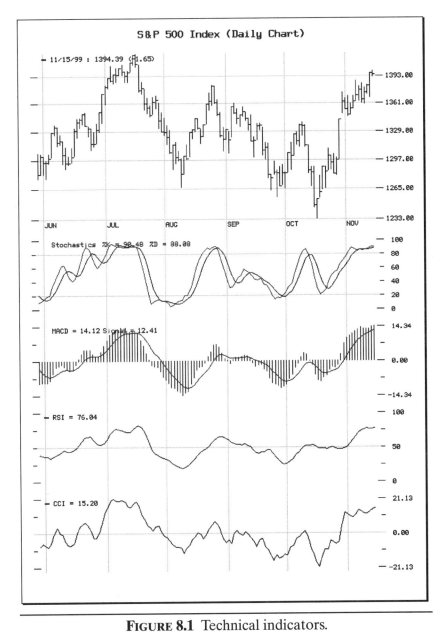

FIGURE 8.1 Technical indicators.
(*Source:* IQC Corp. © 2000 GO2NET, Inc. All rights reserved.
Reprinted with permission.)

the average closing price on down days. This line is plotted on a scale of 0 to 100.

What to watch for: When the line hovers in the area between 20 and 30, it indicates an oversold stock. When in the area between 70 and 80, the stock might be overbought. This index has a tendency to give its indication a few days earlier than stochastics and MACD.

Commodity Channel Index (CCI)

This indicator, despite its name, is also useful with individual equities. This indicates how high or low prices are relative to their statistical mean. It's plotted on a graph with zero as a baseline.

What to watch for: When the CCI breaks beyond 10 it is overbought, and when it drops below −10 it is oversold. As with the RSI, the CCI moves a bit earlier than stochastics and MACD.

Conclusions

Remember that our interest in using these technical indicators is to buy into our positions when prices are depressed in the short term. It's not to time the market, buying in at the right indications and selling out at the opposite ones. The purpose of these indicators is to help us buy in only. Take a look at Figure 8.2. Assume that the S & P 500 Index was an individual stock in our portfolio. We have the Boomer couple's $1,500,000 401(k) in early July of 1999. We start examining the charts of all our stocks. We come to the S & P 500 chart. Here's what it tells us on July 19, 1999:

Closing price—1407.65

Stochastics—%K and %D above 80, crossing and heading down

MACD—cylinders excessively high and trigger line showing air

RSI—82

CCI—17.1

Generally we note that the readings are in the nosebleed section and probably don't have much strength to continue. In fact, the S & P 500 is perilously close to a downtrend. So we hold off and watch it every day.

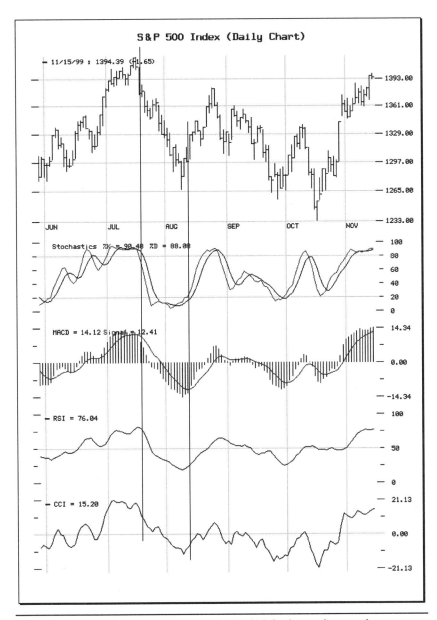

FIGURE 8.2 Standard & Poor's 500 index, when to buy.
(*Source:* IQC Corp. © 2000 GO2NET, Inc. All rights reserved.
Reprinted with permission.)

Here's what the chart tells us on August 10, 1999, the day we actually buy the stock:

Closing price—1281.43

Stochastics—%K and %D below 20, crossed a few days before and heading above the 20 line

MACD—Air between the trigger line and cylinders

RSI—18

CCI—minus 12.6

Again, assuming the S & P 500 was a stock and in our portfolios, by waiting three weeks we were able to take our Boomers' long-term investment position at a price 8.96% below that of the day we began reviewing the market.

Since the goal of using the four indicators is to avoid entering our positions when they are at temporary peaks, or overbought conditions, we would move into those displaying valleys, over-sold characteristics, or neutral indicators:

Stochastics—%K and %D between 20 and 80

MACD—cylinders and trigger moderately off the zero base-line

RSI—between 30 and 70

CCI—between −10 and 10

Step Three: Melding Steps One and Two

Each component of the entry research—Fair Value, STAR, analysts' consensus, indicators—is represented by a number.

Fair Value—5 (undervalued) to 1 (overvalued)

STAR—5 (buy) to 1 (sell)

Analysts' consensus—some percentage of buy, buy/hold, hold, weak-hold, sell

Each indicator—after reading, assign each a 1 (yes, buy) or a 2 (no, wait)

Thus, they can be quantified and combined. If you're handy with a spreadsheet, you can create a program that will present a yes or no response to whether, in the short term, it is suitable to enter a stock position based on the commingling of the four elements. The weight of importance given to each component, as well as to each indicator, is at the discretion of the investment advisor. Refer to Appendix D for a discussion of asset management software.

Backdoor Profit

Occasionally, for whatever reason, a stock will energize and take off, running well beyond Fair Value. Under healthy market conditions, this is not cause for undue suspicion or alarm. However, in a market or an industry with symptoms of frailty, it could be concluded that the lone superstar will soon lose its wings and fall hard and fast.

There are two methods of booking some of the profit generated by this strange conduct: Sell shares of the stock or buy puts. Since long-term investing is the underpinning of our philosophy in the strategic portion of the portfolio, selling shares is inappropriate. As well, it is likely that capital gains tax issues would prevent the use of this technique.

Buying puts, however, is a low-cost means of realizing some profit from the fall. And the risk is fixed at the cost of the put. When buying one, we expect the stock to eventually come off its snooty behavior and decline in price. When (if) it does, the put increases in value and we sell. The value of the stock declined while the value of the put increased: profit protection.

A Little Guesswork

Understandably, calls move opposite puts. After buying one on a stock, we would be pleased if the price of the stock went up. The risk is the same—limited to the loss of the amount paid. The most dominant reasons for buying a call instead of simply buying the stock outright are as a shelter against being a fool and not wanting to own the stock.

If we're wrong and the stock plummets, we do not join in the nastiness. All we've lost is what we've paid for the call. As well, there are infrequent occasions when we believe a stock will rapidly accelerate in value and are not interested in owning shares (or don't have sufficient proceeds in cash) but want to take part. Buying calls allows us this opportunity.

As with tactical management, the use of puts and calls can be declined by clients.

Lightening the Wallet

By constructing and managing these pseudo mutual funds, Boomers save money in two ways, relative to the old method of distributing all their money into a series of retail funds: Lower expenses and lower capital gains taxes. We'll demonstrate these by stacking our portfolios up against a group of 10 matching mutual funds. Each of these mutual fund groups will be identical to each of our portfolios in allocation by category.

Expenses

In our managed portfolios, assume we assign the following fee structure:

$1 to $1,000,000	1.00%
$1,000,001 to $5,000,000	0.75%
$5,000,000	$42,000 per year plus CPI* × 2

But mutual funds are also housed inside our portfolios. They, too, have expenses and must be taken into account. Following are the weighted expenses of the mutual funds used inside our portfolios. These must be added to our management fees.

Portfolio	Weighted Fund Expense
Aggressive	0.149%
Dynamic	0.145%
Moderate	0.129%
Conservative	0.122%
Income	0.031%

---

*Consumer price index

As the total managed amount rises, the management fee drops, while the weighted fund expense remains steady.

The average expense ratio for all loaded funds in each investment category was computed. Though no-loads were also researched, we chose loaded funds because no-loads provide no compensation to the traditional financial advisors (currently, at least). No-load funds actually sported higher average expense ratios.

Category	Number of Loaded Funds	Average Expense Ratio
Large-cap	421	1.20%
Mid-cap	204	1.35%
Small-cap	158	1.63%
Specialty*	36	1.39%
Emerging markets	83	2.07%
International	117	1.68%
Bonds	173	1.01%

Each of our five portfolio allocation distributions is applied to the matching group of mutual fund categories. The average weighted expense ratios are calculated for each category and then summed, providing the total expense ratio. Thus for comparison purposes each of our portfolios is transformed into a mutual fund portfolio of the same categories. See Table 8.1.

So a 1.20% expense ratio is multiplied by 72% (large-cap) of our aggressive portfolio, 1.35% by 3% (mid-cap), 1.63% by 3% (small-cap), and so on. The resulting fragments are summed to arrive at the weighted expense ratio. This is done for each portfolio.

Two final ripples to smooth:

- The effects of the Class A shares' front load on the expense ratio. Though this is an absolute amount that hits once, its ramifications must be included. In all cases, the load was divided by 15 years, converted into a percentage of the total, and added to the expense ratio. Fifteen years was chosen because

*Includes only Technology, Health Care, and Communications.

TABLE 8.1 Weighted Expense Ratios of Equivalent A-Share Mutual Fund Portfolios
The average ratio is multiplied by each objective's percent position in each portfolio.

Number of Funds	Funds Objective	Average Ratio	Aggressive	Weighted Ratio	Dynamic	Weighted Ratio	Moderate	Weighted Ratio	Conservative	Weighted Ratio	Income	Weighted Ratio
421	Large-Cap	1.20%	72.0%	0.864%	65.0%	0.780%	45.0%	0.540%	30.0%	0.360%	25.0%	0.300%
204	Mid-Cap	1.35%	3.0%	0.041%	3.0%	0.041%	3.0%	0.041%	2.0%	0.027%	0.0%	0.000%
158	Small-Cap	1.63%	3.0%	0.049%	3.0%	0.049%	3.0%	0.049%	0.0%	0.000%	0.0%	0.000%
36	Specialty*	1.39%	9.0%	0.125%	9.0%	0.125%	9.0%	0.125%	5.0%	0.070%	0.0%	0.000%
83	Emerging Markets	2.07%	5.0%	0.104%	5.0%	0.104%	5.0%	0.104%	3.0%	0.062%	0.0%	0.000%
117	International	1.68%	5.0%	0.084%	5.0%	0.084%	5.0%	0.084%	5.0%	0.084%	0.0%	0.000%
173	Bonds	1.01%	3.0%	0.030%	10.0%	0.101%	30.0%	0.303%	55.0%	0.556%	75.0%	0.758%
				1.296%		1.283%		1.245%		1.158%		1.058%
			B- and C-Share Addition >	0.7685%		0.7685%		0.7685%		0.7685%		0.7685%
			B- and C-Share Ratio >	2.065%		2.052%		2.014%		1.927%		1.826%

*Technology, Health Care, and Communications.

it equates roughly to the number of years Boomers will spend in retirement. The expense ratio in all Class A mutual fund groups is applied to the total invested minus the load.

- A random selection of 24 A-share mutual funds with companion B and C shares showed that the average increase in expense ratios of these corresponding shares is 0.742% for B shares and 0.795% for C shares. This percentage is added to the A-share expense ratio when calculating the impact of B and C shares during our analysis. The payout on Bs and Cs is roughly 1%, which includes the additional amount plus the base 12b-1 of 0.25%. (Aren't all these commission shenanigans fun? They sure line our pockets while clients scratch their heads.)

Now we have all the converted ingredients to make a parallel comparison of the Boomers' costs to either engage us to actively manage their retirements with one of our portfolios or dump their money into a group of similar retail mutual funds so we can hurry on to the next signature. Let's review:

1. We set an asset management fee.
2. We dug out the weighted fees inside the portfolios' mutual funds.
3. We researched to generate average mutual fund category expense ratios.
4. We reworked our managed portfolios into similar groupings of mutual fund categories.
5. We folded the effects of the Class A load into the expense ratio.
6. We adjusted upward the B- and C-share expense ratio.

Table 8.2 shows all five portfolios in four sizes and compares them with the expenses of comparable mutual fund portfolios.

After all analysis is finished, in every case we save Boomers money. But that could be predicted, because our management fee is lower than the overall average mutual fund expense ratio. The fees vary slightly from portfolio to portfolio, but are quite different for amounts under management. Following are the average annual fees of four investment amounts and the savings.

TABLE 8.2 Portfolio Expenses

	MANAGED				CLASS A		CLASS B & C		ANNUAL SAVINGS MANAGED OVER ALL CLASSES OF FUNDS	
	Management Fee	Weighted Fund Expense	Total Expense	Dollars	Expense %	Dollars	Expense %	Dollars	Class A	Class B & C
$350,000										
Aggressive	1.000%	0.149%	1.149%	$4,022	1.621%	$5,674	2.012%	$7,042	$1,652	$3,021
Dynamic	1.000%	0.145%	1.145%	$4,008	1.597%	$5,590	1.988%	$6,958	$1,582	$2,951
Moderate	1.000%	0.129%	1.129%	$3,952	1.536%	$5,376	1.926%	$6,741	$1,425	$2,790
Conservative	1.000%	0.122%	1.122%	$3,927	1.481%	$5,184	1.871%	$6,549	$1,257	$2,622
Income	1.000%	0.031%	1.031%	$3,609	1.383%	$4,841	1.774%	$6,209	$1,232	$2,601
				$3,903		$5,333		$6,700	$1,429	$2,797
$1,000,000										
Aggressive	1.000%	0.149%	1.149%	$11,490	1.521%	$15,210	2.012%	$20,120	$3,720	$8,630
Dynamic	1.000%	0.145%	1.145%	$11,450	1.497%	$14,970	1.988%	$19,880	$3,520	$8,430
Moderate	1.000%	0.129%	1.129%	$11,290	1.435%	$14,350	1.926%	$19,260	$3,060	$7,970
Conservative	1.000%	0.122%	1.122%	$11,220	1.381%	$13,810	1.871%	$18,710	$2,590	$7,490
Income	1.000%	0.031%	1.031%	$10,310	1.283%	$12,830	1.774%	$17,740	$2,520	$7,430
				$11,152		$14,234		$19,142	$3,082	$7,990
$5,000,000										
Aggressive	0.800%	0.149%	0.949%	$47,450	1.415%	$70,750	2.012%	$100,600	$23,300	$53,150
Dynamic	0.800%	0.145%	0.945%	$47,250	1.391%	$69,550	1.988%	$99,400	$22,300	$52,150
Moderate	0.800%	0.129%	0.929%	$46,450	1.329%	$66,450	1.926%	$96,300	$20,000	$49,850
Conservative	0.800%	0.122%	0.922%	$46,100	1.274%	$63,700	1.871%	$93,550	$17,600	$47,450
Income	0.800%	0.031%	0.831%	$41,550	1.177%	$58,850	1.774%	$88,700	$17,300	$47,150
				$45,760		$65,860		$95,710	$20,100	$49,950
$10,000,000										
Aggressive	0.420%	0.149%	0.569%	$56,900	1.296%	$129,600	2.012%	$201,200	$72,700	$144,300
Dynamic	0.420%	0.145%	0.565%	$56,500	1.283%	$128,300	1.988%	$198,800	$71,800	$142,300
Moderate	0.420%	0.129%	0.549%	$54,900	1.245%	$124,500	1.926%	$192,600	$69,600	$137,700
Conservative	0.420%	0.122%	0.542%	$54,200	1.158%	$115,800	1.871%	$187,100	$61,600	$132,900
Income	0.420%	0.031%	0.451%	$45,100	1.058%	$105,800	1.774%	$177,400	$60,700	$132,300
				$53,520		$120,800		$191,420	$67,280	$137,900

Amount	Managed	Class A (Savings)	Class B or C (Savings
$ 350,000	$ 3,903	$ 5,333 ($ 1,429)	$ 6,700 ($ 2,797)
$ 1,000,000	$11,152	$ 14,234 ($ 3,082)	$ 19,142 ($ 7,990)
$ 5,000,000*	$45,760	$ 65,860 ($20,100)	$ 95,710 ($ 49,950)
$10,000,000*	$53,520	$120,800 ($67,280)	$191,420 ($137,900)

*Generally, Class B shares are prohibited at these total amounts, but Class C shares are not.

What is perhaps more dramatic is the long-term effect of the extra drain by using mutual funds. Retaining the savings in the managed portfolios instead of funneling them to mutual fund managers over 15 years and growing at 12% produces significant accumulated losses. Again, the balances vary slightly from portfolio to portfolio, but are quite different for amounts under management. Following are the average total forfeitures after 15 years of the four investment amounts.

Amount	Class A	Class B or C
$ 350,000	$ 53,288	$ 104,253
$ 1,000,000	$ 114,896	$ 297,865
$ 5,000,000	$ 749,322	$1,862,122
$10,000,000	$2,508,179	$5,140,873

(Take a look at "Expense Comparison Detail" in Appendix B for the calculations.)

Capital Gains Taxes

Since investors have no control over buying or selling positions in the mutual funds they own, every year they receive an out-of-sight, out-of-mind Form 1099—capital gains they must figure into their already hefty tax bill.

In our managed portfolios, there is far less, if any, activity. Whatever activity there is, we will have engaged Boomers in a discussion about its necessity and impact on their tax posture. The same groupings of funds were analyzed to determine average capital gains distributions.

Category	Number of Loaded Funds	Average Capital Gains Distribution
Large-cap	421	2.74%
Mid-cap	204	5.21%
Small-cap	158	5.70%
Specialty*	36	4.92%
Emerging markets	83	4.85%
International	117	2.00%

* Includes only Technology, Health Care, and Communications.

These distribution percentages are applied to the investment amount in each category in our comparative mutual fund portfolios to determine the annual amount in capital gains that would be paid out, which is then multiplied by 20%. Unlike expense ratios, there is a significant difference between the portfolio and the amount invested.

Portfolio	$350,000	$1,000,000	$5,000,000	$10,000,000
Aggressive	$2,004	$5,704	$28,523	$57,046
Dynamic	$1,851	$5,268	$26,341	$52,682
Moderate	$1,462	$4,171	$20,857	$41,715
Conservative	$ 938	$2,681	$13,405	$26,810
Income	$ 480	$1,370	$ 6,850	$13,700
Average	$1,347	$3,839	$19,195	$38,391

Marry these numbers (averages from preceding table) to losses due to mutual fund expense ratios and after 15 years at our 12% annual growth rate the client has developed a quiet but enormous monetary hemorrhage:

Amount	Class A	Class B or C
$ 350,000	$ 103,503	$ 154,468
$ 1,000,000	$ 258,005	$ 440,974
$ 5,000,000	$1,464,914	$2,577,713
$10,000,000	$3,939,370	$6,572,063

For more detail (as if it's needed), please refer to "Capital Gains Taxes" in Appendix B.

Realized gains inside mutual funds are not the only threat to our clients' long-range balances. Potential capital gains residing inside mutual fund assets on the books strike an imposing figure. Averaging 883 equity mutual funds shows potential capital gains of 21%. This is a percentage of the average assets under management, which in this circumstance is $794,000,000. Potential capital gain on the books of the average equity mutual funds is $166,555,000, a hefty tax bill.

Certainly incurring it would mean the mass liquidation of all mutual fund positions that held gains—an unlikely scenario. Yet these gains stand to get even more massive through time, and when Boomers retire and start liquidating, the taxes will begin to hit the books.

We'll inspect the compensation energies of management fees and mutual fund payouts in Chapter 11. However, appetites can be whetted by mentioning that these huge chunks of dollars denied to the mutual fund companies and the IRS after we take matters into our own hands are not all returned to the Boomers. After all, we did elaborate the strategy that saved them all this money. A fair amount finds its way to us.

Winners: Boomers and us. Hooray!

Losers: Mutual fund companies and the IRS. Tsk. Tsk.

Battle in the Trenches

Millions of Boomer couples with $1 million 401(k) balances will very soon face three choices:

1. Working with a team that has a process for planning and monitoring and a sensible and methodical investment policy that charges $11,152 per year

2. Working with one person who purchases a series of mutual funds for them and charges $19,142 per year, then quickly moves on to the next signature (to win the free trip)

3. Working alone, purchasing no-load mutual funds on the Internet, and being charged $14,613 in mutual fund expenses

Who will win in the trenches?

Variations on the Theme

For those financial advisors who specifically ply the market below the $350,000 mark, the same mechanics and procedures can apply with fewer positions. For example, in the aggressive and dynamic portfolios for assets between $100,000 and $350,000, instead of two stocks in each S & P sector we might choose none in the stodgy ones—Utilities, Energy, Materials, Industrials—and redistribute into the zippier ones. We then switch the category philosophy for our conservative and income portfolios, coming out of the more nervous sectors—Information Technology, Health Care, and perhaps Telecommunications Services. As well, in the aggressive and dynamic sectors we choose fewer of the volatile securities, and then only those that have been embedded in our scenery for some time. Finally, with the moderate portfolio, in order to retain its rock-solid diversification, we would have to retain thin positions throughout.

And for those clients dropping less than $100,000 before us? Remember the work Lewis Tyler did for Brian when Brian sold his tavern to Bill Randall for $2 million? Brian paid Lewis hourly to research and construct a portfolio of no-load mutual funds. Brian then hopped on the Internet and bought and monitored them himself.

With blocks of money below the $100,000 mark, a similar but enhanced method should be employed. Research and establish five portfolios of varying risk, populated with no-load, low-expense mutual funds or S & P Depository Receipts (SPDRs). Or design a portfolio based on the client's particular risk level and needs. Prepare meticulous documentation and presentation materials that address the rationale and performance of the selections. This packet demonstrates to the client the process and research followed in the design. Establish a fixed amount that you will charge clients for providing each portfolio—say, $1,000.

Just purchasing a researched portfolio is not the end of our work with these clients. We offer to do the legwork in opening an on-line account on their behalf, showing them how to navigate the site. Once the funds have been deposited, the assets are purchased. We then strongly encourage (some might insist on this as part of the relationship) that the clients return annually to review the performance of the portfolio and make decisions about rebalancing and other adjustments. For this review, we again charge a fixed amount—say, $250.

Back to the Initial Interview

How much of the preceding our triangle group will demonstrate to the client in the initial interview is a function of personalities—both the advisor's and the client's. But certainly the bare fundamentals would be fitting: the exhaustive research that has already been done, the ongoing strategic monitoring of the portfolios, the investigation leading to the tactical management decisions, the quarterly reviews, the annual planning reviews.

These painstaking steps add value to a comprehensive process that shames the tired, clichéd sales attempt. Yes, more work must be done, but this will deliver the Holy Grail.

CHAPTER

9

Distribution and Composition

Getting Your Arms around the Choices

Once we've made our choices, determining distribution and composition is the next step. If we're adept at spreadsheet construction, we can pull together our choices across those hundreds of little cells and make management of our portfolios a matter of tapping a few keyboard buttons. It makes an impressive presentation to clients, allowing us to examine the impact of each portfolio with a few keystrokes.

Our choices are gathered in Figure 9.1, and allocation percentages and historic yields wait to be assigned.

#1—core stocks

#2—volatile stocks

#3—disruptive stocks

#4—supplementals

#5—mutual funds

#6—income positions

#7—composite snapshot

Each of these categories has a column for the percentage we

will assign and a column for the annual historic yield generated from the position, which is updated quarterly. This figure is essential in determining how much income our portfolios create, which is reported in two places: the total in #7, the composite snapshot, and in #8, the performance box.

The performance box identifies for the client the capital gains tax savings relative to a similar portfolio of mutual funds, as discussed in Chapter 8. It shows historic performance, income, and positions held.

In the core stock positions (#1) and the supplementals (#4), each S & P sector corresponds to the S & P sector box and is separated by a dotted line, allowing clients to easily discern which stocks fall into which sectors.

On the next few pages are our five portfolios with the stock allocation and yield assignments for a $1 million portfolio. We've set our trigger at $999,999 for the supplementals to join the portfolios. For simplicity's sake, we chose not to engage tactical management. Following is a summary of the portfolios, comparing yields, annual capital gains tax savings, equity/debt mix, and total positions for each portfolio:

Portfolio	Annual Tax Savings	Yield	Equity/Debt	Positions
Aggressive	$5,705	0.58%	97.5/2.5	43
Dynamic	$5,268	1.34%	90/10	52
Moderate	$4,171	2.61%	70.5/29.5	57
Conservative	$2,681	4.45%	45/55	44
Income	$1,370	6.14%	25/75	20

Note that in the aggressive portfolio (see Figure 9.2) the total distribution into all volatile stocks is 30%, divided equally among the seven positions at 4.2857% each. That amount is sliced in half as it moves to the dynamic portfolio (Figure 9.3) and then in half again for the moderate portfolio (Figure 9.4). If a decision is made to assume an eighth volatile position, enough profit would be taken from the existing seven to purchase the shares and still maintain the total 30% exposure. Each position would thus represent 3.75% of the total.

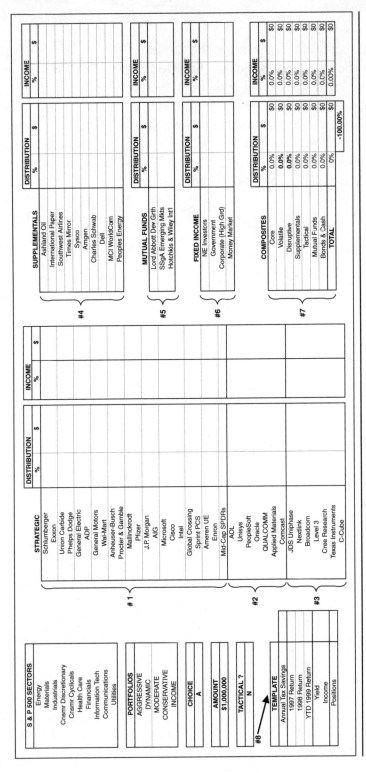

FIGURE 9.1 Investment policy template.

S & P 500 SECTORS
Energy
Materials
Industrials
Cnsmr Discretionary
Cnsmr Cyclicals
Health Care
Financials
Information Tech
Communications
Utilities

PORTFOLIOS	
AGGRESSIVE	
DYNAMIC	
MODERATE	
CONSERVATIVE	
INCOME	

CHOICE	
A	

AMOUNT	
$1,000,000	

TACTICAL ?	
N	

AGGRESSIVE	
Annual Tax Savings	$5,705
1997 Return	41.6%
1998 Return	91.6%
YTD 1999 Return	29.9%
Yield	0.58%
Income	$5,752
Positions	43

STRATEGIC	DISTRIBUTION %	$	INCOME %	$
Schlumberger	1.7%	$16,667	1.3%	$208
Exxon	1.0%	$10,000	2.4%	$241
Union Carbide	0.0%		1.5%	
Phelps Dodge	0.0%		3.6%	
General Electric	1.5%	$15,000	1.1%	$159
ADP	1.8%	$18,333	0.7%	$119
General Motors	0.5%	$5,000	2.9%	$145
Wal-Mart	1.8%	$18,333	0.4%	$66
Anheuser-Busch	1.2%	$11,667	1.7%	$194
Procter & Gamble	1.2%	$11,667	1.2%	$142
Mallinckrodt	1.5%	$15,000	1.9%	$287
Pfizer	2.1%	$20,833	0.9%	$179
J.P. Morgan	0.0%		3.0%	
AIG	1.5%	$15,000	0.2%	$30
Microsoft	2.3%	$22,500	0.0%	$0
Cisco	2.3%	$22,500	0.0%	$0
Intel	2.3%	$22,500	0.2%	$50
Global Crossing	2.1%	$20,833	0.0%	$0
Sprint PCS	2.1%	$20,833	0.0%	$0
Ameren UE	0.0%		6.8%	
Enron	1.2%	$11,667	1.3%	$152
Mid-Cap SPDRs	3.0%	$30,000	0.0%	$0
AOL	4.3%	$42,857	0.0%	$0
Unisys	4.3%	$42,857	0.0%	$0
PeopleSoft	4.3%	$42,857	0.0%	$0
Oracle	4.3%	$42,857	0.0%	$0
QUALCOMM	4.3%	$42,857	0.0%	$0
Applied Materials	4.3%	$42,857	0.0%	$0
Comcast	4.3%	$42,857	0.3%	$111
Uniphase	2.0%	$20,000	0.0%	$0
Nextlink	2.0%	$20,000	0.0%	$0
Broadcom	2.0%	$20,000	0.0%	$0
Level 3	2.0%	$20,000	0.0%	$0
Cree Research	2.0%	$20,000	0.0%	$0
Texas Instruments	2.0%	$20,000	0.0%	$0
C-Cube	2.0%	$20,000	0.0%	$0

SUPPLEMENTALS	DISTRIBUTION %	$	INCOME %	$
Ashland Oil	0.0%		3.3%	
International Paper	1.0%	$10,000	1.9%	$188
Southwest Airlines	1.0%	$10,000	0.1%	$13
Times Mirror	1.3%	$13,333	1.1%	$152
Sysco	1.3%	$13,333	1.3%	$167
Amgen	1.0%	$10,000	0.0%	$0
Charles Schwab	1.0%	$10,000	0.1%	$13
Dell	1.5%	$15,000	0.0%	$0
MCI WorldCom	1.5%	$15,000	0.0%	$0
Peoples Energy	0.0%		5.1%	

MUTUAL FUNDS	DISTRIBUTION %	$	INCOME %	$
Lord Abbott Dev Grth	3.0%	$30,000	0.0%	$0
SSgA Emerging Mkts	6.0%	$60,000	2.6%	$1,560
Hotchkis & Wiley Int'l	4.0%	$40,000	1.0%	$380

FIXED INCOME	DISTRIBUTION %	$	INCOME %	$
NE Investors	0.0%		9.2%	
Government	0.0%		6.1%	
Corporate (High Grd)	0.0%		6.8%	
Money Market	2.5%	$25,000	4.8%	$1,198

COMPOSITES	DISTRIBUTION %	$	INCOME %	$
Core	30.8%	$308,333	0.6%	$1,971
Volatile	30.0%	$300,000	0.0%	$111
Disruptive	14.0%	$140,000	0.6%	$0
Supplementals	9.7%	$96,667	0.6%	$533
Tactical	0.0%	$0	0.0%	$0
Mutual Funds	13.0%	$130,000	1.5%	$1,940
Bonds & Cash	2.5%	$25,000	4.8%	$1,198
TOTAL	100%	$1,000,000	0.58%	$5,752
	0.00%			

FIGURE 9.2 Aggressive portfolio.

S & P 500 SECTORS

S & P 500 SECTORS		
Energy		
Materials		
Industrials		
Cnsmr Discretionary		
Cnsmr Cyclicals		
Health Care		
Financials		
Information Tech		
Communications		
Utilities		

PORTFOLIOS	
AGGRESSIVE	
DYNAMIC	
MODERATE	
CONSERVATIVE	
INCOME	

CHOICE	
D	

AMOUNT	
$1,000,000	

TACTICAL ?	
N	

DYNAMIC	
Annual Tax Savings	$5,268
1997 Return	31.6%
1998 Return	39.9%
YTD 1999 Return	20.4%
Yield	1.34%
Income	$13,436
Positions	52

STRATEGIC

STRATEGIC	DISTRIBUTION %	DISTRIBUTION $	INCOME %	INCOME $
Schlumberger	1.5%	$15,000	1.3%	$188
Exxon	1.5%	$15,000	2.4%	$362
Union Carbide	1.5%	$15,000	1.5%	$218
Phelps Dodge	1.0%	$10,000	3.6%	$360
General Electric	1.5%	$15,000	1.1%	$159
ADP	1.5%	$15,000	0.7%	$98
General Motors	1.5%	$15,000	2.9%	$434
Wal-Mart	1.8%	$17,500	0.4%	$63
Anheuser-Busch	1.3%	$12,500	1.7%	$208
Procter & Gamble	1.5%	$15,000	1.2%	$183
Mallinckrodt	1.5%	$15,000	1.9%	$287
Pfizer	1.8%	$18,333	0.9%	$158
J.P. Morgan	1.0%	$10,000	3.0%	$301
AIG	1.5%	$15,000	0.2%	$30
Microsoft	1.5%	$15,000	0.0%	$0
Cisco	2.0%	$20,000	0.0%	$0
Intel	2.0%	$20,000	0.2%	$44
Global Crossing	2.0%	$20,000	0.0%	$0
Sprint PCS	2.0%	$20,000	0.0%	$0
Ameren UE	1.0%	$10,000	6.8%	$680
Enron	1.5%	$15,000	1.3%	$195
Mid-Cap SPDRs	3.0%	$30,000	0.0%	$0
AOL	3.2%	$32,143	0.0%	$0
Unisys	3.2%	$32,143	0.0%	$0
PeopleSoft	3.2%	$32,143	0.0%	$0
Oracle	3.2%	$32,143	0.0%	$0
QUALCOMM	3.2%	$32,143	0.0%	$0
Applied Materials	3.2%	$32,143	0.0%	$0
Comcast	3.2%	$32,143	0.3%	$84
Uniphase	1.0%	$10,000	0.0%	$0
Nextlink	1.0%	$10,000	0.0%	$0
Broadcom	1.0%	$10,000	0.0%	$0
Level 3	1.0%	$10,000	0.0%	$0
Cree Research	1.0%	$10,000	0.0%	$0
Texas Instruments	1.0%	$10,000	0.0%	$0
C-Cube	1.0%	$10,000	0.0%	$0

SUPPLEMENTALS

SUPPLEMENTALS	DISTRIBUTION %	DISTRIBUTION $	INCOME %	INCOME $
Ashland Oil	1.0%	$10,000	3.3%	$327
International Paper	1.0%	$10,000	1.9%	$188
Southwest Airlines	1.0%	$10,000	0.1%	$13
Times Mirror	1.5%	$15,000	1.1%	$171
Sysco	1.5%	$15,000	1.3%	$188
Amgen	0.5%	$5,000	0.0%	$0
Charles Schwab	1.5%	$15,000	0.1%	$20
Dell	1.3%	$13,333	0.0%	$0
MCI WorldCom	1.3%	$13,333	0.0%	$0
Peoples Energy	1.5%	$15,000	5.1%	$762

MUTUAL FUNDS

MUTUAL FUNDS	DISTRIBUTION %	DISTRIBUTION $	INCOME %	INCOME $
Lord Abbott Dev Grth	3.0%	$30,000	0.0%	$0
SSgA Emerging Mkts	5.0%	$50,000	2.6%	$1,300
Hotchkis & Wiley Int'l	5.0%	$50,000	1.0%	$475

FIXED INCOME

FIXED INCOME	DISTRIBUTION %	DISTRIBUTION $	INCOME %	INCOME $
NE Investors	0.0%	$0	9.2%	$3,050
Government	5.0%	$50,000	6.1%	$1,698
Corporate (High Grd)	2.5%	$25,000	6.8%	$1,698
Money Market	2.5%	$25,000	4.8%	$1,198

COMPOSITES

COMPOSITES	DISTRIBUTION %	DISTRIBUTION $	INCOME %	INCOME $
Core	35.3%	$353,333	1.1%	$3,964
Volatile	22.5%	$225,000	0.0%	$84
Disruptive	7.0%	$70,000	0.0%	$0
Supplementals	12.2%	$121,667	1.4%	$1,668
Tactical	0.0%	$0	0.0%	$0
Mutual Funds	13.0%	$130,000	1.4%	$1,775
Bonds & Cash	10.0%	$100,000	5.9%	$5,945
TOTAL	100%	$1,000,000	1.34%	$13,436
	0.00%			

FIGURE 9.3 Dynamic portfolio.

S & P 500 SECTORS

S & P 500 SECTORS
Energy
Materials
Industrials
Cnsmr Discretionary
Cnsmr Cyclicals
Health Care
Financials
Information Tech
Communications
Utilities

PORTFOLIOS
AGGRESSIVE
DYNAMIC
MODERATE
CONSERVATIVE
INCOME

CHOICE
M

AMOUNT
$1,000,000

NOT AVAILABLE
N

MODERATE	
Annual Tax Savings	$4,171
1997 Return	16.0%
1998 Return	20.4%
YTD 1999 Return	15.9%
Yield	2.61%
Income	$26,115
Positions	57

STRATEGIC

STRATEGIC	DISTRIBUTION %	DISTRIBUTION $	INCOME %	INCOME $
Schlumberger	0.7%	$6,667	1.3%	$83
Exxon	1.0%	$10,000	2.4%	$241
Union Carbide	1.5%	$15,000	1.5%	$218
Phelps Dodge	1.5%	$15,000	3.6%	$540
General Electric	1.0%	$10,000	1.1%	$106
ADP	1.0%	$10,000	0.7%	$65
General Motors	1.5%	$15,000	2.9%	$434
Wal-Mart	1.3%	$13,333	0.4%	$48
Anheuser-Busch	1.3%	$13,333	1.7%	$221
Procter & Gamble	1.5%	$15,000	1.2%	$183
Mallinckrodt	1.0%	$10,000	1.9%	$191
Pfizer	1.3%	$13,333	0.9%	$115
J.P. Morgan	0.7%	$6,667	3.0%	$201
AIG	1.3%	$13,333	0.2%	$27
Microsoft	1.3%	$13,333	0.0%	$0
Cisco	1.3%	$13,333	0.0%	$0
Intel	1.3%	$13,333	0.2%	$29
Global Crossing	1.3%	$13,333	0.0%	$0
Sprint PCS	1.3%	$13,333	0.0%	$0
Ameren UE	1.4%	$14,167	6.8%	$963
Enron	1.8%	$17,500	1.3%	$228
Mid-Cap SPDRs	3.0%	$30,000	0.0%	$0
AOL	2.1%	$21,429	0.0%	$0
Unisys	2.1%	$21,429	0.0%	$0
PeopleSoft	2.1%	$21,429	0.0%	$0
Oracle	2.1%	$21,429	0.0%	$0
QUALCOMM	2.1%	$21,429	0.0%	$0
Applied Materials	2.1%	$21,429	0.3%	$56
Comcast	0.5%	$5,000	0.0%	$0
Uniphase	0.5%	$5,000	0.0%	$0
Nextlink	0.5%	$5,000	0.0%	$0
Broadcom	0.5%	$5,000	0.0%	$0
Level 3	0.5%	$5,000	0.0%	$0
Cree Research	0.5%	$5,000	0.0%	$0
Texas Instruments	0.5%	$5,000	0.0%	$0
C-Cube	0.5%	$5,000	0.0%	$0

SUPPLEMENTALS

SUPPLEMENTALS	DISTRIBUTION %	DISTRIBUTION $	INCOME %	INCOME $
Ashland Oil	1.0%	$10,000	3.3%	$327
International Paper	1.3%	$13,333	1.9%	$251
Southwest Airlines	1.0%	$10,000	0.1%	$13
Times Mirror	1.3%	$13,333	1.1%	$152
Sysco	1.3%	$13,333	1.3%	$167
Amgen	1.3%	$13,333	0.0%	$0
Charles Schwab	1.3%	$13,333	0.1%	$17
Dell	1.3%	$13,333	0.0%	$0
MCI WorldCom	1.0%	$10,000	0.0%	$0
Peoples Energy	1.0%	$10,000	5.1%	$508

MUTUAL FUNDS

MUTUAL FUNDS	DISTRIBUTION %	DISTRIBUTION $	INCOME %	INCOME $
Lord Abbott Dev Grth	3.0%	$30,000	0.0%	$0
SSgA Emerging Mkts	2.5%	$25,000	2.6%	$650
Hotchkis & Wiley Int'l	5.0%	$50,000	1.0%	$475

FIXED INCOME

FIXED INCOME	DISTRIBUTION %	DISTRIBUTION $	INCOME %	INCOME $
NE Investors	2.5%	$25,000	9.2%	$2,293
Government	7.5%	$75,000	6.1%	$4,575
Corporate (High Grd)	17.0%	$170,000	6.8%	$11,543
Money Market	2.5%	$25,000	4.8%	$1,198

COMPOSITES

COMPOSITES	DISTRIBUTION %	DISTRIBUTION $	INCOME %	INCOME $
Core	29.5%	$295,000	1.3%	$3,892
Volatile	15.0%	$150,000	0.0%	$56
Disruptive	3.5%	$35,000	0.0%	$0
Supplementals	12.0%	$120,000	1.2%	$1,435
Tactical	0.0%	$0	0.0%	$0
Mutual Funds	10.5%	$105,000	1.1%	$1,125
Bonds & Cash	29.5%	$295,000	6.6%	$19,608
TOTAL	100%	$1,000,000	2.61%	$26,115
	0.00%			

FIGURE 9.4 Moderate portfolio.

STRATEGIC

	DISTRIBUTION %	DISTRIBUTION $	INCOME %	INCOME $
Schlumberger	2.5%	$25,000	2.4%	$603
Exxon	1.5%	$15,000	1.5%	$218
Union Carbide	1.0%	$10,000	3.6%	$360
Phelps Dodge	1.0%	$10,000	1.1%	$106
General Electric	1.0%	$10,000	0.7%	
ADP	0.0%		0.0%	$0
General Motors	2.0%	$20,000	2.9%	$578
Wal-Mart	0.5%	$5,000	0.4%	$18
Anheuser-Busch	1.0%	$10,000	1.7%	$166
Procter & Gamble	2.5%	$25,000	1.2%	$305
Mallinckrodt	0.5%	$5,000	1.9%	$96
Pfizer	1.0%	$10,000	0.9%	$86
J.P. Morgan	4.0%	$40,000	3.0%	$1,204
AIG	0.5%	$5,000	0.2%	$10
Microsoft	1.0%	$10,000	0.0%	$0
Cisco	1.0%	$10,000	0.0%	$0
Intel	0.7%	$6,667	0.2%	$15
Global Crossing	0.7%	$6,667	0.0%	$0
Sprint PCS	0.7%	$6,667	0.0%	$0
Ameren UE	3.5%	$35,000	6.8%	$2,380
Enron	0.0%		1.3%	$0
Mid-Cap SPDRs	2.0%	$20,000	0.0%	$0
AOL	0.0%		0.0%	
Unisys	0.0%		0.0%	
PeopleSoft	0.0%		0.0%	
Oracle	0.0%		0.0%	
QUALCOMM	0.0%		0.0%	
Applied Materials	0.0%		0.0%	
Comcast	0.0%		0.3%	
Uniphase	0.0%		0.0%	
Nextlink	0.0%		0.0%	
Broadcom	0.0%		0.0%	
Level 3	0.0%		0.0%	
Cree Research	0.0%		0.0%	
Texas Instruments	0.0%		0.0%	
C-Cube	0.0%		0.0%	

S & P 500 SECTORS

- Energy
- Materials
- Industrials
- Cnsmr Discretionary
- Cnsmr Cyclicals
- Health Care
- Financials
- Information Tech
- Communications
- Utilities

PORTFOLIOS

- AGGRESSIVE
- DYNAMIC
- MODERATE
- CONSERVATIVE
- INCOME

CHOICE — C

AMOUNT — $1,000,000

NOT AVAILABLE — N

CONSERVATIVE

Annual Tax Savings	$2,681
1997 Return	5.3%
1998 Return	12.4%
YTD 1999 Return	8.2%
Yield	4.45%
Income	$44,488
Positions	44

SUPPLEMENTALS

	DISTRIBUTION %	DISTRIBUTION $	INCOME %	INCOME $
Ashland Oil	1.3%	$13,333	3.3%	$436
International Paper	1.3%	$13,333	1.9%	$251
Southwest Airlines	0.5%	$5,000	0.1%	$7
Times Mirror	0.5%	$5,000	1.1%	$57
Sysco	0.5%	$5,000	1.3%	$63
Amgen	0.7%	$6,667	0.0%	$0
Charles Schwab	0.7%	$6,667	0.1%	$9
Dell	0.7%	$6,667	0.0%	$0
MCI WorldCom	0.7%	$6,667	0.0%	$0
Peoples Energy	0.7%	$6,667	5.1%	$339

MUTUAL FUNDS

	DISTRIBUTION %	DISTRIBUTION $	INCOME %	INCOME $
Lord Abbott Dev Grth	2.5%	$25,000	0.0%	$0
SSgA Emerging Mkts	2.5%	$25,000	2.6%	$650
Hotchkis & Wiley Int'l	5.0%	$50,000	1.0%	$475

FIXED INCOME

	DISTRIBUTION %	DISTRIBUTION $	INCOME %	INCOME $
NE Investors	2.5%	$25,000	9.2%	$2,293
Government	20.0%	$200,000	6.1%	$12,200
Corporate (High Grd)	30.0%	$300,000	6.8%	$20,370
Money Market	2.5%	$25,000	4.8%	$1,198

COMPOSITES

	DISTRIBUTION %	DISTRIBUTION $	INCOME %	INCOME $
Core	27.5%	$275,000	2.2%	$6,143
Volatile	0.0%	$0	0.0%	$0
Disruptive	0.0%	$0	0.0%	$0
Supplementals	7.5%	$75,000	1.5%	$1,160
Tactical	0.0%	$0	0.0%	$0
Mutual Funds	10.0%	$100,000	1.1%	$1,125
Bonds & Cash	55.0%	$550,000	6.6%	$36,060
TOTAL	100%	$1,000,000	4.45%	$44,488
	0.00%			

FIGURE 9.5 Conservative portfolio.

S & P 500 SECTORS

S & P 500 SECTORS	DISTRIBUTION %	DISTRIBUTION $	INCOME %	INCOME $
Energy				
Materials				
Industrials				
Cnsmr Discretionary				
Cnsmr Cyclicals				
Health Care				
Financials				
Information Tech				
Communications				
Utilities				

PORTFOLIOS

PORTFOLIOS
AGGRESSIVE
DYNAMIC
MODERATE
CONSERVATIVE
INCOME

CHOICE

CHOICE
I

AMOUNT	
$1,000,000	

NOT AVAILABLE	
N	

INCOME	
Annual Tax Savings	$1,370
1997 Return	2.3%
1998 Return	6.9%
YTD 1999 Return	4.1%
Yield	6.14%
Income	$61,440
Positions	20

STRATEGIC

STRATEGIC	DISTRIBUTION %	DISTRIBUTION $	INCOME %	INCOME $
Schlumberger	0.0%		1.3%	
Exxon	0.0%		2.4%	
Union Carbide	0.0%		1.5%	
Phelps Dodge	5.0%	$50,000	3.6%	$1,800
General Electric	0.0%		1.1%	
ADP	0.0%		0.7%	
General Motors	5.0%	$50,000	2.9%	$1,445
Wal-Mart	0.0%		0.4%	
Anheuser-Busch	0.0%		1.7%	
Procter & Gamble	0.0%		1.2%	
Mallinckrodt	0.0%		1.9%	
Pfizer	0.0%		0.9%	
J.P. Morgan	5.0%	$50,000	3.0%	$1,505
AIG	0.0%		0.2%	
Microsoft	0.0%		0.0%	
Cisco	0.0%		0.0%	
Intel	0.0%		0.2%	
Global Crossing	0.0%		0.0%	
Sprint PCS	0.0%		0.0%	
Ameren UE	10.0%	$100,000	6.8%	$6,800
Enron	0.0%		1.3%	
Mid-Cap SPDRs	0.0%		0.0%	
AOL	0.0%		0.0%	
Unisys	0.0%		0.0%	
PeopleSoft	0.0%		0.0%	
Oracle	0.0%		0.0%	
QUALCOMM	0.0%		0.0%	
Applied Materials	0.0%		0.3%	
Comcast	0.0%		0.0%	
Uniphase	0.0%		0.0%	
Nextlink	0.0%		0.0%	
Broadcom	0.0%		0.0%	
Level 3	0.0%		0.0%	
Cree Research	0.0%		0.0%	
Texas Instruments	0.0%		0.0%	
C-Cube	0.0%		0.0%	

SUPPLEMENTALS

SUPPLEMENTALS	DISTRIBUTION %	DISTRIBUTION $	INCOME %	INCOME $
Ashland Oil	0.0%		3.3%	
International Paper	0.0%		1.9%	
Southwest Airlines	0.0%		0.1%	
Times Mirror	0.0%		1.1%	
Sysco	0.0%		1.3%	
Amgen	0.0%		0.0%	
Charles Schwab	0.0%		0.1%	
Dell	0.0%		0.0%	
MCI WorldCom	0.0%		0.0%	
Peoples Energy	0.0%		5.1%	

MUTUAL FUNDS

MUTUAL FUNDS	DISTRIBUTION %	DISTRIBUTION $	INCOME %	INCOME $
Lord Abbott Dev Grth	0.0%		0.0%	
SSgA Emerging Mkts	0.0%		2.6%	
Hotchkis & Wiley Int'l	0.0%		1.0%	

FIXED INCOME

FIXED INCOME	DISTRIBUTION %	DISTRIBUTION $	INCOME %	INCOME $
NE Investors	5.0%	$50,000	9.2%	$4,585
Government	25.0%	$250,000	6.1%	$15,250
Corporate (High Grd)	42.5%	$425,000	6.8%	$28,858
Money Market	2.5%	$25,000	4.8%	$1,198

COMPOSITES

COMPOSITES	DISTRIBUTION %	DISTRIBUTION $	INCOME %	INCOME $
Core	25.0%	$250,000	4.6%	$11,550
Volatile	0.0%	$0	0.0%	$0
Disruptive	0.0%	$0	0.0%	$0
Supplementals	0.0%	$0	0.0%	$0
Tactical	0.0%	$0	0.0%	$0
Mutual Funds	0.0%	$0	0.0%	$0
Bonds & Cash	75.0%	$750,000	6.7%	$49,890
TOTAL	100%	$1,000,000	6.14%	$61,440
	0.00%			

FIGURE 9.6 Income portfolio.

The same systematic reduction of risk is applied to the disruptive stocks. The beginning total distribution in the aggressive portfolio is 14%, sliced in half each time we step down one portfolio. The identical calculation applies if we accept an eighth position. Combining the volatiles and the disruptives, the aggressive portfolio holds 44% at risk, the dynamic drops to 29.5%, and the moderate slides further to 18.5%. The conservative and income portfolios do not participate in the volatile or the disruptive stocks. See Figures 9.5 and 9.6.

Note that in the aggressive portfolio we avoid all high-income stocks—Phelps Dodge, J.P. Morgan, Ameren, Ashland Oil, and Peoples Energy. Not only are these inappropriate for an aggressive portfolio, but they produce unwanted income. As we move down the risk slide, participation increases.

All this is but another signal to the Boomer client that a systematic process is in place to manage their assets at retirement. Comfort sets in rather quickly.

Refer to Appendix D for a more complete discussion of the distribution model.

Crucial Tools

Old Stuff

Certainly the old-guard software programs are still necessary and useful. For research and data analysis, Morningstar and Lipper Analytical are essential. Financial planning software runs the gamut from simple and basic to complex and thorough.

What these programs don't do is:

- Provide a single, instantaneous location where we can manage every aspect of our Boomer clients' financial lives 24 hours a day, 365 days a year, from anywhere on earth.

- Handle portfolio analysis, construction, and presentation

- Create hundreds of customized reports from current prices and activity

- Supply company-specific valuation and recommendations

- Provide technical information

- Allow analysis of company fundamentals

- Furnish up-to-date analysts' reports and pricing information on puts and calls

New Stuff

For the most part, the Old Stuff did not evolve into the New Stuff. Rather, the New Stuff consists of unique creations primarily as the result of technological advancements, specifically computer related. In fact, much of the Old Stuff, already briefly touched upon, has been forced to adapt to remain competitive.

The Internet

Out of our hands, an enemy. In our hands, an ally.

All the essentials that we discussed in Chapter 8 are managed, to some degree, through the Internet. This is the same Internet that is available to Boomers in their living rooms.

As we've already discussed, the Internet is an incredibly potent force of historic magnitude. It parallels no other advancement in its potential to disrupt the current foundation and fabric within the realm of commerce. We can try to beat it away with a stick and a flurry of foul language or we can learn it, consolidate a list of the Web sites that benefit our profession, and integrate them with our software, allowing us to better manage the portfolios and financial lives of our Baby Boomer clients.

In other words, we must take the tool that could ruin us, become more proficient at using it than clients could or would, and put it to use on their behalf.

Portfolio Development and Asset Management

The Web site at www.strategicportfolios.com is an excellent location for researching, building, and maintaining our portfolios. It contains numerous tools for asset management, including a hyperlink to www.stockoptionscentral.com. At Stock Options Central, we can thoroughly analyze our clients' company stock option positions by controlling such variables as:

- Previous year's issues
- Company growth rate
- Growth rate of the proceeds after clients exercise their stock options and turn the funds over to us to manage
- Total net taxes, if clients do or do not exercise their options, including Medicare, Social Security, and state taxes

Once all these variables are plugged in, "what-ifs" can be run. We can exercise any single block of issues in any given future year. And if our Boomer clients don't manually exercise, they automatically do so in the tenth year, as most stock options require. Or if need be, all can be exercised in the current year. Upon exercise, the tax rate is calculated and applied to the exercise proceeds to determine the net tax impact.

These what-ifs allow us to compare scenarios to help determine when and how much to exercise versus waiting for automatic exercise when a client's tax rate might be higher. Being able to manipulate both the growth of the stock options and of our managed portfolios allows us the opportunity to show a client that if his or her company has reached its growth plateau and the client wants to take part in an aggressive portfolio, exercising would be a good source of funds.

For the mutual funds in our portfolios, an excellent source for research and information is www.knowloads.com. This site brings together into one spot the 50 most prominent no-load mutual fund families.

Portfolio Analysis, Construction, and Presentation

A critical tool in asset management is software that assembles securities into a portfolio and analyzes them individually and as a unit using historical prices. Wilson International's Power Optimizer (www.wilsonintl.com) performs these functions, and more, quite well. Once we have developed our models, Power Optimizer (POP) stores and updates them. Updates include raw price and net asset value (NAV) growth, excluding dividend reinvest.

Among other tasks, POP can also perform the following analytical functions for individual stocks during and after the construction of our models:

- Beta/alpha comparisons
- Correlation
- Risk-adjusted return
- Risk/return scattergraphing

We can assign four probability values to performance: 80%, 90%, 95%, and 99%. In addition, POP allows us to toggle on and off the individual or combined impact of taxes, fees, and inflation.

Power Optimizer lets us change, for each security, the income and capital tax rates, yields, management fees and transfer fees, and, for mutual funds, expense ratios and turnover rates. (However, the program has an annoying bug whereby it does not save all the changes made. Once you leave a model and then reopen it, all numbers return to default values. This can induce hair-pulling.) These elements affect the outcome of cash flow analysis.

Once a client's retirement amount is dropped into the model we've created that best fits the individual's risk level, unlimited cash flow scenarios can be built to demonstrate the effect of withdrawals (or contributions to nonqualified assets) on future balances.

The balances generated from the cash flow components are net of gains, withdrawal amounts, income taxes, capital gains taxes, and management fees. Power Optimizer gives us 11 portfolio reports:

- Rate of return

- Values

- Recommendations

- Analysis

- Cash flow

- Asset class information

- Asset class statistics

- Implementation

- Assets return

- Correlation

- Status

and three historical reports:

- Monthly rate of return

- Growth of a dollar

- Rolling period rates of return

Then there's the Efficient Frontier mechanism, whereby the computer software distributes the assets into the most ideal mix of securities inside our portfolios based on rate of return relative to standard deviation. The computer is so good at this that it almost always dumps the money into a single security displaying the most ideal combination of the two components. In order to override this, we must make minimum/maximum choices for each security. In other words, we must tell the software we want, for example, at least 1.25% but no more than 2.5% of the total assets to go into ABC Corporation. Note that this nuance is not a Wilson International problem. It's simply the way the Efficient Frontier operates.

Perhaps the most significant impact that POP delivers is its client presentation ability. Most charts and graphs are excellent; some are merely good. All graphs show five-year minimum and maximum values and rates of return, based on historical standard deviation.

The pie charts are sizeable, both three-dimensional and 2-dimensional. Pieces of the pie can be pulled away from the whole. There are 49 colors from which to choose for the slices.

Four charts are offered: rate of return, range of returns, standard deviation, and range of values. These can be shown in bar, line, or mountain style and also offer 49 colors from which to choose for the components and the background.

Three line charts present dollar growth, monthly rate of return, and rolling rate of return over a chosen time period. Each shows the number of high periods and the number of low periods.

Finally there is the scattergraph, which plots all individual securities in a portfolio on an x-axis/y-axis graph, with x equaling rate of return and y representing standard deviation. This graph also pinpoints the location of the average x and y values for the entire portfolio.

There are a few annoyances: The date selection in the cash flow input process manufactures a table with an erroneous start date. In addition, only 1- to 5-year periods are available for charting and graphing, although the portfolio analysis report shows 10 and 15 years.

Daily Client Portfolio Tracking and Customized Reporting

The four primary suppliers of this software are Advent, dbCams, Centerpoint, and CapTool. All offer the same service with minor variations. They are a means of constructing a multitude of client portfolio reports using the previous day's closing prices as a base for the entire history. This is accomplished by data downloads that occur every day. All client activity is brought into the database: buys, sells, dividends, capital gains, transfers, cash infusions, cash disbursements. Plunking down in one handy spot the entire universe of client activity swings open the door to an unimaginable number of reports.

Asset reports

Financial statements and net worth

Statement of financial position

Financial summary

Current position

Unrealized increase/decrease

Percentage of total

Detail positions

Position comparison

Asset allocation

Performance reports

With any date range

With multiple date ranges

With period returns

With annualized returns

By internal rate of return

By time-weighted rate of return

By category

By portfolio within a client's account

This software also includes IRS Schedule B (dividend income) and IRS Schedule D (capital gains) for any time periods. And if we're not pleased as punch with any of the standard reports, we can design our own by manipulating any of the variables as we see fit.

Each of these versions also integrates client management into the base software or offers it as an add-on.

Company Valuation and Recommendations

Standard & Poor's hosts an Internet site at www.advisorinsight .com. Unlike Morningstar, Valueline, Lipper, and some others, this Web page is accessible only to professional investment advisors, locking out the general public. With the resources S & P can muster, it's no wonder this site splits the monitor's seams with information about and recommendations for each of the positions in our portfolios.

A section titled "Marketscope" offers market commentary, economic analysis, technical analysis, special investment ideas, their STAR ratings, and Fair Value calculations; it maintains specific portfolios, market statistics, stock splits, earnings forecasts, takeover news, new issues (in case we want to expand our volatile picks), and more. Standard & Poor's also puts up general analysts' recommendations and compares them to their own proprietary advice.

In a second section, called "Stock Reports," you can nose around in all the fundamentals of our companies as well as read an overview, a valuation synopsis, and a business summary. You can pull up news on a particular stock (although it's not as current as it could be), the Wall Street consensus on the stock, and an industry outlook. In this section, you can also devise screens using one or a combination of over 200 variables. Ongoing research can be burdensome and frustrating, however, because you can't save favorite screens, so you have to perpetually rebuild them. Furthermore, the site doesn't allow you to input and save portfolios for future analysis.

A third location is called "Fund Advisor." As the title implies, this is where you can execute the search for portfolio funds. However, for reasons similar to those mentioned in conjunction with the troublesome chore of picking screen criteria, Morningstar is a more likely and suitable source for these funds. Once funds are selected, this location offers little of value because its choices are arbitrary. This would change if S & P's site were to offer the ability to save a group of funds for continued analysis.

This Web site has no distracting clutter of banner ads. It's a nice quiet place to do research.

Technical Analysis

As discussed in Chapter 9, technical analysis is useful for short-term determination of when to buy into securities. Technical analysis software and sites are plentiful on the Internet. Some of them are designed for day traders, those folks who remain attached to their poor computer mice throughout the day as they jump in and out of trading positions. Their investment time frame is measured in minutes, not weeks or months, and until the majority go bankrupt, much of the software is aimed at them and constructed for such maximum use by showing microtrends in pricing behavior.

Decisionpoint.com and IQC.com are two Web sites that seem to offer all the necessary elements to accomplish the goal of most appropriate market entry. The charting is free on the Internet, although it does not come in as real-time. Real-time charting is nice but not essential.

Each of these sites allows you to choose technical indicators, with the exception of DecisionPoint, which does not offer the Commodity Channel Index (CCI).

Fundamental Analysis

Spredgar is an excellent software program whose primary feature is its graphic analysis of corporate fundamentals. The name *Spredgar* is a combination of "spreadsheet" and "EDGAR." EDGAR is an acronym for Electronic Data Gathering, Analysis, and Retrieval. It's the SEC's free database Web site for corporate filings of 10-K (annual) and 10-Q (quarterly) reports. Among many other reports, this site includes a balance sheet and a cash flow statement, both of which produce an army of performance ratios. It's about as official and accurate as you can find.

Spredgar reaches into EDGAR and seamlessly pulls into a spreadsheet the balance sheet and cash flow reports of any company you choose and then displays subsequent performance ratios as bar charts. It also compares the company's performance with others in the same Standard Industrial Classification (SIC) code. You can assemble and store all your equity choices inside Spredgar so that ratios are updated upon the companies' quarterly filings with the SEC.

Whereas Spredgar is a numeric and graphic assistant, Multex .com is a qualitative shopping spot. Multex is a site for professional investment advisors that brings to us hundreds of analysts' reports on our companies. (And the word "shopping" is intended literally.) Most reports cost money—anywhere from $5 to $300. An occasional report is free; however, these are often of little significance. Also available are video interviews with people who are experts on or who track particular companies. In addition, you can enter and save the list of selected companies so that Multex displays the available reports on only those designated.

In order to manage puts and calls properly, you can visit the Chicago Board of Options Exchange Web site (CBOE.com). Valuable mostly for quotes and options chains, it is also an exceptional information and education center for derivatives.

Surely Wilson International, IQCharts, Standard & Poor's, Spredgar.com, and Multex.com have competitors. It would be prudent to investigate them, as well.

CHAPTER

11

Mythologies

I
f we are compensated by fee only, in generally smaller amounts on an ongoing basis as opposed to being paid once and up front, we think we'll make less money, have to work harder, and have less time. In fact, we'll make more money and work the same amount of time or less.

The data to prove these assertions is hovering out there in the public domain for anyone to grab. All that's necessary is an impartial, careful look at it. Tables 11.1 through 11.5 show five comparisons into the future between compensation patterns of the traditional salesperson and that of the future advisor.

The assumptions are as follows:

1. Every client of the salesperson results in a $500,000 annuity that pays net up-front 5% commission, or $25,000.

2. Every client of the advisor results in a $500,000 managed account with a 1% annual management fee.

3. Every penny of their compensation is invested.

4. The market grows at 12% per year.

The only variable we'll control is the number of clients added per year. After all, this is the ultimate measure of quality service. It is easier to take microscopic care of 50 clients than 150 clients.

Adding Five Clients per Year

Refer to Table 11.1. If the advisor and the salesperson add five clients a year, somewhere in the first quarter of the fourth year, their per-year compensation is equal. After 10 years, the annual paycheck of the advisor is $438,718 compared to the salesperson's $125,000—a 251% difference. After 15 years, the advisor makes $931,993 and the salesperson is still at $125,000.

True, relative to the salesperson the advisor takes it on the compensation chin the first few years. So in order to demonstrate the cumulative effect of the income streams, which accounts for the advisor's slow start, we force our two titans to invest every penny. Just toward the end of the eighth year, the advisor's ending invested balance passes the salesperson's. After the tenth year, the advisor has 28% more than the salesperson. After 15 years, the advisor has twice as much tucked away, with a balance of $10,458,880 to the salesperson's $5,219,160.

Salesperson Adding Clients to Match Advisor's Compensation

Refer to Table 11.2. We increase the number of clients the salesperson must add annually to force his or her income to keep pace with that of the advisor. After 10 years, the advisor, continuing to add only five clients a year, has an annual income of $438,718 and 50 clients to keep happy. During the same 10 years, the salesperson's paycheck is almost the same as the advisor's, but the salesperson has accepted almost 90 clients. The difference is even more dramatic in five additional years. The advisor and the salesperson are making about the same amount, but the advisor has 75 clients and the salesperson has more than three times that, at 232.

Who is offering superior service more efficiently?

Advisor Stops Adding Clients in Attempt to Match Salesperson's Compensation

Refer to Table 11.3. This is the antithesis of Table 11.2: Out of politeness to the salesperson, we reduce the number of clients the advisor takes on in an attempt to keep their compensation equal

TABLE 11.1 Adding Five Clients per Year

SALESPERSON

Yr	Clients Added per Year	Compensation per Client	Compensation per Year	Investment Beginning Balance	Investment Growth	Investment Ending Balance
1	5	$25,000	$125,000	$125,000	$15,000	$140,000
2	5	$25,000	$125,000	$265,000	$31,800	$296,800
3	5	$25,000	$125,000	$421,800	$50,616	$472,416
4	5	$25,000	$125,000	$597,416	$71,690	$669,106
5	5	$25,000	$125,000	$794,106	$95,293	$889,399
6	5	$25,000	$125,000	$1,014,399	$121,728	$1,136,126
7	5	$25,000	$125,000	$1,261,126	$151,335	$1,412,462
8	5	$25,000	$125,000	$1,537,462	$184,495	$1,721,957
9	5	$25,000	$125,000	$1,846,957	$221,635	$2,068,592
10	5	$25,000	$125,000	$2,193,592	$263,231	$2,456,823
11	5	$25,000	$125,000	$2,581,823	$309,819	$2,891,642
12	5	$25,000	$125,000	$3,016,642	$361,997	$3,378,639
13	5	$25,000	$125,000	$3,503,639	$420,437	$3,924,075
14	5	$25,000	$125,000	$4,049,075	$485,889	$4,534,964
15	5	$25,000	$125,000	$4,659,964	$559,196	$5,219,160
	50	< 10-year Total Client Base				
	75	< 15-year Total Client Base				

ADVISOR

Yr	Clients Added per Year	Compensation per Client	Compensation per Year	Investment Beginning Balance	Investment Growth	Investment Ending Balance
1	5	$2,500,000	$25,000	$25,000	$3,000	$28,000
2	5	$5,300,000	$53,000	$81,000	$9,720	$90,720
3	5	$8,436,000	$84,360	$175,080	$21,010	$196,090
4	5	$11,948,320	$119,483	$315,573	$37,869	$353,442
5	5	$15,882,118	$158,821	$512,263	$61,472	$573,734
6	5	$20,287,973	$202,880	$776,614	$93,194	$869,808
7	5	$25,222,529	$252,225	$1,122,033	$134,644	$1,256,677
8	5	$30,749,233	$307,492	$1,564,169	$187,700	$1,751,870
9	5	$36,939,141	$369,391	$2,121,261	$254,551	$2,375,812
10	5	$43,871,838	$438,718	$2,814,531	$337,744	$3,152,274
11	5	$51,636,458	$516,365	$3,668,639	$440,237	$4,108,876
12	5	$60,332,833	$603,328	$4,712,204	$565,464	$5,277,668
13	5	$70,072,773	$700,728	$5,978,396	$717,408	$6,695,804
14	5	$80,981,506	$809,815	$7,505,619	$900,674	$8,406,293
15	5	$93,199,287	$931,993	$9,338,286	$1,120,594	$10,458,880
	50	< 10-year Total Client Base				
	75	< 15-year Total Client Base				

TABLE 11.2 Salesperson Adding Clients to Match Advisor's Compensation

SALESPERSON

Yr	Clients Added per Year	Compensation per Client	Compensation per Year	Investment Beginning Balance	Investment Growth	Investment Ending Balance
1	5.0	$25,000	$125,000	$125,000	$15,000	$140,000
2	5.0	$25,000	$125,000	$265,000	$31,800	$296,800
3	5.0	$25,000	$125,000	$421,800	$50,616	$472,416
4	5.0	$25,000	$125,000	$597,416	$71,690	$669,106
5	6.4	$25,000	$158,750	$827,856	$99,343	$927,199
6	8.1	$25,000	$202,750	$1,129,949	$135,594	$1,265,542
7	10.1	$25,000	$252,500	$1,518,042	$182,165	$1,700,208
8	12.3	$25,000	$307,500	$2,007,708	$240,925	$2,248,632
9	14.8	$25,000	$369,500	$2,618,132	$314,176	$2,932,308
10	17.6	$25,000	$438,750	$3,371,058	$404,527	$3,775,585
11	20.7	$25,000	$516,250	$4,291,835	$515,020	$4,806,856
12	24.1	$25,000	$603,125	$5,409,981	$649,198	$6,059,178
13	28.0	$25,000	$700,500	$6,759,678	$811,161	$7,570,840
14	32.4	$25,000	$809,750	$8,380,590	$1,005,671	$9,386,260
15	37.3	$25,000	$931,875	$10,318,135	$1,238,176	$11,556,312
	89	< 10-Year Total Client Base				
	232	< 15-Year Total Client Base				

ADVISOR

Yr	Clients Added per Year	Compensation per Client	Compensation per Year	Investment Beginning Balance	Investment Growth	Investment Ending Balance
1	5	$2,500,000	$25,000	$25,000	$3,000	$28,000
2	5	$5,300,000	$53,000	$81,000	$9,720	$90,720
3	5	$8,436,000	$84,360	$175,080	$21,010	$196,090
4	5	$11,948,320	$119,483	$315,573	$37,869	$353,442
5	5	$15,882,118	$158,821	$512,263	$61,472	$573,734
6	5	$20,287,973	$202,880	$776,614	$93,194	$869,808
7	5	$25,222,529	$252,225	$1,122,033	$134,644	$1,256,677
8	5	$30,749,233	$307,492	$1,564,169	$187,700	$1,751,870
9	5	$36,939,141	$369,391	$2,121,261	$254,551	$2,375,812
10	5	$43,871,838	$438,718	$2,814,531	$337,744	$3,152,274
11	5	$51,636,458	$516,365	$3,668,639	$440,237	$4,108,876
12	5	$60,332,833	$603,328	$4,712,204	$565,464	$5,277,668
13	5	$70,072,773	$700,728	$5,978,396	$717,408	$6,695,804
14	5	$80,981,506	$809,815	$7,505,619	$900,674	$8,406,293
15	5	$93,199,287	$931,993	$9,338,286	$1,120,594	$10,458,880
	50	< 10-Year Total Client Base				
	75	< 15-Year Total Client Base				

TABLE 11.3 Advisor Stops Adding Clients in Attempt to Match Salesperson's Compensation

SALESPERSON

Yr	Clients Added per Year	Compensation per Client	Compensation per Year	Investment Beginning Balance	Investment Growth	Investment Ending Balance
1	5.0	$25,000	$125,000	$125,000	$15,000	$140,000
2	5.0	$25,000	$125,000	$265,000	$31,800	$296,800
3	5.0	$25,000	$125,000	$421,800	$50,616	$472,416
4	5.0	$25,000	$125,000	$597,416	$71,690	$669,106
5	5.0	$25,000	$125,000	$794,106	$95,293	$889,399
6	5.0	$25,000	$125,000	$1,014,399	$121,728	$1,136,126
7	5.0	$25,000	$125,000	$1,261,126	$151,335	$1,412,462
8	5.0	$25,000	$125,000	$1,537,462	$184,495	$1,721,957
9	5.0	$25,000	$125,000	$1,846,957	$221,635	$2,068,592
10	5.0	$25,000	$125,000	$2,193,592	$263,231	$2,456,823
11	5.0	$25,000	$125,000	$2,581,823	$309,819	$2,891,642
12	5.0	$25,000	$125,000	$3,016,642	$361,997	$3,378,639
13	5.0	$25,000	$125,000	$3,503,639	$420,437	$3,924,075
14	5.0	$25,000	$125,000	$4,049,075	$485,889	$4,534,964
15	5.0	$25,000	$125,000	$4,659,964	$559,196	$5,219,160
	50	< 10-year Total Client Base				
	75	< 15-year Total Client Base				

ADVISOR

Yr	Clients Added per Year	Compensation per Client	Compensation per Year	Investment Beginning Balance	Investment Growth	Investment Ending Balance
1	5	$2,500,000	$25,000	$25,000	$3,000	$28,000
2	5	$5,300,000	$53,000	$81,000	$9,720	$90,720
3	5	$8,436,000	$84,360	$175,080	$21,010	$196,090
4	5	$11,948,320	$119,483	$315,573	$37,869	$353,442
5	0	$13,382,118	$133,821	$487,263	$58,472	$545,734
6	0	$14,987,973	$149,880	$695,614	$83,474	$779,088
7	0	$16,786,529	$167,865	$946,953	$113,634	$1,060,587
8	0	$18,800,913	$188,009	$1,248,596	$149,832	$1,398,428
9	0	$21,057,022	$210,570	$1,608,998	$193,080	$1,802,078
10	0	$23,583,865	$235,839	$2,037,917	$244,550	$2,282,467
11	0	$26,413,929	$264,139	$2,546,606	$305,593	$2,852,199
12	0	$29,583,600	$295,836	$3,148,035	$377,764	$3,525,799
13	0	$33,133,632	$331,336	$3,857,135	$462,856	$4,319,991
14	0	$37,109,668	$371,097	$4,691,088	$562,931	$5,254,019
15	0	$41,562,828	$415,628	$5,669,647	$680,358	$6,350,005
	20	< 10-year Total Client Base				
	20	< 15-year Total Client Base				

through the years. Note that it's not possible. The advisor accepts no more clients after the original 20 and after 10 years is making $235,839. The salesperson is still making $125,000 but has added 50 clients. After 15 years, the advisor still has 20 clients and is making $415,628, while the salesperson maintains $125,000 with 75 clients.

Advisor Adds Clients to Match Salesperson's 10-Year Accumulated Ending Balance

Refer to Table 11.4. Because the advisor gets off to a slow cash flow start, he or she will have to add 77 total clients over 10 years in order to bring his or her invested balance equal to that of the salesperson. During that same time, the salesperson has added almost 89 clients. The advisor reverts to adding 5 clients per year in the tenth year, so that after 15 years he or she has 102 clients but his or her invested base has grown to $13,317,788. While the salesperson continues to bloat his or her base to 232, with an invested balance of $11,556,312.

Advisor Matches Salesperson's Client Additions

Refer to Table 11.5. In Table 11.2, we saw how the salesperson would have to increase client base in order to keep up with the advisor's compensation as the advisor adds only five clients a year. A competitive itch hits the advisor, who decides to match the salesperson's client additions. After 10 years, the advisor has the same number of clients but is making $674,212 per year to the salesperson's $438,750. After 15 years, the advisor's annual income is $2,063,627 and the salesperson's is $931,875.

Conclusion

We've eyed this compensation issue from every angle and discovered that it is pure folly to assume that we will make more money if we receive it once and up front rather than in a continuous stream. We will experience some painful blips in the first few years, but our income will pick up steam exponentially thereafter. It would not be a great leap of reason to assume that since

TABLE 11.4 Advisor Adds Clients to Match Salesperson's 10-Year Accumulated Ending Balance

SALESPERSON

Yr	Clients Added per Year	Compensation per Client	Compensation per Year	Investment Beginning Balance	Investment Growth	Investment Ending Balance
1	5.0	$25,000	$125,000	$125,000	$15,000	$140,000
2	5.0	$25,000	$125,000	$265,000	$31,800	$296,800
3	5.0	$25,000	$125,000	$421,800	$50,616	$472,416
4	5.0	$25,000	$125,000	$597,416	$71,690	$669,106
5	6.4	$25,000	$158,750	$827,856	$99,343	$927,199
6	8.1	$25,000	$202,750	$1,129,949	$135,594	$1,265,542
7	10.1	$25,000	$252,500	$1,518,042	$182,165	$1,700,208
8	12.3	$25,000	$307,500	$2,007,708	$240,925	$2,248,632
9	14.8	$25,000	$369,500	$2,618,132	$314,176	$2,932,308
10	17.6	$25,000	$438,750	$3,371,058	$404,527	$3,775,585
11	20.7	$25,000	$516,250	$4,291,835	$515,020	$4,806,856
12	24.1	$25,000	$603,125	$5,409,981	$649,198	$6,059,178
13	28.0	$25,000	$700,500	$6,759,678	$811,161	$7,570,840
14	32.4	$25,000	$809,750	$8,380,590	$1,005,671	$9,386,260
15	37.3	$25,000	$931,875	$10,318,135	$1,238,176	$11,556,312

89	< 10-year Total Client Base
232	< 15-year Total Client Base

ADVISOR

Yr	Clients Added per Year	Compensation per Client	Compensation per Year	Investment Beginning Balance	Investment Growth	Investment Ending Balance
1	5.0	$2,500,000	$25,000	$25,000	$3,000	$28,000
2	5.0	$5,300,000	$53,000	$81,000	$9,720	$90,720
3	5.0	$8,436,000	$84,360	$175,080	$21,010	$196,090
4	5.0	$11,948,320	$119,483	$315,573	$37,869	$353,442
5	6.4	$16,557,118	$165,571	$519,013	$62,282	$581,294
6	8.1	$22,598,973	$225,990	$807,284	$96,874	$904,158
7	10.1	$30,360,849	$303,608	$1,207,767	$144,932	$1,352,699
8	12.3	$40,154,151	$401,542	$1,754,240	$210,509	$1,964,749
9	14.8	$52,372,649	$523,726	$2,488,475	$298,617	$2,787,092
10	5.0	$61,157,367	$611,574	$3,398,666	$407,840	$3,806,506
11	5.0	$70,996,251	$709,963	$4,516,468	$541,976	$5,058,445
12	5.0	$82,015,802	$820,158	$5,878,603	$705,432	$6,584,035
13	5.0	$94,357,698	$943,577	$7,527,612	$903,313	$8,430,925
14	5.0	$108,180,621	$1,081,806	$9,512,732	$1,141,528	$10,654,259
15	5.0	$123,662,296	$1,236,623	$11,890,882	$1,426,906	$13,317,788

77	< 10-year Total Client Base
102	< 15-year Total Client Base

TABLE 11.5 Advisor Matches Salesperson's Client Additions from Table 11.2

SALESPERSON

Yr	Clients Added per Year	Compensation per Client	Compensation per Year	Investment Beginning Balance	Investment Growth	Investment Ending Balance
1	5.0	$25,000	$125,000	$125,000	$15,000	$140,000
2	5.0	$25,000	$125,000	$265,000	$31,800	$296,800
3	5.0	$25,000	$125,000	$421,800	$50,616	$472,416
4	5.0	$25,000	$125,000	$597,416	$71,690	$669,106
5	6.4	$25,000	$158,750	$827,856	$99,343	$927,199
6	8.1	$25,000	$202,750	$1,129,949	$135,594	$1,265,542
7	10.1	$25,000	$252,500	$1,518,042	$182,165	$1,700,208
8	12.3	$25,000	$307,500	$2,007,708	$240,925	$2,248,632
9	14.8	$25,000	$369,500	$2,618,132	$314,176	$2,932,308
10	17.6	$25,000	$438,750	$3,371,058	$404,527	$3,775,585
11	20.7	$25,000	$516,250	$4,291,835	$515,020	$4,806,856
12	24.1	$25,000	$603,125	$5,409,981	$649,198	$6,059,178
13	28.0	$25,000	$700,500	$6,759,678	$811,161	$7,570,840
14	32.4	$25,000	$809,750	$8,380,590	$1,005,671	$9,386,260
15	37.3	$25,000	$931,875	$10,318,135	$1,238,176	$11,556,312
89	< 10-year Total Client Base					
232	< 15-year Total Client Base					

ADVISOR

Yr	Clients Added per Year	Compensation per Client	Compensation per Year	Investment Beginning Balance	Investment Growth	Investment Ending Balance
1	5.0	$2,500,000	$25,000	$25,000	$3,000	$28,000
2	5.0	$5,300,000	$53,000	$81,000	$9,720	$90,720
3	5.0	$8,436,000	$84,360	$175,080	$21,010	$196,090
4	5.0	$11,948,320	$119,483	$315,573	$37,869	$353,442
5	6.4	$16,557,118	$165,571	$519,013	$62,282	$581,294
6	8.1	$22,598,973	$225,990	$807,284	$96,874	$904,158
7	10.1	$30,360,849	$303,608	$1,207,767	$144,932	$1,352,699
8	12.3	$40,154,151	$401,542	$1,754,240	$210,509	$1,964,749
9	14.8	$52,362,649	$523,626	$2,488,375	$298,605	$2,786,980
10	17.6	$67,421,167	$674,212	$3,461,192	$415,343	$3,876,535
11	20.7	$85,836,707	$858,367	$4,734,902	$568,188	$5,303,090
12	24.1	$108,199,612	$1,081,996	$6,385,087	$766,210	$7,151,297
13	28.0	$135,193,566	$1,351,936	$8,503,233	$1,020,388	$9,523,621
14	32.4	$167,611,794	$1,676,118	$11,199,738	$1,343,969	$12,543,707
15	37.3	$206,362,709	$2,063,627	$14,607,334	$1,752,880	$16,360,214
89	< 10-year Total Client Base					
232	< 15-year Total Client Base					

the advisor has fewer clients and is keeping annual additions steady compared to the salesperson, the advisor can tend to them more scrupulously.

If we assume Table 11.2 to be the most realistic, our advisor has 75 clients after 15 years, whereas our salesperson has 232. The year has roughly 2,000 hours of labor in it. If the salesperson is consuming 80% of this time still rustling up new clients, then a mere 400 hours each year are devoted to pampering those already on the roster—less than 1 hour and 45 minutes per existing client. The advisor has 75 clients to keep happy and 80% of 2,000 hours in which to do so, equating to 21 hours and 15 minutes per year for each client. Which is better for each client—1 hour and 45 minutes or 21 hours and 15 minutes?

However, we need to make some adjustments to this analogy because our advisor really functions as just one point of a triangle, which means there is 300% of consumable time. The Bubbler spends 100% of the time wooing clients, and each of the other two points in the triangle spend 100% of their time servicing the client base. Thus the real time dedicated to gaining clients is 33%, not 20%. And, functioning as a triangle, they can absorb three times the 75 clients, or 225 clients. So, as a triangle, they spend 66% of 6,000 labor-hours on pleasing their clients, or 17 hours and 40 minutes a year per client.

Moreover, instead of spending 80% of our time piling on new clients and 20% of our time servicing them after they've joined the heap, we can transpose those numbers and have fewer people to keep happier. We also retain the option of, at some point, transforming that 20% client search time to leisure time. After all, our income continues to rise as we spend 80% of our time taking better care of our current clients.

The same percentage breakdown can be applied to the golf game. We can spend 80% of tee times with current clients—presumably more pleasant than the 20% spent with strangers we're yapping at about how good we are.

So let's take a final tally of the benefits of our new approach:

- More money
- Better service

- Same amount of time working (and potentially less)

- No reduction in time spent on the golf game and this time is probably less stressful

The myths are now on the shelf, out of the way.

Most financial services companies offer compensation choices that fulfill, to some degree, each of these elements. What they don't do is encourage the alternatives.

In fact, a few financial services company chiefs have addressed the perceived virtues of commission versus fees, attempting to convince a monolithic market that the direction in which it is barreling toward fees happens to be wrong. Surely, there have been past corporate leaders who believed they possessed the power to manipulate the consumer market in the face of incontrovertible disruptive change. And just as surely, they have led their companies down a dangerous path of crippling disability or even ruin.

Then there are some financial company captains who have demonstrated the requisite vision. They not only are aware of the force of the new approach, but they are harnessing it. As of this writing, two such firms are Merrill Lynch and Morgan Stanley Dean Witter. They offer on-line, fee-based programs that combine no-commission trading with the guidance of an advisor, all for an annual fee charged directly and up front. Now a Merrill or MSDW advisor can actually be compensated for telling a client to do nothing. Can you imagine being paid for a calming, unbiased piece of advice? What's next? Free luxurious trips based on how well we take care of our clients rather than how many we can herd through the door?

It's coming. The market will see to it.

CHAPTER

12

The Purity Scale

acts surrounding financial advisors' compensation have historically been heavily guarded, tucked away in the fine print
of the contract. It's so much easier on us if the client never
sees what we make or how we make it. That way we can fill our
pockets without explaining anything, leaving clients sitting
across the conference tables perplexed about how we're paid.
How often have we explained to them, "I get paid by the [prod-
uct] company. You don't have to worry. Nothing comes directly
out of your pocket or your account."

This proclamation takes great courage.

Then there are those moments when we leave meetings with
prospects, wondering how they could muster the audacity to
relentlessly burrow into our means of compensation with
those bothersome questions. Why couldn't they just accept the
fact that they're not supposed to see how much we make off
them?

The matter is not much more distinct with stockbrokers. As a
party to a transaction-based relationship, a stockbroker conducts
nearly all trades through phone conversations or a series of
e-mails. When was the last time a client came to the office to discuss a trade? Thus, when transactions happen, clients are not

always immediately aware of the commission. They know it's there, but overshadowing it is the momentary, raw psychological power of the chance to make instant money: "You've got to get in on this stock. The analysts think its ready to blow the roof off." Or to protect profit: "We should get out of this thing. It looks like it's topped out."

Because, at the moment of the transaction, clients are perched somewhere near one end or the other of the profit spectrum—in the grip of either greed or panic—commission is at least temporarily irrelevant. For us, client greed equals commission. Likewise, client panic equals commission.

Sure, we had to engage with clients in the initial dance about the commission issue when they were still just prospects. We had to be competitive and deliver a tad more value than the stockbroker down the block. But we now know that the commission waltz is about to run out of music, because rates have been slashed 90% by the Internet. So all we have left to bring to the dance is value, and the amount we bring better be more than just a tad.

There are four means by which compensation is delivered to us, divided into two categories:

Fee-based	Direct and one-time
	Direct over time
Commission-based	Indirect and one-time
	Indirect over time

From out perspective, fee-based compensation has not been the most cherished method and being compensated indirectly over time is only slightly less galling. But fee-based compensation is just over the horizon, accompanied by the thundering herd of Baby Boomer retirees, who will demand to be informed of and have the right to compare outright the payment method and amount and the promised value received in return. They'll want to be certain they are getting their money's worth. And once they verify this, they will pay top dollar for the superior service that is their Holy Grail.

Commission-based compensation that traps Boomer clients in particular products leaves them cold and they will refuse to participate. Though compensation that is indirect over time is palatable to them, they cannot see its effects and will forever be suspicious of it. The more open we become to recognizing these urges and the more likely we are to switch compensation methods, the more momentum the drive toward fee-based compensation will gain until it overpowers commission-based compensation.

In Chapter 4, we reviewed in detail the methods of indirect compensation. Now we'll delve into two methods that our Boomer clients will increasingly prefer. The first is designed for the triangles that operate inside the independent arena. The second is for the triangles that work as captive employees of large financial services companies.

There are two primary differences between the independents and the captives. The first is who works for whom. The financial services company serving the independent works for the independent and can be invited to stop being a vendor at any time without financial ramifications. The captive works for the financial services outfit and can be invited to leave at any time with financial consequences. Though this rarely occurs if the person in question is profitable for the company.

The second difference is payout level—compensation. Independents receive, on average, over 40% more in compensation than captive employees, although in the independent's realm nothing is free—not office space, clerical assistance, receptionist, office machinery, software, or stationery. Breakeven generally lies somewhere around $120,000 of the gross concession barrier. So if an individual were a captive employee making around $60,000 to $70,000, he or she would make the same amount, net of expenses, as an independent. But as an independent, what happens after breaking that barrier is momentous: For every $1,000 generated in gross concessions beyond the $120,000, the independent keeps $400 more than the captive employee.

From a psychological perspective, independents must have the entrepreneurial spirit. Captive employees need the corporate umbrella in order to remain focused on their sole purpose of generating revenue with the sale of products.

Moreover, a number of financial services corporations still demand that their captive employees offer only homegrown products. Many, however, have introduced "product networks" that allow their captive employees to place before their clients the products of many competitors. At first blush this appears honorable and objective until the captive employees discover that their company runs interference on the competition's payout and claims as its own up to 50% of it. So the choice as a captive employee is to be paid half of 100% of the company's stuff or half of 50% of some other company's. Given captive employees' foremost priority of creating revenue, there's little doubt which approach will be used. It's a great marketing tool to dangle objectivity in front of clients and then pull it away at the last minute.

A final reason for making these distinctions is that, due to more liberal and varied compensation choices, the independents can deliver a purer version of fee work than can captive employees.

Independents

There are nearly 40,000 of us toiling away on our own. Independents associate with brokers who provide the same service as a large financial services employer supplies to its captive employees. They make available the products—mutual funds, life insurance, and annuities—and the ability to trade equities through a clearinghouse. Financial Network Investment Corporation (FNIC), Linsco/Private Ledger (LPL), Raymond James, and Royal Alliance are a few of the larger brokers serving independents. There are 10, including the 4 mentioned, that boast at least 1,000 or more advisors and serve almost 63% of all independents. There are roughly an additional 30 that retain at least 100 advisors and pick up the remaining percentage.

The average payout of the top 30 brokers is 86.7% on all investment-related products. Of the compensation received for all other work, 100% is retained by the independent. This includes the compilation of financial plans, health insurance, whole life and term insurance, and long-term care insurance. Although these are fringe products relative to those that are investment related, they do create revenue. Thus, depending upon the level of activity in them, the net payout can be some figure higher than 86.7%.

Because the payout level applies to all the products brought to independents by their brokers, any variations that occur among products of the same nature are the direct result of the compensation structures of the products themselves. But since most brokers gather thousands of products together under their roof for the independents' use, such disparity is minor.

The One-Stop Fee

Our goal is to satisfy the three requirements our Boomer clients have regarding how they pay us:

- The method of compensation must be direct.
- The method of compensation must be ongoing.
- The method of compensation must allow them to maintain their freedom.

In the managed portfolio examples from Chapter 8, we charge the client based on the following fee structure (which is outlined in our ADV II, the document the SEC requires Registered Investment Advisors to provide to clients):

$1 to $1,000,000	1.00%
$1,000,001 to $5,000,000	0.75%
$5,000,000	$42,000 per year plus CPI* × 2.

A client with $1 million pays us $10,000 annually. The client signs the engagement letter, which clearly outlines the fee structure. The fees are removed from the client's account quarterly by the broker. After siphoning off the house cut, the broker forwards the remainder to the financial advisor. A letter is sent to the client every quarter outlining the fee withdrawal.

---

*Consumer price index

Therefore, clients are able to recognize the fees when they begin working with their financial advisors—every quarter by special notification, every quarter as reported on the brokerage statement.

The engagement letter not only defines the fee structure, it lets the client know that the engagement with the financial advisor can be terminated by either party with a 30-day written notice.

- The fees are always clear and apparent.

- They are ongoing.

- Clients are free to walk at will.

Since we have so simply and so efficiently achieved client fee nirvana, why complicate or sully it with the commission streams of other products they will surely need—life insurance, specifically? We won't. At this point we stop charging our Boomer clients money. Everything else is gratis. No fees involved. Financial planning, annuities, life insurance—all at no additional cost.

We can hear the old guard howl its disapproval. But if we contend that our goal is to offer the Holy Grail, then why not make the process as simple as possible? This does not mean that we have to forfeit compensation in the other areas. We merely adjust the management fees to reflect our mix of advice. But beware of those healthy market forces that maintain equilibrium between price and value. We've already demonstrated that, by charging a streaming fee, we save our clients money while making more ourselves. How does this phenomenon take place? Take a look at Table 12.1.

Clients' money goes to three entities: the financial advisor, the broker, and the mutual fund families. Note that by using an average from the managed portfolios as opposed to using an average of the group of A-share mutual funds, we accomplish two nifty goals, one benefiting the client and the other us: The client saves almost $20,000 ($28,584 versus $48,890) and we retain 73.8% of the total the client paid versus only 16.8% in A shares. Compared to the B- or C-share arrangement, the client saves over $48,000 ($28,584 versus $76,828) and we keep 30.4% (73.8% − 43.4%) more of the total client charges.

TABLE 12.1 Who Gets What Every Year: Independents

					PAYOUT 86.7%		

MANAGED	Total from Clients	Fee to Us	Kept by Funds	To Our Broker	To Us	Percent to Us	
$350,000	$3,903	$3,035	$323	$489	$3,092	79.2%	
$1,000,000	$11,152	$8,670	$1,986	$1,396	$7,770	69.7%	
$5,000,000	$45,760	$26,010	$4,608	$5,845	$35,307	77.2%	
$10,000,000	$53,520	$36,414	$9,216	$6,041	$38,263	71.5%	
	$28,584	$18,532	$4,033	$3,443	$21,108	73.8%	

A Shares	From Clients	Load Annlzd over 15 Yrs	Total from Clients	Kept by Funds	To Our Broker	To Us	Percent to Us
$350,000	$4,166	$1,167	$5,333	$3,508	$947	$878	16.5%
$1,000,000	$11,817	$2,417	$14,234	$9,816	$2,047	$2,371	16.7%
$5,000,000	$58,777	$7,083	$65,860	$48,084	$6,642	$11,134	16.9%
$10,000,000	$120,800	$0	$120,800	$96,640	$3,213	$20,947	17.3%
	$48,890	$2,667	$51,557	$39,512	$3,212	$8,832	16.8%

B or C Shares	Total from Clients	Kept by Funds	To Our Broker	To Us	Percent to Us
$350,000	$6,700	$3,350	$446	$2,904	43.4%
$1,000,000	$19,142	$9,571	$1,273	$8,298	43.4%
$5,000,000	$95,710	$47,855	$6,365	$41,490	43.4%
$10,000,000	$185,760	$92,880	$12,353	$80,527	43.4%
	$76,828	$38,414	$5,109	$33,305	43.4%

So which of this triumvirate is the loser in these cases? Brokers should be pleased to observe that their revenues remain somewhat level. Since the revenues for financial advisors are elevating and those of brokers are static, that means the mutual fund companies are the losers. They forfeit an average of $33,000 in both instances.

It should be noted that the compensation levels for financial advisors with the managed portfolios are quite close to those of the B and C shares. This is because mutual fund companies are standing squarely between us and our clients. But we let them do so. In the B- and C-share arrangement, we pull in the same amount, while our clients are being bled to death financially. We drag the fund company in front of us simply to hide our own compensation.

But we can change that—in all instances.

Financial Planning

Many of us already fold the financial plans that we offer into the fee for clients for whom we already manage assets. And for those clients who simply want a plan written, then the compensation is made once and up front.

Annuities

Limited research has uncovered American Skandia as the only insurance company offering an annuity (Choice 2000) to registered investment advisors that does not throw off a commission of some sort. No up-front 6%. No trail. No client contingent deferred sales charge (CDSC). With a combined administration and mortality and expense (M&E) charge of only 0.65%, this annuity is the least expensive on the market. Having as money managers the likes of Alger, AIM, Janus, T. Rowe Price, PIMCo, Lord Abbott, and 14 other banner names will fortify the possibility of benchmark beatings. When we explain the tidiness of this contract to our Boomer clients and that our asset fee covers the management of the subaccounts also, they will appreciate the simplicity.

For clients who have only an annuity with us, we apply the fee to the total under management in the subaccounts. They write a quarterly check. A receivables department could conceivably become a thorn, but there aren't too many folks whose only assets reside in annuities. And, of course, we all know the moral and ethical issues of plopping 401(k) proceeds into an annuity.

Life Insurance

Unlike the scarcity of no-commission annuities, there is a whopping total of two no-commission life insurance companies from which to choose: Ameritas and Paragon Life. In these policies, Boomers incur no charges associated with the commission paid the life insurance salesperson—there is none. Therefore, there are no surrender charges. The sales charges diminish the premium payment share that is diverted into the subaccounts, which drastically reduces the overall growth rate.

Aside from the clear advantages to our clients of not being affected by the commissions pulled out of surrender value, Boomers also have that freedom to exit the arrangement at no further cost to them. They get all the cash value. It's like having term insurance and building investment value all at once. Would we buy a house at the cost of renting it if we could?

The impact on clients of not having major portions of their premiums removed to satisfy commissions is striking. Compare policy surrender values on level option $500,000 contracts, each with an annual premium of $5,370 for the first three years and $3,883 thereafter for 17 years on a male, age 45, and with a gross rate of return of 10%.

	No-Commission	*Traditional*
3 years	$ 15,534	$ 13,728
5 years	$ 24,173	$ 21,190
10 years	$ 51,474	$ 44,249
15 years	$ 92,117	$ 76,224
20 years	$147,954	$121,408

Refer to Appendix A for a complete ledger and all the comparative particulars of these two policies.

The no-commission policy puts no money into our pockets, but we're already charging the client an asset management fee, including the work to install the policies. Besides the information gathering time, which we would do anyway as a part of the financial plan, in general it takes up to five hours of hard labor to put a client into a life insurance policy. We have to determine the suitable policy factors, complete the application, schedule the physical, follow the underwriting and respond to their questions and requests for additional paperwork, and finish by delivering the policy and getting the receipt signed.

On the aforementioned commission policy, the target premium is $3,913. We would have to regard this as worthy of our compensation attention. If, as suggested, it takes an average of five hours of work to install a life insurance policy and the financial advisor is operating at the average independent 86% payout mark, that drops $3,365 into the advisor's lap, or $673 an hour. But let's assume that after the planning session the client suddenly decides to triple the death benefit, and the target goes to $11,739. Now, for the same amount of legwork, the commission jumps to $10,096, or $2,019 per hour. Even if the advisor claims 10 hours of work, the hourly rates are $336.50 and $1,009.50, respectively. Sounds a bit like our buddy from Chapter 2, Lewis Tyler. For the sake of normalcy, we would have to conclude that these scenarios are a bit extreme and that they smack of product pay, a condition that causes severe nervousness about when and if we can push the next product and continue a steady pay stream. So, pushing products, we squeeze too hard at each opportunity.

In this instance, what we squeeze from our clients is $15,896 after 15 years. This is the year at which our Boomer clients can finally claim full ownership of the policy's value, or it is when the surrender value equals the cash value. Freedom at last, after 15 years of confinement.

We're already charging the client $10,000 a year on $1,000,000 under management. Doesn't it seem obnoxious to gouge out an additional $3,870 for five hours of work? Are they clients or are they suckers? If we see them as the latter, our Boomer clients will quickly catch on to this and take their financial interests to the Internet, where new opportunities continually beckon.

And what of those Boomers who seek our advice on life insurance and also have not a dime parked under our sage management? Our ADV II clearly outlines our financial planning services and what we charge hourly for the execution— say, $150 per hour.

Imagine the surprised and gleeful expressions on our clients' faces when we inform them in the initial interview that, according to the way we do business, they will pay nothing to get into the least expensive annuity on the market and will use life insurance that never has a surrender charge. Even if they never need these, the very notion of working with someone who offers these options in such an untainted (nonproduct) form is proof that the Holy Grail is within their grasp.

Treating assets, annuities, and life insurance in this manner transforms them from products into services. If we really believe that the Holy Grail is the goal, then we must reshape our practices, not merely in the hollowness of word but in the essence of deed, and the most potent and final deed is means of compensation. Our goal can no longer be the selling of a product. It must be the delivery of a service.

The independent's score on the Purity Scale:

Direct = 3.0 (assets, annuities, life insurance)

Ongoing = 3.0 (assets, annuities, life insurance)

Freedom = 3.0 (assets, annuities, life insurance)

Purity Scale = 9.0

Captive Employees

Because we don't hold all the strings, those of us who are captive employees are unable to structure our practices to provide access to the Holy Grail in its purest form. There are two general captive populations: stockbrokers and people working for life insurance companies. Each group makes available the same kinds of products and, increasingly, the same products themselves. The difference between these two groups is the core business that generates the greatest revenue stream. Stockbrokers are paid primarily to buy and sell individual equities or to gather assets, so they generate ticket charges and commission for their companies. Life insurance salespeople are paid primarily to sell life insurance and annuities, so they generate subaccount management fees, mortality and administrative fees, and policy loan interest. Overlaying both equally is the gross concession form of A-share, B-share, and C-share mutual fund sales.

Stockbrokers

Since many brokerage firms are launching assets under management programs whereby clients pay a quarterly fee and no transaction commission, and since the main source of fee creation in a financial advisor's practice is also assets under management, stockbrokers have the opportunity to deliver the pure Holy Grail of service more easily than do life insurance folks.

Two factors prevent stockbrokers from presenting no-commission annuities or no-commission life insurance: Because they have no control over compensation structures, there are no means to adjust their pay to account for it, and their companies do not make them available. There are no commission, no dealer concession, and no profit. However, guts and creativity could be mustered in the future to incrementally increase the quarterly fee in the asset management account based on the total amount in all subaccounts of either the annuity policy or the life policy. The first brokerage house that puts this on the table will be operating high on the Purity Scale.

But as brokers wait for corporate courage and ingenuity, they must slightly tarnish the purity by offering one of the dozen annuities on the market that produce a 1% annual fee with no CDSC. With one of these, clients pay covertly and the fee gradually drifts from their memory. And by choosing an annuity with no CDSC, clients retain their freedom. Selecting 1% annually instead of 6%, brokers are paid in an ongoing fashion, knowing very well that in order for the fee to continue they must always trot out the Holy Grail.

Life insurance is another matter. The vast majority of the compensation to brokers is on a one-time basis, with an inconsequential trickle of trails on future premiums.

The stockbroker score on the Purity Scale:

Direct = 1.0 (assets)

On-going = 2.0 (assets, annuities)

Freedom = 2.0 (assets, annuities)

Purity Scale = 5.0

Life Insurance Salespeople

Most life insurance companies have assets under management programs but only allow them to be populated with mutual funds. They're called *wrap* accounts and operate under strict guidelines regarding the funds that are available, the fee structure, and reporting. The fees are generally so steep as to be prohibitive. After all, three parties must divvy them—the insurance salesperson, the broker-dealer, and the life insurance company.

In addition, some insurance companies won't even pay the salesperson's deserved cut, or will pay only a portion of the cut, unless life insurance sales goals are reached first—a practice that could be regarded as illegal and ought to be reviewed by the NASD and/or the SEC.

Because of these stringent mechanisms, assets under management programs in this dismally pure form are, for all practical purposes, nonexistent at most life insurance agencies. They are token programs put into place to present the façade of asset management in order to lure high-net-worth folks into the life insurance and annuity traps—the revenue generators. Simply put, fee-based assets under management programs at life insurance agencies are loss leaders.

Some may tout the notion that using C shares is equivalent to assets under management because the compensation methods are similar—both are ongoing (though dissimilar in that assets under management are conspicuous). The freedom factor is still intact as well: Clients can exit at any time. A few may even exercise poetic license by saying that they have "X amount of assets under management," parked in C shares. But they are managing nothing—except spin. They are merely mutual fund salespeople using an obscure way of making money, and the clients will pay dearly.

Although structural resemblances do exist between the two programs—asset management and C shares—it is a huge stretch to claim they are the same, considering that C shares, in our average $1 million case, bleed from the client $297,865 over 15 years in additional fees, relative to our managed portfolios. Refer to Table 12.2.

Where's the $297,865 of value: in 15 years of brokerage statements? Yawn. Note that in both independent and captive arrangements, once portfolios jump past $1 million, our compensation accelerates dramatically in the B- and C-share funds relative to the managed portfolio, where the fees, at $5 million, no longer move up with the balance but with twice the consumer price index. Thus, the increase to the client is far less dramatic. And rest assured that it takes considerably more work to actively manage a portfolio of individual securities than to lounge back and haul in the 12b-1s. So Boomers are paying less for more. Where's the value? Where's the Holy Grail?

If you think that $1 million is too large a case to present as an example, think again. The average 401(k) balance for a 50-year-old is $110,000. Table 12.3 indicates that it won't take long for that to grow substantially. At 12% annual growth, with contributions and company matching at 9%, and salary growing at 2.5%,

TABLE 12.2 Expense Comparison Detail

$350,000	Managed Expenses	Class A Expenses	Difference from Mngd	Percent Savings	15 Years @ 12%	Class B or C Expenses	Difference from Mngd	Percent Savings	15 Years @ 12%
Aggressive	$4,022	$5,674	$1,652	29.1%	$61,586	$7,042	$3,021	42.89%	$112,603
Dynamic	$4,008	$5,590	$1,582	28.3%	$58,977	$6,958	$2,951	42.40%	$109,994
Moderate	$3,952	$5,376	$1,425	26.5%	$53,105	$6,741	$2,790	41.38%	$103,992
Conservative	$3,927	$5,184	$1,257	24.2%	$46,842	$6,549	$2,622	40.03%	$97,729
Income	$3,609	$4,841	$1,232	25.5%	$45,929	$6,209	$2,601	41.88%	$96,946
	$3,903	$5,333	$1,429	26.8%	$53,288	$6,700	$2,797	41.74%	$104,253

$1,000,000	Managed Expenses	Class A Expenses	Difference from Mngd	Percent Savings	15 Years @ 12%	Class B or C Expenses	Difference from Mngd	Percent Savings	15 Years @ 12%
Aggressive	$11,490	$15,210	$3,720	24.5%	$138,681	$20,120	$8,630	42.89%	$321,724
Dynamic	$11,450	$14,970	$3,520	23.5%	$131,225	$19,880	$8,430	42.40%	$314,268
Moderate	$11,290	$14,350	$3,060	21.3%	$114,076	$19,260	$7,970	41.38%	$297,119
Conservative	$11,220	$13,810	$2,590	18.8%	$96,554	$18,710	$7,490	40.03%	$279,225
Income	$10,310	$12,830	$2,520	19.6%	$93,945	$17,740	$7,430	41.88%	$276,988
	$11,152	$14,234	$3,082	21.7%	$114,896	$19,142	$7,990	41.74%	$297,865

$5,000,000	Managed Expenses	Class A Expenses	Difference from Mngd	Percent Savings	15 Years @ 12%	Class C Expenses	Difference from Mngd	Percent Savings	15 Years @ 12%
Aggressive	$47,450	$70,750	$23,300	32.9%	$868,617	$100,600	$53,150	52.83%	$1,981,417
Dynamic	$47,250	$69,550	$22,300	32.1%	$831,338	$99,400	$52,150	52.46%	$1,944,137
Moderate	$46,450	$66,450	$20,000	30.1%	$745,594	$96,300	$49,850	51.77%	$1,858,394
Conservative	$46,100	$63,700	$17,600	27.6%	$656,123	$93,550	$47,450	50.72%	$1,768,922
Income	$41,550	$58,850	$17,300	29.4%	$644,939	$88,700	$47,150	53.16%	$1,757,739
	$45,760	$65,860	$20,100	30.5%	$749,322	$95,710	$49,950	52.19%	$1,862,122

$10,000,000	Managed Expenses	Class A Expenses	Difference from Mngd	Percent Savings	15 Years @ 12%	Class C Expenses	Difference from Mngd	Percent Savings	15 Years @ 12%
Aggressive	$56,900	$129,600	$72,700	56.1%	$2,710,235	$201,200	$144,300	71.72%	$5,379,463
Dynamic	$56,500	$128,300	$71,800	56.0%	$2,676,684	$198,800	$142,300	71.58%	$5,304,903
Moderate	$54,900	$124,500	$69,600	55.9%	$2,594,668	$192,600	$137,700	71.50%	$5,133,417
Conservative	$54,200	$115,800	$61,600	53.2%	$2,296,430	$187,100	$132,900	71.03%	$4,954,474
Income	$45,100	$105,800	$60,700	57.4%	$2,262,879	$177,400	$132,300	74.58%	$4,932,106
	$53,520	$120,800	$67,280	55.7%	$2,508,179	$185,760	$123,440	66.45%	$5,140,873

TABLE 12.3 Baby Boomers' Retirement Balances

Employee Income	Beginning Balance	Inflation	Growth Rate	Employee Contribution	Employer Match	Total Invested
$85,000	$110,000	2.5%	15.0%	6.0%	3.0%	9.0%
				$5,100	$2,550	$7,650

Age	Opening Balance	Salary	Annual Contribution	Balance Growth	Contribution Growth	Ending Balance
50	$110,000	$87,125	$7,841	$16,500	$588	$134,929
51	$134,929	$89,303	$8,037	$20,239	$603	$163,809
52	$163,809	$91,536	$8,238	$24,571	$618	$197,236
53	$197,236	$93,824	$8,444	$29,585	$633	$235,899
54	$235,899	$96,170	$8,655	$35,385	$649	$280,588
55	$280,588	$98,574	$8,872	$42,088	$665	$332,214
56	$332,214	$101,038	$9,093	$49,832	$682	$391,821
57	$391,821	$103,564	$9,321	$58,773	$699	$460,614
58	$460,614	$106,153	$9,554	$69,092	$717	$539,977
59	$539,977	$108,807	$9,793	$80,997	$734	$631,500
60	$631,500	$111,527	$10,037	$94,725	$753	$737,016
61	$737,016	$114,316	$10,288	$110,552	$772	$858,628
62	$858,628	$117,173	$10,546	$128,794	$791	$998,759
63	$998,759	$120,103	$10,809	$149,814	$811	$1,160,193
64	$1,160,193	$123,105	$11,079	$174,029	$831	$1,346,132
65	$1,346,132	$126,183	$11,356	$201,920	$852	$1,560,260
66	$1,560,260	$129,338	$11,640	$234,039	$873	$1,806,812
67	$1,806,812	$132,571	$11,931	$271,022	$895	$2,090,660
68	$2,090,660	$135,885	$12,230	$313,599	$917	$2,417,406
69	$2,417,406	$139,282	$12,535	$362,611	$940	$2,793,493

at age 65 a Baby Boomer will have more than $1 million. At 15%, the ending balance would be more than $1.5 million.

And 401(k)s won't constitute the entirety of our clients' savings. They will have nonqualified accounts as well. Dipping into these taxable dollars first allows the 401(k) balances under our control to grow rapidly, while the mutual fund companies bloat and we happily and quietly sneak away with our mammoth 12b-1s.

Many years from now, with this siphoning in full effect, these clients will be trapped by a low tax basis and unable to flee. Whether we enjoy it or not, we will be hauling in huge sums of money so thoroughly disproportionate to the quality of service delivered that shame will overcome us—or *should* overcome us.

Unfortunately, annuities offer no more relief for the life insurance captives. Home offices thrust their homegrown policies down the pipe and make their compensation so much more attractive relative to the "network" versions that choosing these alternatives induces snickers. But most of these plans do offer optional payout schedules, which usually include 1% annually. We may reply that this satisfies the ongoing compensation element of our Purity Scale. Sorry.

The reason: Nearly all our proprietary annuities are burdened with CDSCs, or backloads, in the vicinity of nine years. They render the substitute payout a mere cash flow issue for us and our company and provide nothing toward the delivery of the Holy Grail. In fact, the CDSC strips away our clients' freedom, an act we know they abhor. A backload is a jail cell in which we place our clients. With them safely trapped, we can run off and collect more bottom-line signatures toward winning free trips, knowing that every bit of the lump sum in commission we just hauled in will remain our property.

The life insurance compensation issues are identical to those faced by the stockbroker.

Life insurance sales score on the Purity Scale:

Direct = 0.0

Ongoing = 0.0

Freedom = 1.0 (assets in C shares)

Purity Scale = 1.0

The Captive's Cut

On average, stockbrokers receive 40% to 50% of the commissions generated. Life insurance salespeople receive 50% to 60%. Table 12.4 uses 50% to demonstrate how much of our clients' money we get to keep. Again, captive employees' clients' money goes to three entities: the captive employee, his or her employer, and the mutual fund families. This analysis also uses an average from the managed portfolios versus the average of the mutual fund groups.

Comparing managed portfolios with the mutual fund groups, clients save the same amount as if they were working with an independent: more than $20,000 in A shares and more than $48,000 in B and C shares. Table 12.4 outlines the captive employee's take.

The difference is the distribution of these charges among the three parties. In the managed portfolio arrangement, the captive employee pockets 38.8% of the clients' fees versus 12.1% in A shares (independents, 73.8% versus 16.8%). Compared to the B-

TABLE 12.4 Who Gets What Every Year: Captive Employees

				PAYOUT 50.00%		
MANAGED	Total from Our Clients	Fee to Us	Kept by Funds	To Our Employer	To Us	Percent to Us
$350,000	$3,903	$1,750	$323	$1,965	$1,615	41.4%
$1,000,000	$11,152	$5,000	$922	$5,615	$4,615	41.4%
$5,000,000	$45,760	$15,000	$4,608	$23,076	$18,076	39.5%
$10,000,000	$53,520	$21,000	$9,216	$24,252	$20,052	37.5%
	$28,584	$10,688	$3,767	$13,727	$11,090	38.8%

A Shares	From Clients	Load Annlzd over 15 Yrs	Total from Our Clients	Kept by Funds	To Our Employer	To Us	Percent to Us
$350,000	$4,166	$1,167	$5,333	$3,508	$825	$1,000	18.8%
$1,000,000	$11,817	$2,417	$14,234	$9,816	$2,028	$2,390	16.8%
$5,000,000	$58,777	$7,083	$65,860	$48,084	$8,357	$9,419	14.3%
$10,000,000	$120,800	$0	$120,800	$96,640	$12,080	$12,080	10.0%
	$48,890	$2,667	$51,557	$39,512	$5,822	$6,222	12.1%

B or C Shares	Total from Our Clients	Kept by Funds	To Our Employer	To Us	Percent to Us
$350,000	$6,700	$3,350	$1,675	$1,675	25.0%
$1,000,000	$19,142	$9,571	$4,786	$4,786	25.0%
$5,000,000	$95,710	$47,855	$23,928	$23,928	25.0%
$10,000,000	$185,760	$92,880	$46,440	$46,440	25.0%
	$76,828	$38,414	$19,207	$19,207	25.0%

or C-share arrangement, captive employees who use managed portfolios keep over 13.8% more of the clients' fees (independent, 30.4%).

Who are the winners? Who are the losers? The captive employee sharing differences are less striking than those of the independents. On portfolio size average, as captive employees, we're paid more if we use B- and C-share mutual funds rather than managed portfolios—$19,207 versus $11,090. Note, however, that this average is the result of the $10 million portfolio. On portfolio balance up to that point, compensation is nearly a dead heat. Again, the cause of the sharp increase is the fact that the managed portfolio fee structure increases by CPI times two past $5 million instead of tracking the balance.

With managed portfolios relative to mutual funds, the fund families are the biggest losers. They give up the same amount—about $35,000 of income in both captive and independent instances.

Following is a snapshot of independents and captive employees, showing what the client pays and what we keep on a $1 million portfolio.

	Client Pays	*Independent Keeps*	*Captive Employee Keeps*
Managed	$11,152	$7,770	$4,615
A shares	$14,234	$2,371	$2,390
B and C shares	$19,142	$8,298	$4,786

One wonders if there is any truth to the fundamental and venerable belief on Wall Street that those businesses that can reduce prices (managed), increase service (managed), and make more money (managed) than their competitors (A and B shares) will gorge on market share until those competitors change or perish.

Alterations

Let's review. Purity Scale summary:

Independents	9
Stockbrokers	5
Life insurance salespeople	1

The simple core issue is how we receive pay from clients. Showing them how we do it and every time we do it, hiding nothing, is the fairest and most forthright approach. Allowing them to cease the relationship with us and walk away without forfeiting a single dollar puts complete freedom in their hands. It drastically reduces the potential for criminal behavior on our part and will be the impetus behind the elimination of the crooked element in our profession. After all, it is quite difficult to cheat and lie when all compensation is reported clearly every time it happens.

Since asset accumulation has become a dominant part of life insurance and annuities, this clear and unequivocal way of taking money from clients to manage these subaccounts should be put into place by financial services companies.

For brokerage firms, doing so is quite simple. They can offer no-commission annuities and no-commission life insurance to financial advisors and place and report their subaccounts in fee-based brokerage accounts, to which the advisors can charge their quarterly fees.

In many life insurance companies, real fee-based management programs must first be made available to financial advisors rather than gimmicky arrangements that pay out only when someone sells the right amount of life insurance. Then they must make available the no-commission vehicles.

With the Internet and technology burning along, all this can be accomplished swiftly and simply.

Please avoid the canned corporate argument that all fees are made clear in the prospectus. Nothing in the prospectus is clear. Those of us working in the trenches can assure CEOs that prospectuses are plopped in front of the client with a hollow encouragement to cozy up before the fire with them. Most clients roll their eyes at the prospect.

CHAPTER

13

All That Rationale

It's our goal as financial advisors to deliver the Holy Grail of service as quickly and thoroughly as possible, thereby plundering market share from those who are latecomers or who simply refuse to evolve.

There are various reasons, economic and psychological, that might stop us from transitioning our practice from the current decaying system to one that promises success, makes us more money, and serves Baby Boomer clients more scrupulously while saving them money. We tend to assume we're loners. But remember, the transition includes creating triangle relationships, which consist of offsetting strengths and companionship.

The following reasons for not changing have their roots in the nature of our compensation. Our means of pay is the backbone of quality service, our clients' Holy Grail. Triangles can be formed initially, irrespective of pay issues—that is, the process of constructing them can be started, followed later by compensation transition. Often, however, the other two points of the triangle (CPAs and attorneys) are already operating under fee-only structures and might be less inclined to become involved in commission work.

Fear of Change

Fear of change is probably the greatest obstacle that needs to be overcome. Change presents the possibility of an endless number of unknown monsters. Fear can cause us to seize up and render us incapable of making any decision at all. Then, when we are forced into action for the sake of survival, it is too late and the fears that previously halted us in our tracks have become self-fulfilling prophecies.

The two supreme fears of financial advisors are losing clients as a result of the transition and the inability to get new clients because we are not practiced at presenting the information that our compensation will be removed right from their pockets for services rendered. We are so accustomed to hiding comfortably behind the prospectus that the thought of exposing our method of payment to the public is as dreadful as the thought of exposing *ourselves* to the public.

These fears must be purged as a result of courage and vision, which assemble in the soul after a great deal of searching. From a practical perspective, however, keep in mind that there are only four types of client assets that should be transitioned: qualified money, high-tax-basis dollars, new assets hauled to the investment table, and equities sold whose gains are offset by any losses the client can carry forward on his or her income tax return. Primarily because of tax consequences, all other assets are taboo unless clients consent for other reasons.

With prospective Boomer clients, merely dangling before them the Holy Grail of good service, the prospect of lower fees, and the fact that we are selective about our clientele will have them salivating, as long as we are firm in our own conviction. If the soul-searching process has not yet been finished, you should not try this. You should finish the groundwork first. But do so quickly—you must get to the market with your new wares.

Being Logistically Trapped

We might have to leave one company and join another. If someone is a captive employee at a financial services company that shows dangerous signs of calcification with regard to offering creative compensation programs, that person might be forced to become a captive employee at a more progressive company. On the other hand, if the person is the entrepreneurial sort, he or she can punch through into independence, where there is a good chance of moving to the pinnacle of the Purity Scale.

Making such a move is often easier said than done. Many people would have to walk away from some compensation trails from previous life insurance policies and, perhaps, annuities if they chose to be paid on an ongoing basis versus up-front compensation on occasions in the past. Moreover, many financial services companies now use those handy stock options with a vesting schedule attached to discourage migration to other firms.

In addition, the thought of having to meet with existing clients to explain the reason for the move is somewhat unnerving. How will they react? And just thinking about all the paperwork that would have to be completed to finalize clients' transition with us is an absolute burden on the mind, so we say, "What a pain. Just forget it," and continue on.

Greed

Many people have an intense need to amass as much money as possible. There are those who are about as altruistic as Ebenezer Scrooge and are driven almost to the point of panic to accumulate as much money in the shortest period of time. Up-front compensation is the narcotic that satisfies that craving. The notion of receiving pay in amounts that dribble in causes them to walk in circles, mumbling to themselves. They have even been known to suggest not attending the free trips in exchange for an equivalent payment in cash. Service is just above a root canal on their priority list.

This tiny contingent is a lost cause. However, because of blind passion, most of its members will succeed and retire before the Boomer trend has completely washed over the financial services industry. The clients they leave standing in the service desert, scratching their heads and holding their products, will be the losers.

Compensation Structure

As pointed out in Chapter 11, the first few years of working within the ongoing compensation structure are leaner than those working within the up-front model. If someone is new in the business and starts a practice cold using the streaming compensation method, having a considerate working spouse is marvelous, if not downright essential. Also helpful is recognizing that sacrifice is a virtue leading to far more generous future years. Patience and determination are also valuable ingredients for success.

Veterans with more than 10 years left to toil most likely have (or should have) assets in reserve that they can count on to make up for deficits in their living standard until the lean years pass and they move into the stronger times. Comparing the total depleted from current assets to fund the shortfall with the total added beyond the breakeven point should help to determine whether the transition is financially worthwhile. Remember, however, that all assets added after the transition continue to provide income, even after a practice succeeds, which we'll discuss later.

For those who have less than 10 years left to run, the transition moves from the personal financial arena to the personal preference arena.

Inflexible Traditionalism

Those who are bound by inflexible traditionalism can't accept or comprehend change. These people are the source of the grousing about the impudence of suggesting that our business be conducted some other way. Such people question the value of recognizing and identifying changes in market trends. They believe that as financial advisors we control the market and therefore should tell clients what they want and need. Likewise, *we* should determine how we're paid. We are in charge. The Internet is a fad to them, as are computers and technological innovation in general.

Fortunately for those of us who are willing to make the transition, many of our cohorts fall into this traditionalist category, removing a healthy measure of competition and leaving us to pick and choose the best clients.

Too Broad a Market

A market that is too broad means that we are selling everyone everywhere everything. Some people cannot pass up a sale, so if one presents itself, they feel compelled to act, to capture the moment and convert it to glory. Financial advisors who operate in too broad a market have no definition to their practice, no direction, no focus. They are jacks-of-all-trades and the masters of none, but they don't care about that. They have grown accustomed to spanning the buying market, representing every conceivable product for which they can get licensed and which they can legally represent.

The business mix for such advisors is so splintered that organizing and conducting a transition to fee-based assets under management does not make sense and is likely impossible. In fact, the notion of managing assets at all is foreign to their core, because service is an afterthought to the impulse to close the sale. Contests and free trips are not their main motivations. What powers such people is an uncontrollable, instinctive need to be in front of people, selling them something that they truly believe will better their lives.

These financial advisors are from the old-line sales fleet that gets its fire from the belly, not from the business plan.

Ego

The price of a large ego is an insatiable hunger for awards, recognition, and free trips. There is nothing grander than standing on stage and being greeted by a sea of applause. These people feel they have won the most cherished gift: their peers' recognition. They can hardly wait to move among them, providing autographs and hearing the whispered adorations, "There he is. He is number three in the entire country. Can we get close to him? Touch him?"

Meanwhile, the clients behind the 387 signatures this superstar secured in the past 12 months that landed him on stage are wondering why he hasn't returned their calls. He explains that, because of sheer volume, they will have to wait in line. In the meantime, please don't bother him while he's on his free trip getting awards and gliding among his admirers.

Such people cannot survive in the fee-only, managed assets realm, where success is based not on product signatures, but on delivering the Holy Grail. The only applause offered in this arrangement is represented by the continued quarterly fees from clients, indicating that they, not our employers, are pleased. You can't hang this applause on the office walls or strut among your peers, flashing it about. But you can tuck it away in your soul, knowing you have truly satisfied, from every perspective, the most important group of people in your business life—Baby Boomer clients.

Unwieldy Client Base

A client base that is too large is difficult to transfer to a fee-based system. If you've been humming along for a number of years, adding client after client to your roster, you might think you're not a candidate for a transition because moving such a mammoth bulk would be a like wedging an elephant into a beer mug. But, in fact, you may be a very good candidate. How often have you complained that your client base has grown too massive to offer consistently good service? Here's your opportunity.

First, focus on clients with nonqualified assets who have a balance of at least $350,000—those who can be repositioned into the new model with no tax consequences. Decide which 20% of these clients you most enjoy working with and who would transition with ease. Second, examine the balance sheets of your entire client base to identify which clients will retire within five to seven years with a future 401(k) value of over $500,000. And third, verify which clients hold strong stock option positions (after strike price) that are exercisable within five to seven years.

Once you've designed your fee structure, you can do the simple math to determine your ongoing compensation level as soon as you hit the ground on the other side of the fence. To determine if it's doable, you need to consider the increase of fees based on the market, the consumer price index, and adding clients.

If you decide to make the transition, meet with each of these clients to explain very thoroughly your reasons for switching to noncommissioned, fee-based work: It costs them less and you can deliver a much healthier dose of quality service. (It's a personal decision whether to inform them of the increase in compensation.) This presents the ideal opportunity to request referrals.

Meet with the clients who don't push through the three screens but who have been active participants in your relationship and explain what you're doing and why. Introduce them to a solid rookie who is breaking into the business and who will step in as your replacement. For those clients who have not been so involved in the relationship, a letter will suffice.

Complacency

Your own lifestyle is the central focus. "Don't bother me with that fee stuff. Can't you see I'm being fitted for a suit?"

Succession

etirement from the day-to-day corporate office is a breeze. The responsibilities these folks shouldered for years are handed off to the people replacing them as they pass at the door. They grab their 401(k)s, deferred compensation plans, and perhaps a handful of stock options and away they go. The corporation left behind remains intact and in motion. They take nothing that is the corporation's and the corporation withholds nothing that is theirs. It is a clean break with no disorder.

The customers and clients with whom they developed powerful relationships belong to the mother ship and are assured of continued superior service by the fresh face planted on the case. The focused might of the corporation will see to that.

These tidy, definitive maneuvers are not so clear for financial advisors who manage assets for fees. When we start thinking seriously about ambling off into the sunset, we realize we've got this $75,000,000-under-management problem sitting over in the corner. What do we do with it? How do we responsibly and transparently shift our clients into a different set of qualified hands? These questions are just starting to percolate in the profession. Commencing in 2010, the retirements of Baby Boomer financial advisors, who are managing their fellow Boomers' money, will bring the issue to a full boil.

From a profit perspective, upon the retirement of a financial advisor who manages assets for a fee, the employer (if the advisor is a captive employee) or broker (for independents) wants to ensure that the assets being managed remain in-house. Employers have devised a better means of accomplishing this than brokers who serve independents. Reason: Brokers have no control over independents. Remember, brokers are employed by independents. They are vendors, not employers.

Retirement departure for a captive employee is similar to that of the corporate retiree. There is limited control over the clients' destinies. Despite all the huffing and puffing by financial advisors, employers regard clients as their property and thus assign them to other captive employees, thereby ensuring that their assets remain on board. Yet we might believe these clients would be better served by a colleague we long ago befriended—perhaps an employee of a different employer or an independent. The ultimate decision, of course, lies with the clients. But their path of least resistance is to remain with the current employer, who will be vigorous in an effort to preserve control of the assets.

From the survival perspective, like corporate retirees, financial advisors have 401(k)s, deferred compensation money, and vested stock options that they take with them. Revenue streams from these buckets offset the loss of ongoing management fees. Succession complete and smooth, the retired advisor is free to roam to Phoenix, Arizona, or Naples, Florida.

Independents, however, cook in a different kitchen. Since they're not employees, they have complete control, which can either complicate or enhance their voyage into retirement. If they're not geared up far in advance, they'll scramble to secure their clients' futures. Starting preparations at least three years prior to their departure date allows them to rest easy and creates additional income.

Preparing is a matter of finding a qualified and younger replacement at least three years before retirement. Whether operating alone or as part of an internal triangle, replacing the retiree early is essential. Getting the new face and equivalent talent in front of clients repeatedly over time establishes confidence in the replacement. The stipulation with the understudy should be that during the three-year learning curve, the compensation split will be in the vicinity of 80%-20% on all assets, existing and new. Then, upon departure, since the retiree will always remain registered with the NASD, reversing that split will ensure that a portion of the fee is directed toward the retiree's address in Phoenix or Naples and will cause our understudy to be giddy with excitement, a condition surely anticipated throughout the three-year stint as a novice. This fee stream adds to that from a SEP and maybe from a deferred compensation plan as well (if the retiree had such foresight).

If the candidate for retirement is part of a firm with partners who are together merely to share expenses, matters get a bit trickier. The initial step is to move beyond expense sharing and install a means of placing value on owning a partner position.

Market value is based on what someone would pay for something. The value of any company on the market is one to three years of predictable revenue streams or profits plus hard assets. Assume the firm held $100 million of client assets. If the partners achieved this over time by selling nothing but Class A mutual funds, annual 12b-1 revenue would be $250,000, minus the broker's cut. So the firm would be worth $250,000 to $750,000. Value cannot be placed on something that is fleeting, such as revenue from sales. No one is going to buy something that has not happened yet, so there is no value to it.

On the other hand, if the $100 million was exposed to a net 0.85% management fee, single-year revenues would be $850,000, creating a value of $850,000 and $2,550,000. Someone will buy a steady, ongoing flow of cash, so it holds value. However, perhaps the partner really doesn't want to sell at this point. The purpose of establishing a means of valuation is to create a smooth avenue for partner retirements later.

Recurring income (RI), or management fees, is a marketable basis for determining each partner's portion of value in the firm. Although operating at a level of nine on the Purity Scale is the finest of Holy Grails, partners must recognize and account for past methods. Therefore RI includes all passive income generated every quarter. These include fee-based income, 12b-1 income, annuity trails, third-party income, timing income, health insurance trails, life insurance trails, consulting fees, or any other income that is ongoing because of a partner's management of client assets or financial lives.

This does not include income generated once on the sale of an asset or financial instrument, such as up-front commission on annuities, Class A and Class B mutual funds, the purchase or sale of a stock or bond, life insurance, health insurance, or anything that is singular in nature.

Ownership should be broken into two parts: *absolute* and *variable*. With the absolute portion, we share in each other's success. There will be monetary incentive to help each other. With the variable portion, the lion's share of each person's ownership is still in his or her own hands.

Formulas

Absolute Portion

The absolute portion is a percentage of the unchanged ownership by each partner. It's based on the annual RI. For example, the partners decide that a total of 40% of the RI should be the absolute portion. This 40% is divided among, say, four partners. Suppose the whole firm's year-ending RI is $2,000,000. Each partner owns 10% of $2,000,000 (irrespective of its origin), or $200,000. This 10% never changes. Thus, $800,000 of the firm's $2,000,000 RI is accounted for, leaving $1,200,000.

Variable Portion

Assignment of the remaining nonabsolute portion ($1,200,000) is based on each partner's three-year average RI relative to the three-year average total RI of the whole firm. For example, the firm's three-year average RI is $1,000,000. A partner's three-year average RI is $150,000, or 15% of the firm's average RI. The partner would own 15% of the remaining $1,200,000 of RI, or $180,000. This partner owns 19% of the firm, or $380,000 worth of the RI—$200,000 (absolute) plus $180,000 (variable).

Ascertaining specific ownership values paves two separate paths for partner retirements: straight buyout or a steady cash payout.

Straight Buyout

Part of the firm's ownership arrangement should be a predetermined multiplier, or range, that will be applied to the retiring partner's total value in a straight buyout arrangement. In the preceding example, the partner who owns $380,000 of the firm's RI decides to retire. The predetermined multiplier is 2.5. The remaining partners buy the retiring partner out for $950,000, or 2½ years of RI.

Steady Cash Payout

Once again, part of the firm's arrangement should include an agreed-upon split, or a range, for the steady cash payout method. Continuing the example, if the retiring partner chooses this means of buyout, and the initial agreement calls for the payout portion to be 33%, the retiree will receive $125,400 per year and the firm will retain the balance—$254,600. Simple actuarial runs would help determine the most appropriate and fairest multipliers and splits.

In each case, the departing partner's clients become the firm's house accounts and are divided among the remaining partners for service. All future RI from these clients will be split, with 50% going to the partner servicing the case and 50% going to the house pot. This further builds real core value in the firm because a portion of the retired partner's RI remains in the firm's general revenue pot, a portion which all the partners determined by their variable ownership share. In the straight buyout case, 100% of the RI is split, meaning the servicing partner receives 50% of 100% and the firm retains the other 50%. In the steady cash payout method, 66% of the RI is split, with the servicing partner receiving 50% of it and the firm's pot the balance.

Not only is our delivery of the Holy Grail better for the clients and better for us, it facilitates smooth succession.

External Triangle Compensation

Recall the independents' relationship with external triangles, CPAs, and attorneys? From the CPAs' and attorneys' perspective, two compensation management methods were discussed: (1) all parties register with the NASD and (2) only a single partner from each of the other firms in the triangle registers and revenue flows through that partner to the others.

A relationship forged between an independent financial advisory firm and these other professional firms can be a highly successful pact. But managing compensation flow and client flow as they enter the independent financial advisory firm from the other two can be tricky. If there is no equity ownership agreement of some type, how do the incoming clients get distributed and how does the independent firm itself generate value from the referral relationship?

If the partners are merely together in an expense-sharing arrangement, they will fall all over each other to take that divorcée worth $5 million who has been referred to them by the law firm. This could be an ugly scene, causing deep animosities that would certainly destroy the firm. The lack of a means of distributing compensation according to an agreed-upon arrangement, whereby all the partners benefit to some degree, spells trouble.

The equity ownership agreement outlined here provides just that. When clients are funneled to the independent firm, they can be assigned to a partner by sequence—the first referral goes to partner A, the second to partner B, and so forth, in a continuous cycle. If we're true believers in the notion that, over time, all things even out, this is the most favorable process. A portion of the asset management fee thrown off annually by all these cases—say, 50%—becomes the property of the entire firm. The remaining 50% belongs to the partner who has taken the case. In addition, with the absolute portion of ownership, each partner shares in the 50% that's dumped into the firm's general pot.

Let's examine that wealthy divorcée from the perspective of the servicing partner and the firm. If we put the divorcée into the moderate portfolio, the fee on a $5 million portfolio would be $46,450. This is the total cost to the client, including mutual fund expense ratio fees. Our immediately collectible fee would be $42,500 ($40,000 + CPI $\times$ 2). We'll avoid the minor distraction of mutual fund 12b-1s in this analysis. The servicing partner receives $21,250, while the firm claims the other half. Yet the servicing partner also owns 10% of the firm's accumulated assets, an additional $2,125.

Every time a client is added, the asset management fee, or recurring income according to our formula of absolute and variable ownership, affects one and all. The question then arises as to the treatment of the asset accumulated within the year. Is it distributed as income to the partners proportionate to the variable ownership percentage, or does it sit on the books as retained earnings and thus appear on each partner's balance sheet? Much of the answer to this question depends on the corporate structure the firm assumes.

A final note of caution: If there are any partners in the firm who have instinctive tendencies toward greed or cancerous suspicions that someone else on the planet (much less in the firm itself) is unfairly doing better than they are, vote them off the team—immediately. This arrangement requires calm trust among professionals, an accepted attitude that each member will gradually benefit from continuity.

CHAPTER 15

Graveside

I t's cloudy but not raining—a good sign.

There stands the tent. Beneath it stand the Baby Boomers, out of respect. Stretched taut over the rectangular hole are the canvas straps that suspend the casket. The headstone is deep, blood-colored granite. Some would say it's a gaudy depiction of an annoying but honorable profession. It's a statue of a man in a double-breasted suit, hollow smile, briefcase in hand, leaning forward, arm outstretched for a handshake. On the base is inscribed, "Hi there, my name is . . ."

As the casket is lowered, the sighs are difficult to classify—mourning or relief?

The sun breaks through and creeps across the gravesite. The Boomers are liberated. They are seasoned veterans, patient, methodical. Their incessant and unwavering demands have paid off.

Across the grassy way, near the long string of parked cars curling down the drive, a young woman waits piously and with all due respect. As the ceremony ends, the Boomers move from under the tent, visibly content as they approach the woman.

She is part of a triangular team that holds the Holy Grail.

Summary

M ajor components of the financial services profession are in
upheaval, causing us to seriously review old practices. We're
being assaulted by Baby Boomers, the Internet, technology,
compensation restructuring, and more.

Baby Boomers long for their Holy Grail: impeccable service.
Their rearing planted the seeds of this craving deep within their
souls. As they assumed control of the world of commerce, it flourished into a passion. Accepting less than superior service was
barely tolerable during their working years. When they retire, they
will put their demand for the Holy Grail on the table before us
and they will not negotiate. If we deliver, we succeed. If we can't,
they walk.

Through those glowing monitors in our homes we can reach
into every corner of the world, instantly, for free. The Internet
eliminates all obstacles to the purchase of all goods from all over
the world. It opens every book, makes available every bit of
knowledge. In the name of efficiency, intermediaries that once
profited from commercial flows because they held and sheltered
key pieces of information are brushed aside. Information can no
longer be protected. We, as financial advisors, are the intermediaries. To succeed, we must redefine the value we generate and
reshape our practices to take advantage of the Internet.

Technology itself—computer software and hardware—also plays a role in eliminating the middleman. Its effects reach the depths of the financial services industry: the old trading floor, where buyer met seller through the intervention of a human being. Technology replaces the human being with a computer and saves the buyer and seller money.

Finally, compensation methods must be reviewed and questioned. If we are to present the Holy Grail to our Baby Boomer clients, the means by which we are paid, including the fluff of freebies, must be seriously examined. The entire structure must be redesigned to accommodate and encourage the delivery of service rather than the sale of product.

The Internet has killed the salesperson.

We must form triangles inside our operations, the three points of which are held by three persons with three distinct strengths: people skills to find clients, analytical skills for comprehensive planning, and analytical skills for investment management. Systematizing procedures within these triangles ensures thorough, quality work for the clients. They comprehend and appreciate that a process and a staff are in place to specifically tend to their retirement needs. Doing this moves the relationship from being product-based to being service-based. It creates an atmosphere of ease throughout contact with the Baby Boomer clients, who will surely respond more favorably to a string of coordinated services on their behalf than to the purchase of a product. It adds strength to inherent weaknesses and creates a humming whole, essential for delivering the Holy Grail. It also relieves the stress, the clutter, and the cost of adding new clients.

When possible, external triangles should be formed with CPAs and attorneys (when and if this group allows fee sharing). These pros invading our field are here to stay. We should coordinate, reciprocate, share the wealth, and maintain the level of service quality represented by the Holy Grail.

The old method of randomly grabbing at funds, or assembling them based on the shallow precept that the funds rather than the managers perform, will perish. Structuring portfolios from individual stocks and bonds and offering a complete spectrum of risk levels is the replacement. In other words, we will create and manage mutual funds (in concept) for our Boomers clients. This costs them less. Sure, we will work harder, but we will likewise enhance our compensation.

Pushing aside some of the old technologies are software packages and Internet sites and services specifically designed to assist us in managing these portfolios. In fact, they are indispensable to our work. And harnessing the Internet instead of defying it is our solution to meeting this challenge.

The notion that we will make less money if we accept compensation that is streaming versus that which occurs one time and up front is dead. The reverse is the new reality. We will make more money with fewer clients, and this means that delivering their Holy Grail is much easier. The practice of piling clients on is a sure formula for service disaster.

Flowing all no-commission investment products, including life insurance and annuities, through a managed account and applying a fee to the subaccounts ensures the purest form of compensation—payment that is up front and ongoing, and that allows clients the freedom to exit at will. Unfortunately, not all financial services arms (namely, life insurance companies) are serious about managed assets. Their compensation structures guarantee this. Individually, there are numerous reasons why we can't transition to noncommission, fee-only work, and all of them are rationalizations.

Because we develop deeply intertwined relationships with our clients, walking away from them for retirement is difficult. Captive employees have a smooth means of transition in place, but they exercise less control. Independents must engage in complex business agreements that, once in place, offer greater flexibility, rewards, and wealth accumulation opportunities.

Appendix A

No-Commission Life Insurance

Consider the economic difference between a no-commission variable universal life insurance policy and one offered by the traditional agent. (Refer to Tables A.1 and A.2.)

Here are the details. With two exceptions, they are identical in each contract.

Death benefit	$500,000
Death benefit option	Level
Age	45
Gender	Male
Status	Preferred, nonsmoker
Initial premium	$5,370 (years 1–3)
Subsequent premium	$3,883 (years 4–20)
Lump-sum premium	0
1035 exchange	0
Subaccount expense ratio	0.28%
Gross rate of return	10.0%

TABLE A.1 Great A-B-C Life Insurance Company No-Commission Variable Universal Life

End of Year	Age	Premium	Surrender Value
1	46	$5,370	$ 4,892
2	47	5,370	10,082
3	48	5,370	15,534
4	49	3,883	19,744
5	50	3,883	24,173
6	51	3,883	28,860
7	52	3,883	33,827
8	53	3,883	39,219
9	54	3,883	45,086
10	55	3,883	51,474
11	56	3,883	58,437
12	57	3,883	65,960
13	58	3,883	74,101
14	59	3,883	82,836
15	60	3,883	92,117
16	61	3,883	101,971
17	62	3,883	112,431
18	63	3,883	123,547
19	64	3,883	135,369
20	65	3,883	147,954
21	66		157,270
22	67		167,086
23	68		177,434
24	69		188,347
25	70		199,868
26	71		212,047
27	72		224,957
28	73		238,690
29	74		253,346
30	75		269,050

(*continues*)

TABLE A.1 Great A-B-C Life Insurance Company
No-Commission Variable Universal Life (*continued*)

End of Year	Age	Premium	Surrender Value
31	76		285,958
32	77		304,251
33	78		324,163
34	79		345,997
35	80		370,140
36	81		397,094
37	82		427,413
38	83		461,977
39	84		501,375
40	85		544,165
41	86		590,354
42	87		640,159
43	88		693,804
44	89		751,522
45	90		813,552
46	91		880,209
47	92		953,240
48	93		1,033,553
49	94		1,122,220
50	95		1,220,511
51	96		1,329,935
52	97		1,449,173
53	98		1,579,108
54	99		1,720,697
55	100		1,874,987

TABLE A.2 Great A-B-C Life Insurance Company Commission
Variable Universal Life

End of Year	Age	Premium	Surrender Value
1	46	$5,370	$ 4,293
2	47	5,370	8,861
3	48	5,370	13,728
4	49	3,883	17,354
5	50	3,883	21,190
6	51	3,883	25,257
7	52	3,883	29,570
8	53	3,883	34,159
9	54	3,883	39,043
10	55	3,883	44,249
11	56	3,883	49,806
12	57	3,883	55,746
13	58	3,883	62,106
14	59	3,883	68,917
15	60	3,883	76,224
16	61	3,883	84,064
17	62	3,883	92,482
18	63	3,883	101,516
19	64	3,883	111,197
20	65	3,883	121,408
21	66		128,383
22	67		135,602
23	68		143,057
24	69		150,741
25	70		158,642
26	71		166,747
27	72		175,057
28	73		183,573
29	74		192,290
30	75		201,202

(continues)

TABLE A.2 Great A-B-C Life Insurance Company Commission
Variable Universal Life (*continued*)

End of Year	Age	Premium	Surrender Value
31	76		210,305
32	77		219,579
33	78		229,007
34	79		238,582
35	80		248,300
36	81		258,166
37	82		267,970
38	83		277,697
39	84		587,339
40	85		296,845
41	86		306,166
42	87		315,258
43	88		324,086
44	89		332,641
45	90		340,934
46	91		349,013
47	92		357,331
48	93		366,118
49	94		375,718
50	95		386,598
51	96		399,438
52	97		415,262
53	98		435,577
54	99		462,665
55	100		500,035

Exceptions:

Current asset charges	1.03% for life of policy (no-commission)
Current asset charges	0.98% years 1–20 (commission)
	0.73% years 20 and up (commission)

These two exceptions alter the effective rate of return for each policy:

| Net rate of return | 8.97% (no-commission) |
| Net rate of return | 9.02% (commission) |

Appendix B

Charts and Tables

Individual Compensation Factors

Given Baby Boomers' craving for superior service and our national insistence on independence it is assumed that, of the four conditions (direct compensation, continuous compensation, Holy Grail service, and freedom to end a relationship at no cost), service and freedom are the most cherished. Take a look at Table B.1. Only 35% (7 of 20) of all fees and charges are attached to a service, and only 45% (9 of 20) leave investors with their freedom. In addition, note that all those fees that are attached to a service are also associated with freedom. And all but one of those (flat fee for a comprehensive plan) are continuous.

S & P Sectors of Our Core Choices

Table B.2 is a complete S & P breakdown indicating where each of our core S & P choices falls. Note that a few industries are not represented. Since there are only so many slots to fill, the advisor responsible for constructing the portfolios must make choices. (The core choices do not have to be limited to a certain number in each sector, although it is recommended that each sector be represented.)

TABLE B.1 Individual Compensation Factors

	Fee or Charge	Key	Product / Service	Free / Trapped	Direct / Indirect	Once / Continous
1	Asset-based management fees	1	Service	Free	Direct	Continuous
2	Net-worth-based management fees	1	Service	Free	Direct	Continuous
3	Consulting fees	1	Service	Free	Direct	Continuous
4	C-share 12b-1s	2	Service	Free	Indirect	Continuous
5	Management and administrative fees within C-share mutual funds	2	Service	Free	Indirect	Continuous
6	A- & B-share 12b-1s	3	Product	Trapped	Indirect	Continuous
7	Management and administrative fees within A- & B-share mutual funds	3	Product	Trapped	Indirect	Continuous
8	Back loads on Class B mutual fund shares for early withdrawal	3	Product	Trapped	Direct	Once
9	Front loads on Class A mutual fund shares	3	Product	Trapped	Direct	Once
10	Extra expense on Class B mutual funds shares until conversion	3	Product	Trapped	Indirect	Continuous
11	Commission on securities trades	4	Product	Free	Direct	Once
12	Ticket charges on securities trades	4	Product	Free	Direct	Once
13	Fee-only comprehensive financial planning	5	Service	Free	Direct	Once
14	Surrender charges on life insurance contracts for early termination	6	Product	Trapped	Direct	Once
15	Mortality and expense charges in life insurance contracts	6	Product	Trapped	Indirect	Continuous
16	Subaccount management fees in life insurance contracts	6	Product	Trapped	Indirect	Continuous
17	Surrender charges on annuities for early termination	7	Product	Trapped	Direct	Once
18	Mortality and expense charges in annuity contracts	7	Product	Trapped	Indirect	Continuous
19	Subaccount management fees in annuity contracts	7	Product	Trapped	Indirect	Continuous
20	Trust account fees	8	Service	Free	Direct	Continuous

TABLE B.2 S & P Sectors for Our Core Choices

10	Sector—Energy	
1010	Industry group—Energy	
101010	Industry—Energy Equipment & Services	
10101010	Subindustry—Oil & Gas Drilling	None
10101020	Subindustry—Oil & Gas Equipment & Services	Schlumberger
101020	Industry—Oil & Gas	
10102010	Subindustry—Integrated Oil & Gas	Exxon
10102020	Subindustry—Oil & Gas Exploration & Production	None
10102030	Subindustry—Oil & Gas Refining & Marketing	Ashland Oil
15	Sector—Materials	
1510	Industry group—Materials	
151010	Industry—Chemicals	Union Carbide
151020	Industry—Construction Materials	None
151030	Industry—Containers & Packaging	None
151040	Industry—Metals & Mining	Phelps Dodge
151050	Industry—Paper & Forest Products	International Paper
20	Sector—Industrials	
2010	Industry group—Capital Goods	General Electric
2020	Industry group—Commercial Services & Supplies	ADP
2030	Industry group—Transportation	Southwest Airlines
25	Sector—Consumer Discretionary	
2510	Industry group—Automobiles & Components	General Motors
2520	Industry group—Consumer Durables & Apparel	None
2530	Industry group—Hotels, Restaurants & Leisure	None
2540	Industry group—Media	Times Mirror
2550	Industry group—Retailing	Wal-Mart

(*continues*)

30	Sector—Consumer Staples	
3010	Industry group—Food & Drug Retailing	Sysco
3020	Industry group—Food Beverage & Tobacco	Anheuser-Busch
3030	Industry group—Household & Personal Products	Procter & Gamble
35	Sector—Health Care	
3510	Industry group—Health Care Equipment & Services	
351010	Industry—Health Care Equipment & Supplies	Mallinckrodt
351020	Industry—Health Care Providers & Services	None
3520	Industry group—Pharmaceuticals & Biotechnology	
352010	Industry—Biotechnology	Amgen
352020	Industry—Pharmaceuticals	Pfizer
40	Sector—Financials	
4010	Industry group—Banks	J.P. Morgan
4020	Industry group—Diversified Financials	Charles Schwab
4030	Industry group—Insurance	AIG
45	Sector—Information Technology	
4510	Industry group—Software & Services	
451010	Industry—Internet Software & Services	None
451020	Industry—IT Consulting & Services	None
451030	Industry—Software	Microsoft
4520	Industry group—Technology Hardware & Equipment	
452010	Industry—Communications Equipment	Cisco
452020	Industry—Computers & Peripherals	Dell

(*continues*)

TABLE B.2 S & P Sectors for Our Core Choices (*continued*)

452030	Industry—Electronic Equipment & Instruments	None
452040	Industry—Office Electronics	None
452050	Industry—Semiconductor Equipment & Products	Intel
50	Sector—Telecommunication Services	
5010	Industry group—Telecommunication Services	
501010	Industry—Diversified Telecom Services	
50101010	Subindustry—Alternative Carriers	Global Crossing
50101020	Subindustry—Integrated Telecom Services	MCI WorldCom
501020	Industry—Wireless Telecom Services	
50102010	Subindustry—Wireless Telecom Services	Sprint PCS
55	Sector—Utilities	
5510	Industry group—Utilities	
551010	Industry—Electrical	ConEd
551020	Industry—Gas	Peoples Energy
551030	Industry—Multi	Enron

In the Energy sector, we had to dig all the way down into the subindustry stratum to find our picks.

Expense Comparison Detail

Understanding the long-term impact of our practice on our clients' financial strength is imperative. It's simple to place them in today's and yesterday's common investment vehicles, take our commission, and feel warm and fuzzy that over the long haul our clients are in the best possible arrangement.

Without the unequivocal quantitative facts, we cannot be assured that this is happening. Following are the quantitative

TABLE B.3 Expense Comparison Detail

$350,000	Managed Expenses	Class A Expenses	Difference from Mngd	Percent Savings	15 Years @ 12%	Class B or C Expenses	Difference from Mngd	Percent Savings	15 Years @ 12%
Aggressive	$4,022	$5,674	$1,652	29.1%	$61,586	$7,042	$3,021	42.89%	$112,603
Dynamic	$4,008	$5,590	$1,582	28.3%	$58,977	$6,958	$2,951	42.40%	$109,994
Moderate	$3,952	$5,376	$1,425	26.5%	$53,105	$6,741	$2,790	41.38%	$103,992
Conservative	$3,927	$5,184	$1,257	24.2%	$46,842	$6,549	$2,622	40.03%	$97,729
Income	$3,609	$4,841	$1,232	25.5%	$45,929	$6,209	$2,601	41.88%	$96,946
	$3,903	$5,333	$1,429	26.8%	$53,288	$6,700	$2,797	41.74%	$104,253

$1,000,000	Managed Expenses	Class A Expenses	Difference from Mngd	Percent Savings	15 Years @ 12%	Class B or C Expenses	Difference from Mngd	Percent Savings	15 Years @ 12%
Aggressive	$11,490	$15,210	$3,720	24.5%	$138,681	$20,120	$8,630	42.89%	$321,724
Dynamic	$11,450	$14,970	$3,520	23.5%	$131,225	$19,880	$8,430	42.40%	$314,268
Moderate	**$11,290**	**$14,350**	**$3,060**	**21.3%**	**$114,076**	**$19,260**	**$7,970**	**41.38%**	**$297,119**
Conservative	$11,220	$13,810	$2,590	18.8%	$96,554	$18,710	$7,490	40.03%	$279,225
Income	$10,310	$12,830	$2,520	19.6%	$93,945	$17,740	$7,430	41.88%	$276,988
	$11,152	$14,234	$3,082	21.7%	$114,896	$19,142	$7,990	41.74%	$297,865

$5,000,000	Managed Expenses	Class A Expenses	Difference from Mngd	Percent Savings	15 Years @ 12%	Class C Expenses	Difference from Mngd	Percent Savings	15 Years @ 12%
Aggressive	$47,450	$70,750	$23,300	32.9%	$868,617	$100,600	$53,150	52.83%	$1,981,417
Dynamic	$47,250	$69,550	$22,300	32.1%	$831,338	$99,400	$52,150	52.46%	$1,944,137
Moderate	$46,450	$66,450	$20,000	30.1%	$745,594	$96,300	$49,850	51.77%	$1,858,394
Conservative	$46,100	$63,700	$17,600	27.6%	$656,123	$93,550	$47,450	50.72%	$1,768,922
Income	$41,550	$58,850	$17,300	29.4%	$644,939	$88,700	$47,150	53.16%	$1,757,739
	$45,760	$65,860	$20,100	30.5%	$749,322	$95,710	$49,950	52.19%	$1,862,122

$10,000,000	Managed Expenses	Class A Expenses	Difference from Mngd	Percent Savings	15 Years @ 12%	Class C Expenses	Difference from Mngd	Percent Savings	15 Years @ 12%
Aggressive	$56,900	$129,600	$72,700	56.1%	$2,710,235	$201,200	$144,300	71.72%	$5,379,463
Dynamic	$56,500	$128,300	$71,800	56.0%	$2,676,684	$198,800	$142,300	71.58%	$5,304,903
Moderate	$54,900	$124,500	$69,600	55.9%	$2,594,668	$192,600	$137,700	71.50%	$5,133,417
Conservative	$54,200	$115,800	$61,600	53.2%	$2,296,430	$187,100	$132,900	71.03%	$4,954,474
Income	$45,100	$105,800	$60,700	57.4%	$2,262,879	$177,400	$132,300	74.58%	$4,932,106
	$53,520	$120,800	$67,280	55.7%	$2,508,179	$185,760	$123,440	66.45%	$5,140,873

TABLE B.4 Expense Comparison Detail, with Capital Gains Impact

EXPENSE COMPARISON DETAIL - WITH CAPITAL GAINS IMPACT

$350,000	Managed Expenses	Class A Expenses	Difference from Mngd	Avg Cap Gain Loss	Percent Savings	15 Years @ 12%	Class B or C Expenses	Difference from Mngd	Avg Cap Gain Loss	Percent Savings	15 Years @ 12%
Aggressive	$4,022	$5,674	$1,652	$2,004	64.44%	$136,295	$7,042	$3,021	$2,004	71.35%	$187,312
Dynamic	$4,008	$5,590	$1,582	$1,851	61.42%	$127,981	$6,958	$2,951	$1,851	69.01%	$168,999
Moderate	$3,952	$5,376	$1,425	$1,462	53.69%	$107,608	$6,741	$2,790	$1,462	63.07%	$158,495
Conservative	$3,927	$5,184	$1,257	$938	42.34%	$81,810	$6,549	$2,622	$938	54.36%	$132,697
Income	$3,609	$4,841	$1,232	$480	35.37%	$63,823	$6,209	$2,601	$480	49.61%	$114,840
	$3,903	$5,333	$1,429	$1,347	52.06%	$103,503	$6,700	$2,797	$1,347	61.85%	$154,468

$1,000,000	Managed Expenses	Class A Expenses	Difference from Mngd	Avg Cap Gain Loss	Percent Savings	15 Years @ 12%	Class B or C Expenses	Difference from Mngd	Avg Cap Gain Loss	Percent Savings	15 Years @ 12%
Aggressive	$11,490	$15,210	$3,720	$5,704	61.96%	$351,324	$20,120	$8,630	$5,704	71.24%	$534,367
Dynamic	$11,450	$14,970	$3,520	$5,268	58.70%	$327,614	$19,880	$8,430	$5,268	68.90%	$510,658
Moderate	**$11,290**	**$14,350**	**$3,060**	**$4,171**	**50.39%**	**$269,570**	**$19,260**	**$7,970**	**$4,171**	**63.04%**	**$452,613**
Conservative	$11,220	$13,810	$2,590	$2,681	38.17%	$196,501	$18,710	$7,490	$2,681	54.36%	$379,172
Income	$10,310	$12,830	$2,520	$1,370	30.32%	$145,018	$17,740	$7,430	$1,370	49.61%	$328,061
	$11,152	$14,234	$3,082	$3,839	48.62%	$258,005	$19,142	$7,990	$3,839	61.80%	$440,974

$5,000,000	Managed Expenses	Class A Expenses	Difference from Mngd	Avg Cap Gain Loss	Percent Savings	15 Years @ 12%	Class C Expenses	Difference from Mngd	Avg Cap Gain Loss	Percent Savings	15 Years @ 12%
Aggressive	$47,450	$70,750	$23,300	$28,523	73.25%	$1,931,947	$100,600	$53,150	$28,523	81.19%	$3,044,746
Dynamic	$47,250	$69,550	$22,300	$26,341	69.94%	$1,813,323	$99,400	$52,150	$26,341	78.96%	$2,926,122
Moderate	$46,450	$66,450	$20,000	$20,857	61.49%	$1,523,137	$96,300	$49,850	$20,857	73.42%	$2,635,937
Conservative	$46,100	$63,700	$17,600	$13,405	48.67%	$1,155,858	$93,550	$47,450	$13,405	65.05%	$2,268,657
Income	$41,550	$58,850	$17,300	$6,850	41.04%	$900,305	$88,700	$47,150	$6,850	60.88%	$2,013,105
	$45,760	$65,860	$20,100	$19,195	59.66%	$1,464,914	$95,710	$49,950	$19,195	72.24%	$2,577,713

$10,000,000	Managed Expenses	Class A Expenses	Difference from Mngd	Avg Cap Gain Loss	Percent Savings	15 Years @ 12%	Class C Expenses	Difference from Mngd	Avg Cap Gain Loss	Percent Savings	15 Years @ 12%
Aggressive	$56,900	$129,600	$72,700	$57,046	100.11%	$4,836,894	$201,200	$144,300	$57,046	100.07%	$7,506,121
Dynamic	$56,500	$128,300	$71,800	$52,682	97.02%	$4,640,653	$198,800	$142,300	$52,682	98.08%	$7,268,873
Moderate	$54,900	$124,500	$69,600	$41,715	89.41%	$4,149,791	$192,600	$137,700	$41,715	93.15%	$6,688,540
Conservative	$54,200	$115,800	$61,600	$26,810	76.35%	$3,295,900	$187,100	$132,900	$26,810	85.36%	$5,953,943
Income	$45,100	$105,800	$60,700	$13,700	70.32%	$2,773,611	$177,400	$132,300	$13,700	82.30%	$5,442,838
	$53,520	$120,800	$67,280	$38,391	87.48%	$3,939,370	$191,420	$137,900	$38,391	92.10%	$6,572,063

TABLE B.5 Compensation Patterns of Salesperson versus Financial Advisor

Block 1

		SALESPERSON						ADVISOR				
Yr	Added	Comp Each	Annual Comp	Invested Beginning	Growth	Ending	Added	Amount Managed	Annual Comp	Investment Beginning	Growth	Ending
1	5	$25,000	$125,000	$125,000	$15,000	$140,000	5	$2,500,000	$25,000	$25,000	$3,000	$28,000
2	5	$25,000	$125,000	$265,000	$31,800	$296,800	5	$5,300,000	$53,000	$81,000	$9,720	$90,720
3	5	$25,000	$125,000	$421,800	$50,616	$472,416	5	$8,436,000	$84,360	$175,080	$21,010	$196,090
4	5	$25,000	$125,000	$597,416	$71,690	$669,106	5	$11,948,320	$119,483	$315,573	$37,869	$353,442
5	5	$25,000	$125,000	$794,106	$95,293	$889,399	5	$15,882,118	$158,821	$512,263	$61,472	$573,734
6	5	$25,000	$125,000	$1,014,399	$121,728	$1,136,126	5	$20,287,973	$202,880	$776,614	$93,194	$869,808
7	5	$25,000	$125,000	$1,261,126	$151,335	$1,412,462	5	$25,222,529	$252,225	$1,122,033	$134,644	$1,256,677
8	5	$25,000	$125,000	$1,537,462	$184,495	$1,721,957	5	$30,749,233	$307,492	$1,564,169	$187,700	$1,751,870
9	5	$25,000	$125,000	$1,846,957	$221,635	$2,068,592	5	$36,939,141	$369,391	$2,121,261	$254,551	$2,375,812
10	5	$25,000	$125,000	$2,193,592	$263,231	$2,456,823	5	$43,871,838	$438,718	$2,814,531	$337,744	$3,152,274
11	5	$25,000	$125,000	$2,581,823	$309,819	$2,891,642	5	$51,636,458	$516,365	$3,668,639	$440,237	$4,108,876
12	5	$25,000	$125,000	$3,016,642	$361,997	$3,378,639	5	$60,332,833	$603,328	$4,712,204	$565,464	$5,277,668
13	5	$25,000	$125,000	$3,503,639	$420,437	$3,924,075	5	$70,072,773	$700,728	$5,978,396	$717,408	$6,695,804
14	5	$25,000	$125,000	$4,049,075	$485,889	$4,534,964	5	$80,981,506	$809,815	$7,505,619	$900,674	$8,406,293
15	5	$25,000	$125,000	$4,659,964	$559,196	$5,219,160	5	$93,199,287	$931,993	$9,338,286	$1,120,594	$10,458,880
	75	< 15 year					75	< 15 year				
	50	< 10 year					50	< 10 year				

Block 2

		SALESPERSON						ADVISOR				
Yr	Added	Comp Each	Annual Comp	Invested Beginning	Growth	Ending	Added	Amount Managed	Annual Comp	Investment Beginning	Growth	Ending
1	5.0	$25,000	$125,000	$125,000	$15,000	$140,000	5	$2,500,000	$25,000	$25,000	$3,000	$28,000
2	5.0	$25,000	$125,000	$265,000	$31,800	$296,800	5	$5,300,000	$53,000	$81,000	$9,720	$90,720
3	5.0	$25,000	$125,000	$421,800	$50,616	$472,416	5	$8,436,000	$84,360	$175,080	$21,010	$196,090
4	5.0	$25,000	$125,000	$597,416	$71,690	$669,106	5	$11,948,320	$119,483	$315,573	$37,869	$353,442
5	6.4	$25,000	$158,750	$827,856	$99,343	$927,199	5	$15,882,118	$158,821	$512,263	$61,472	$573,734
6	8.1	$25,000	$202,750	$1,129,949	$135,594	$1,265,542	5	$20,287,973	$202,880	$776,614	$93,194	$869,808
7	10.1	$25,000	$252,500	$1,518,042	$182,165	$1,700,208	5	$25,222,529	$252,225	$1,122,033	$134,644	$1,256,677
8	12.3	$25,000	$307,500	$2,007,708	$240,925	$2,248,632	5	$30,749,233	$307,492	$1,564,169	$187,700	$1,751,870
9	14.8	$25,000	$369,500	$2,618,132	$314,176	$2,932,308	5	$36,939,141	$369,391	$2,121,261	$254,551	$2,375,812
10	17.6	$25,000	$438,750	$3,371,058	$404,527	$3,775,585	5	$43,871,838	$438,718	$2,814,531	$337,744	$3,152,274
11	20.7	$25,000	$516,250	$4,291,835	$515,020	$4,806,856	5	$51,636,458	$516,365	$3,668,639	$440,237	$4,108,876
12	24.1	$25,000	$603,125	$5,409,981	$649,198	$6,059,178	5	$60,332,833	$603,328	$4,712,204	$565,464	$5,277,668
13	28.0	$25,000	$700,500	$6,759,678	$811,161	$7,570,840	5	$70,072,773	$700,728	$5,978,396	$717,408	$6,695,804
14	32.4	$25,000	$809,750	$8,380,590	$1,005,671	$9,386,260	5	$80,981,506	$809,815	$7,505,619	$900,674	$8,406,293
15	37.3	$25,000	$931,875	$10,318,135	$1,238,176	$11,556,312	5	$93,199,287	$931,993	$9,338,286	$1,120,594	$10,458,880
	232	< 15 year					75	< 15 year				
	89	< 10 year					50	< 10 year				

Block 3

		SALESPERSON						ADVISOR				
Yr	Added	Comp Each	Annual Comp	Invested Beginning	Growth	Ending	Added	Amount Managed	Annual Comp	Investment Beginning	Growth	Ending
1	5	$25,000	$125,000	$125,000	$15,000	$140,000	5	$2,500,000	$25,000	$25,000	$3,000	$28,000
2	5	$25,000	$125,000	$265,000	$31,800	$296,800	5	$5,300,000	$53,000	$81,000	$9,720	$90,720
3	5	$25,000	$125,000	$421,800	$50,616	$472,416	5	$8,436,000	$84,360	$175,080	$21,010	$196,090
4	5	$25,000	$125,000	$597,416	$71,690	$669,106	5	$11,948,320	$119,483	$315,573	$37,869	$353,442
5	5	$25,000	$125,000	$794,106	$95,293	$889,399	0	$13,392,118	$133,821	$487,263	$58,472	$545,734
6	5	$25,000	$125,000	$1,014,399	$121,728	$1,136,126	0	$14,987,973	$149,880	$695,614	$83,474	$779,088
7	5	$25,000	$125,000	$1,261,126	$151,335	$1,412,462	0	$16,786,529	$167,865	$946,953	$113,634	$1,060,587
8	5	$25,000	$125,000	$1,537,462	$184,495	$1,721,957	0	$18,800,913	$188,009	$1,248,596	$149,832	$1,398,428
9	5	$25,000	$125,000	$1,846,957	$221,635	$2,068,592	0	$21,057,022	$210,570	$1,608,998	$193,080	$1,802,078
10	5	$25,000	$125,000	$2,193,592	$263,231	$2,456,823	0	$23,583,865	$235,839	$2,037,917	$244,550	$2,282,467
11	5	$25,000	$125,000	$2,581,823	$309,819	$2,891,642	0	$26,413,929	$264,139	$2,546,606	$305,593	$2,852,199
12	5	$25,000	$125,000	$3,016,642	$361,997	$3,378,639	0	$29,583,600	$295,836	$3,148,035	$377,764	$3,525,799
13	5	$25,000	$125,000	$3,503,639	$420,437	$3,924,075	0	$33,133,632	$331,336	$3,857,135	$462,856	$4,319,991
14	5	$25,000	$125,000	$4,049,075	$485,889	$4,534,964	0	$37,109,668	$371,097	$4,691,088	$562,931	$5,254,019
15	5	$25,000	$125,000	$4,659,964	$559,196	$5,219,160	0	$41,562,828	$415,628	$5,669,647	$680,358	$6,350,005
	75	< 15 year					20	< 15 year				
	50	< 10 year					20	< 10 year				

Block 4

		SALESPERSON						ADVISOR				
Yr	Added	Comp Each	Annual Comp	Invested Beginning	Growth	Ending	Added	Amount Managed	Annual Comp	Investment Beginning	Growth	Ending
1	5.0	$25,000	$125,000	$125,000	$15,000	$140,000	5.0	$2,500,000	$25,000	$25,000	$3,000	$28,000
2	5.0	$25,000	$125,000	$265,000	$31,800	$296,800	5.0	$5,300,000	$53,000	$81,000	$9,720	$90,720
3	5.0	$25,000	$125,000	$421,800	$50,616	$472,416	5.0	$8,436,000	$84,360	$175,080	$21,010	$196,090
4	5.0	$25,000	$125,000	$597,416	$71,690	$669,106	5.0	$11,948,320	$119,483	$315,573	$37,869	$353,442
5	6.4	$25,000	$158,750	$827,856	$99,343	$927,199	6.4	$16,557,118	$165,571	$519,013	$62,282	$581,294
6	8.1	$25,000	$202,750	$1,129,949	$135,594	$1,265,542	8.1	$22,598,973	$225,990	$807,284	$96,874	$904,158
7	10.1	$25,000	$252,500	$1,518,042	$182,165	$1,700,208	10.1	$30,360,849	$303,608	$1,207,767	$144,932	$1,352,699
8	12.3	$25,000	$307,500	$2,007,708	$240,925	$2,248,632	12.3	$40,154,151	$401,542	$1,754,240	$210,509	$1,964,749
9	14.8	$25,000	$369,500	$2,618,132	$314,176	$2,932,308	14.8	$52,372,649	$523,726	$2,488,475	$298,617	$2,787,092
10	17.6	$25,000	$438,750	$3,371,058	$404,527	$3,775,585	5.0	$66,157,367	$611,574	$3,398,666	$407,840	$3,806,506
11	20.7	$25,000	$516,250	$4,291,835	$515,020	$4,806,856	5.0	$70,996,251	$709,963	$4,516,468	$541,976	$5,058,445
12	24.1	$25,000	$603,125	$5,409,981	$649,198	$6,059,178	5.0	$82,015,802	$820,158	$5,878,603	$705,432	$6,584,035
13	28.0	$25,000	$700,500	$6,759,678	$811,161	$7,570,840	5.0	$94,357,698	$943,577	$7,527,612	$903,313	$8,430,925
14	32.4	$25,000	$809,750	$8,380,590	$1,005,671	$9,386,260	5.0	$108,180,621	$1,081,806	$9,512,732	$1,141,528	$10,654,259
15	37.3	$25,000	$931,875	$10,318,135	$1,238,176	$11,556,312	5.0	$123,662,296	$1,236,623	$11,890,882	$1,426,906	$13,317,788
	232	< 15 year					102	< 15 year				
	89	< 10 year					77	< 10 year				

Block 5

		SALESPERSON						ADVISOR				
Yr	Added	Comp Each	Annual Comp	Invested Beginning	Growth	Ending	Added	Amount Managed	Annual Comp	Investment Beginning	Growth	Ending
1	5.0	$25,000	$125,000	$125,000	$15,000	$140,000	5.0	$2,500,000	$25,000	$25,000	$3,000	$28,000
2	5.0	$25,000	$125,000	$265,000	$31,800	$296,800	5.0	$5,300,000	$53,000	$81,000	$9,720	$90,720
3	5.0	$25,000	$125,000	$421,800	$50,616	$472,416	5.0	$8,436,000	$84,360	$175,080	$21,010	$196,090
4	5.0	$25,000	$125,000	$597,416	$71,690	$669,106	5.0	$11,948,320	$119,483	$315,573	$37,869	$353,442
5	6.4	$25,000	$158,750	$827,856	$99,343	$927,199	6.4	$16,557,118	$165,571	$519,013	$62,282	$581,294
6	8.1	$25,000	$202,750	$1,129,949	$135,594	$1,265,542	8.1	$22,598,973	$225,990	$807,284	$96,874	$904,158
7	10.1	$25,000	$252,500	$1,518,042	$182,165	$1,700,208	10.1	$30,360,849	$303,608	$1,207,767	$144,932	$1,352,699
8	12.3	$25,000	$307,500	$2,007,708	$240,925	$2,248,632	12.3	$40,154,151	$401,542	$1,754,240	$210,509	$1,964,749
9	14.8	$25,000	$369,500	$2,618,132	$314,176	$2,932,308	14.8	$52,362,649	$523,626	$2,488,375	$298,605	$2,786,980
10	17.6	$25,000	$438,750	$3,371,058	$404,527	$3,775,585	17.6	$67,421,167	$674,212	$3,461,192	$415,343	$3,876,535
11	20.7	$25,000	$516,250	$4,291,835	$515,020	$4,806,856	20.7	$85,836,707	$858,367	$4,734,902	$568,188	$5,303,090
12	24.1	$25,000	$603,125	$5,409,981	$649,198	$6,059,178	24.1	$108,199,612	$1,081,996	$6,385,087	$766,210	$7,151,297
13	28.0	$25,000	$700,500	$6,759,678	$811,161	$7,570,840	28.0	$135,193,566	$1,351,936	$8,503,233	$1,020,388	$9,523,621
14	32.4	$25,000	$809,750	$8,380,590	$1,005,671	$9,386,260	32.4	$167,611,794	$1,676,118	$11,199,738	$1,343,969	$12,543,707
15	37.3	$25,000	$931,875	$10,318,135	$1,238,176	$11,556,312	37.3	$206,362,709	$2,063,627	$14,607,334	$1,752,880	$16,360,214
	232	< 15 year					232	< 15 year				
	89	< 10 year					89	< 10 year				

facts, and we are unequivocally not positioning them to the best of our abilities.

In Table B.3 we see that plopping our clients into A shares and B and C shares costs them a certain absolute amount of money. To zero in, note that in our $1 million moderate portfolio, the client pays an annual $11,290 management fee. In a similar portfolio of A-share mutual funds, the client is drained of $14,350. So we remark, "What's three grand out of a million bucks?" Other than the mere fact that it's wasting the client's money, do that for 15 years and you have just squandered a piddling $114,076 of your client's money—and that's without growing the $1 million. B and C shares are more than twice the thief as A shares.

So if we're wilting at the thought of having to actually reveal to our clients how they are paying us, rest assured that our actions are costing them big bucks. Small arguments can be mounted against this analysis, but numbers do not lie.

Up until the past few years, portfolio management suggestions such as those in this book would be difficult if not entirely impossible for most frontline financial advisors. The big guns, the folks who manage bargefuls of money for obscenely wealthy castle dwellers, have been doing it efficiently and properly for a long time.

Now that the Internet is here and large institutions (including the SEC) are pushing us intently into fee-based compensation structures, the midline financial advisor has the tools and the incentive to cast off the burdensome mutual funds and to manage specific portfolios for a fee.

Capital Gains Taxes

Now let's saddle the preceding with a larger burden: uncontrollable capital gains taxes flung off by mutual funds every year beyond those generated by our portfolios. The calamity grows more troubling.

The A-share degradation increases more than twofold. And the B and C share deepens from $297,119 to almost a half a million dollars. See Table B.4.

Table B.5 lines up all the tables from Chapter 11, "Mythologies," for quick comparison.

Appendix C

Internet Addresses

This appendix lists a variety of Web sites that can be useful for the financial advisor.

Crucial Tools

- www.strategicportfolios.com This site allows you to build, monitor, and manage client portfolios in a comprehensive fashion. There are tools in this site, including thorough stock option exercise analysis and retirement distribution strategies, that are indispensable to proper and comprehensive analysis.

- www.stockoptionscentral.com At StockOptionsCentral you can analyze the profit and tax ramifications of exercising your clients' company stock options. You can demonstrate current effects or future effects on one grant or all grants. You can also control the growth rate of the company's shares and the growth rate of reinvested after-tax proceeds after the exercise.

- www.knowloads.com Knowloads.com gathers 50 major no-load mutual fund family sites onto one site. Unlike most mutual fund Web sites, Knowloads doesn't want you to stay on their site. They want you to click through to the mutual fund families.

- www.wilsonintl.com   Portfolio management software from Wilson International.

- www.advisorinsight.com   S & P's Internet site for financial advisors only, unavailable to the public. Provides important fundamental information about companies, including their proprietary STAR and Fair Value ratings.

- www.cboe.com   The Chicago Board Options Exchange site lists options pricing and offers gobs of educational information, instructional seminars, books, and so on.

- www.multex.com   Research site where you can buy reports on any publicly owned company followed by analysts. Also allows you to build and maintain portfolios so that reports on only those companies show up on the menu.

- www.iqc.com   Definable charts for performing technical analysis to help determine the optimal time, short term, to enter the market.

- www.spredgar.com   Spreadsheet software that reaches into EDGAR and pulls out fundamental ratios of companies and then displays them with bar charts.

Data and Research Sources

- www.interactive.wsj.com/documents/bcom-markcal.htm
  Index of over 45 economic reports (link to briefing.com), from Auto Sales and Average Workweek to Unemployment Rate and Wholesale Inventories.

- www.decisionpoint.com/DailyCharts   Advance-decline line in relation to NYSE closes, as well as numerous other market charts.

- www.edgar-online.com/ipoexpress/   This initial public offering center allows us to search, using numerous variables, for upcoming IPOs as well as those recently dropped onto the market. It provides lead underwriter, company description, price range, issue size, and so on.

- www.fairmark.com/   Excellent investor tax guide site. Timely topics as well as search and research capabilities.

- www.spglobal.com/sector-scorecard.html Displays the performance of all the S & P sectors and subsectors. Standard & Poor's also assigns its Fair Value and STAR calculations to each, as well as recommendations on participation.

- www.interactive.wsj.com/edition/resources/documents/ mktindex.htm?fedwatch.htm *Wall Street Journal Interactive*'s Federal Reserve site. Here are the minutes of previous Fed meetings, including a listing of all members, current bias, and previous interest rate changes.

- www.interactive.wsj.com/documents/mktindex.htm?uscal.htm A schedule of official economic announcements due out within the upcoming two weeks. It provides the report name, time, and date of announcement, as well as consensus on the statistic itself.

- www.isld.com/BookViewer/javaversion.htm Island ECN Web site. Watch as afterhours traders put forth bids and asks on stocks.

- www.interactive.wsj.com/documents/mktindex.htm?earncal .htm A *Wall Street Journal Interactive* list of when companies will announce earnings within the upcoming week.

- www.interactive.wsj.com/documents/mktindex.htm?insider1 .htm A listing of insider trading activity, searched by sales, buys, intent to sell, industry leaders, and the largest traders of the previous week.

- www.interactive.wsj.com/documents/mktindex.htm?ipopipe .htm Another list of recent IPOs, in alphabetical order.

- www.cbs.marketwatch.com/data/dbcfiles/indindext.htx?source =htx/http2_mw A list of most market indices, from the airlines and autos to transportation and utilities.

Information Sites

- www.brook.edu/comm/comm_hp.htm The Brookings Institute pressroom. Free.

- www.businessweek.com/contents.htm *Business Week Online*. Cost.

- www.cbs.marketwatch.com/news/newsroom.htx?source=htx/ http2_mw   CBSWatch. Cost.

- http://interactive.wsj.com/pages/front.htm   *Wall Street Journal Interactive.* Cost.

- www.dismal.com/thoughts/archive/archives.asp   The Dismal Scientist, serving up many articles on the economy. Free.

- www.economist.com/   *The Economist,* the prestigious British economics magazine. Cost.

- www.gildertech.com/   Technology newsletter, authored by the respected George Gilder. Cost.

- www.kiplinger.com/clients/   Kiplinger Newsletter (not magazine). Cost.

- www.slate.com/toc/toc.asp   General news and economics magazine. Free.

Major Statistical Sites

- http://interactive.wsj.com/documents/bcom-suboececi.htm Employment cost index (ECI).

- http://interactive.wsj.com/documents/mlab-index_yields.htm Corporate earnings.

- http://interactive.wsj.com/documents/bcom-suboecemploy.htm Hourly wages.

- http://interactive.wsj.com/documents/bcom-suboecstarts.htm Housing starts.

- http://interactive.wsj.com/documents/bcom-suboecnapm.htm National Association of Purchasing Managers—Manufacturing.

- http://interactive.wsj.com/documents/bbnonman.htm   National Association of Purchasing Managers—Service.

- http://interactive.wsj.com/documents/bcom-suboecppi.htm Producer price index (PPI).

- http://stats.bls.gov/eag.table.html   Labor statistics.

- http://interactive.wsj.com/documents/bcom-suboecconf.htm Consumer Confidence, the University of Michigan's and the Conference Board's.

- http://interactive.wsj.com/documents/bcom-suboeccpi.htm Consumer price index (CPI).

- http://interactive.wsj.com/documents/bcom-suboecexist.htm Existing home sales.

- http://interactive.wsj.com/documents/bcom-suboecnewhom .htm   New home sales.

- http://interactive.wsj.com/documents/bcom-suboecclaims.htm Initial unemployment claims.

- http://interactive.wsj.com/documents/bcom-suboecretail.htm Retail sales.

- http://interactive.wsj.com/documents/bcom-suboecemploy .htm   Nonfarm employment.

- http://www.cnnfn.com/markets/bondcenter/rates.html   Bond rates.

- http://www.federalreserve.gov/releases/H15/   Bond rates, Federal Reserve site.

- http://interactive.wsj.com/documents/mlab-money_supply .htm   Money supply.

- http://tfc-charts.w2d.com/custom_menu.php3   Commodity prices.

- http://interactive.wsj.com/documents/mlab-per_share.htm Dow Jones industrial earnings per share (EPS).

- http://interactive.wsj.com/edition/resources/documents/ mktindex.htm?rates.htm   Money rates.

Appendix D

Asset Management Software

Managing and continually valuing five portfolios holding upward of 50 positions—some core, some tactical, and some derivatives—requires a central location that provides ease of movement. In Chapter 9 we reviewed tables that demonstrated the positions held in each of our portfolios. This table is but one of 10 locations in the Microsoft Excel–based spreadsheet constructed and employed by the author.

1. Distribution Assignments
2. Positions
3. Shares to Purchase upon Market Entry
4. Valuation
5. Profile
6. Tactical
7. Options
8. Retirement Distribution
9. Tax Savings
10. Fees

If you are handy with the construction of workbooks, you can develop interrelated worksheets that pull your entire portfolio management into a central location, and with only a few key-strokes you can maintain their integrity daily. Following are depictions of these 10 sites. They will guide the spreadsheet builder in visualizing each location. Along with these, professional experience, and knowledge of Excel's formula components, you can develop a workbook.

If you're not adept at spreadsheet creation, or don't have the time or patience but have an interest in test-driving the concept, e-mail the author at thomasgrady@thomasgrady.com. You can also e-mail any comments you have on this book. But be nice.

Distribution Assignment

Table D.1 is an internal site where the financial advisor constructs each portfolio. Each equity choice is entered, along with the percentage to be held in each position of each portfolio, in addition to the historic yields. The remainder of the program will not function until this site is complete. The aggressive (A) and dynamic (D) portfolios each have a sister entry column with a plus sign. These are alternate percentage assignments that are added to the regular column if the client declines tactical management. In this case the 10% must be folded back into the core equity positions. Such alterations are not made for the supplemental stocks.

The financial advisor also sets the trigger to incorporate the supplementals.

Positions

Table D.2 is our central location and the ideal place to present to our Baby Boomer clients the effects of their participation in any one of the portfolios. This location is fed from the Distribution Assignment site. Only three entries are made here: choice, amount, and tactical. In our sample, $1 million is suggested for our dynamic portfolio, and the client has declined to have 10% of his assets tactically managed. We've set our supplemental trigger at $999,999, so the supplementals become involved in the distribution.

TABLE D.1 Assignments

$999,999

I	C	M	D	D+	A	A+	STRATEGIC	Yld
	2.5%	0.7%	1.0%	0.5%	1.2%	0.5%	Schlumberger	1.3%
		1.0%	1.0%	0.5%	0.5%	0.5%	Exxon	2.4%
5%	1.5%	1.5%	1.0%	0.5%			Union Carbide	1.5%
	1.0%	1.5%	0.5%	0.5%			Phelps Dodge	3.6%
	1.0%	1.0%	1.0%	0.5%	1.0%	0.5%	General Electric	1.1%
		1.0%	1.0%	0.5%	1.3%	0.5%	ADP	0.7%
5%	2.0%	1.5%	1.0%	0.5%	1.3%	0.5%	General Motors	2.9%
	0.5%	1.3%	1.3%	0.5%		0.5%	Wal-Mart	0.4%
	1.0%	1.3%	0.8%	0.5%	0.7%	0.5%	Anheuser-Busch	1.7%
	2.5%	1.5%	1.0%	0.5%	0.7%	0.5%	Procter & Gamble	1.2%
	0.5%	1.0%	1.0%	0.5%	1.0%	0.5%	Mallinckrodt	1.9%
	1.0%	1.3%	1.3%	0.5%	1.3%	0.8%	Pfizer	0.9%
5%	4.0%	0.7%	0.5%	0.5%	1.0%	0.5%	J.P. Morgan	3.0%
	0.5%	1.3%	1.0%	0.5%	1.5%	0.5%	AIG	0.2%
	1.0%	1.3%	1.5%	0.5%	1.5%	0.8%	Microsoft	0.0%
	1.0%	1.3%	1.5%	0.5%	1.5%	0.8%	Cisco	0.0%
	0.7%	1.3%	1.5%	0.5%	1.5%	0.8%	Intel	0.2%
	0.7%	1.3%	1.5%	0.5%	1.3%	0.8%	Global Crossing	0.0%
	0.7%	1.3%	1.5%	0.5%	1.3%	0.8%	Sprint PCS	0.0%
10%	3.5%	1.4%	0.5%	0.5%	0.7%		Ameren UE	6.8%
		1.8%	1.0%	0.5%	0.7%	0.5%	Enron	1.3%
	2.0%	3.0%	3.0%		3.0%		Mid-Cap SPDRs	0.0%
		2.1%	3.2%		4.3%		AOL	
		2.1%	3.2%		4.3%		Unisys	
		2.1%	3.2%		4.3%		PeopleSoft	
		2.1%	3.2%		4.3%		Oracle	
		2.1%	3.2%		4.3%		QUALCOMM	
		2.1%	3.2%		4.3%		Applied Materials	
		2.1%	3.2%		4.3%		Comcast	
		0.5%	1.0%		2.0%		Uniphase	
		0.5%	1.0%		2.0%		Nextlink	
		0.5%	1.0%		2.0%		Broadcom	
		0.5%	1.0%		2.0%		Level 3	
		0.5%	1.0%		2.0%		Cree Research	
		0.5%	1.0%		2.0%		Texas Instruments	
		0.5%	1.0%		2.0%		C-Cube	

I	C	M	D	A	SUPPLEMENTALS	Yld
	1.3%	1.0%	1.0%	1.0%	Ashland Oil	3.3%
	1.3%	1.3%	1.0%	1.0%	International Paper	1.9%
	0.5%	1.0%	1.0%	1.0%	Southwest Airlines	0.1%
	0.5%	1.3%	1.5%	1.3%	Times Mirror	1.1%
	0.5%	1.3%	1.5%	1.3%	Sysco	1.3%
	0.7%	1.3%	0.5%	1.0%	Amgen	0.0%
	0.7%	1.3%	1.5%	1.0%	Charles Schwab	0.1%
	0.7%	1.3%	1.3%	1.5%	Dell	0.0%
	0.7%	1.0%	1.3%	1.5%	MCI WorldCom	0.0%
	0.7%	1.0%	1.5%	1.5%	Peoples Energy	5.1%

I	C	M	D	A	MUTUAL FUNDS	Yld
	2.5%	3.0%	3.0%	3.0%	Lord Abbott Dev Grth	0.0%
	2.5%	2.5%	5.0%	6.0%	SSgA Emerging Mkts	2.6%
	5.0%	5.0%	5.0%	4.0%	Hotchkis & Wiley Int'l	1.0%

I	C	M	D	A	FIXED INCOME	Yld
5.0%	2.5%	2.5%			NE Investors	9.2%
25.0%	20.0%	7.5%	5.0%		Government	6.1%
42.5%	30.0%	17.0%	2.5%		Corporate (High Grd)	6.8%
2.5%	2.5%	2.5%	2.5%	2.5%	Money Market	4.8%

I	C	M	D	A	COMPOSITES
25.0%	35.0%	60.0%	77.0%	84.5%	Strategic
		0.0%	0.0%	0.0%	Tactical
75.0%	55.0%	29.5%	10.0%	2.5%	Bonds & Cash
0.0%	10.0%	10.5%	13.0%	13.0%	Mutual Funds
100%	100%	100%	100%	100%	TOTAL
20	44	57	59	50	Positions

I	C	M	D	A	PERFORMANCE
2%	5%	16%	32%	42%	1997
7%	12%	20%	40%	92%	1998
4%	8%	16%	20%	30%	YTD 1999

0.00%

213

S & P 500 SECTORS

S & P 500 SECTORS
ENERGY
MATERIALS
INDUSTRIALS
CNSMR DISCRETIONARY
CNSMR CYCLICALS
HEALTH CARE
FINANCIALS
INFORMATION TECH
COMMUNICATIONS
UTILITIES

STRATEGIC

STRATEGIC	DISTRIBUTION %	$	INCOME %	$
Schlumberger	1.5%	$15,000	1.3%	$188
Exxon	1.5%	$15,000	2.4%	$362
Union Carbide	1.5%	$15,000	1.5%	$218
Phelps Dodge	1.0%	$10,000	3.6%	$360
General Electric	1.5%	$15,000	1.1%	$159
ADP	1.5%	$15,000	0.7%	$98
General Motors	1.5%	$15,000	2.9%	$434
Wal-Mart	1.8%	$17,500	0.4%	$63
Anheuser-Busch	1.3%	$12,500	1.7%	$208
Procter & Gamble	1.5%	$15,000	1.2%	$183
Mallinckrodt	1.5%	$15,000	1.9%	$287
Pfizer	1.8%	$18,333	0.9%	$158
J.P. Morgan	1.0%	$10,000	3.0%	$301
AIG	1.5%	$15,000	0.2%	$30
Microsoft	1.5%	$15,000	0.0%	$0
Cisco	2.0%	$20,000	0.0%	$0
Intel	2.0%	$20,000	0.2%	$44
Global Crossing	2.0%	$20,000	0.0%	$0
Sprint PCS	2.0%	$20,000	0.0%	$0
Ameren UE	1.0%	$10,000	6.8%	$680
Enron	1.5%	$15,000	1.3%	$195
Mid-Cap SPDRs	3.0%	$30,000	0.0%	$0
AOL	3.2%	$32,143	0.0%	$0
Unisys	3.2%	$32,143	0.0%	$0
PeopleSoft	3.2%	$32,143	0.0%	$0
Oracle	3.2%	$32,143	0.0%	$0
QUALCOMM	3.2%	$32,143	0.0%	$0
Applied Materials	3.2%	$32,143	0.3%	$84
Comcast	1.0%	$10,000	0.0%	$0
Uniphase	1.0%	$10,000	0.0%	$0
Nextlink	1.0%	$10,000	0.0%	$0
Broadcom	1.0%	$10,000	0.0%	$0
Level 3	1.0%	$10,000	0.0%	$0
Cree Research	1.0%	$10,000	0.0%	$0
Texas Instruments	1.0%	$10,000	0.0%	$0
C-Cube	1.0%	$10,000	0.0%	$0

SUPPLEMENTALS

SUPPLEMENTALS	DISTRIBUTION %	$	INCOME %	$
Ashland Oil	1.0%	$10,000	3.3%	$327
International Paper	1.0%	$10,000	1.9%	$188
Southwest Airlines	1.0%	$10,000	0.1%	$13
Times Mirror	1.5%	$15,000	1.1%	$171
Sysco	1.5%	$15,000	1.3%	$188
Amgen	0.5%	$5,000	0.0%	$0
Charles Schwab	1.5%	$15,000	0.1%	$20
Dell	1.3%	$13,333	0.0%	$0
MCI WorldCom	1.3%	$13,333	0.0%	$0
Peoples Energy	1.5%	$15,000	5.1%	$762

MUTUAL FUNDS

MUTUAL FUNDS	DISTRIBUTION %	$	INCOME %	$
Lord Abbott Dev Grth	3.0%	$30,000	0.0%	$0
SSgA Emerging Mkts	5.0%	$50,000	2.6%	$1,300
Hotchkis & Wiley Int'l	5.0%	$50,000	1.0%	$475

FIXED INCOME

FIXED INCOME	DISTRIBUTION %	$	INCOME %	$
NE Investors	0.0%	$0	9.2%	$3,050
Government	5.0%	$50,000	6.1%	$1,698
Corporate (High Grd)	2.5%	$25,000	6.8%	$1,198
Money Market	2.5%	$25,000	4.8%	$1,198

COMPOSITES

COMPOSITES	DISTRIBUTION %	$	INCOME %	$
Core	35.3%	$353,333	1.1%	$3,964
Volatile	22.5%	$225,000	0.0%	$84
Disruptive	7.0%	$70,000	0.0%	$0
Supplementals	12.2%	$121,667	1.4%	$1,668
Tactical	0.0%	$0	0.0%	$0
Mutual Funds	13.0%	$130,000	1.4%	$1,775
Bonds & Cash	10.0%	$100,000	5.9%	$5,945
TOTAL	100%	$1,000,000	1.34%	$13,436
	0.00%			

PORTFOLIOS

PORTFOLIOS
AGGRESSIVE
DYNAMIC
MODERATE
CONSERVATIVE
INCOME

CHOICE
D

AMOUNT
$1,000,000

TACTICAL ?
N

DYNAMIC	
ANNUAL TAX SAVINGS	$5,268
1997 RETURN	31.6%
1998 RETURN	39.9%
YTD 1999 RETURN	20.4%
YIELD	1.34%
INCOME	$13,436
POSITIONS	59

With these entries, all distributions (percentages and dollar amounts), yields, and income calculate automatically. The client sees the total exposure to the volatile and disruptive stocks (which should be color-coded), the total income, the annual tax savings over a similar portfolio of mutual funds, the total yield and annual income, and the total positions held.

Shares to Purchase upon Market Entry

Table D.3 is also an internal location. Once the portfolio is chosen, the financial advisor visits this site to determine the number of shares that will be purchased based on the most current share price. By inserting the current price of each equity (previous day's NAV for mutual funds), the shares calculate.

It also calculates the amount the client will pay in transaction charges. In the "Transaction" box, we must first plug in the per-share cost and flat ticket charge, if any. In our example, the total entry cost is $1,877, or 0.188% of the $1 million.

Mutual fund expense ratios are recorded at this site in order to determine the net fee charged on each of our portfolios. In this example, $1,454 is the annual expense cost from the three funds we use inside our dynamic portfolio.

Valuation

In Table D.4, the financial advisor quantifies the current valuation (fundamental and technical) health of all the equity positions on any given day, including the day the assets are to be entered into the market. The site determines the health of each company's fundamentals, and the amount overvalued or undervalued for each position is based on S & P's Fair Value and STAR conclusions. It does the same for each equity's related S & P sector. The financial advisor can assign weights to each category—single equity and sector—to affect the combined quantitative outcome of the stock's fundamental health.

Once these numbers have been calculated, the financial advisor analyzes the technical short-term vigor of each stock. While reviewing the charts, the advisor plugs in one of two digits: 1 or

Table D.3 Entry

ENTRY
D

	Total Ticket	TRANSACTION per Share	Flat Ticket
	$1,877	$0.05	$25.00
	0.188%		

STOCKS	Shares	$	Price	Ticker	Tckt
Schlumberger	357.14	15,000	$42.00	SLB	$42.86
Exxon	227.27	15,000	$66.00	XON	$36.36
Union Carbide	192.31	15,000	$78.00	UK	$34.62
Phelps Dodge	112.36	10,000	$89.00	PD	$30.62
General Electric	148.51	15,000	$101.00	GE	$32.43
ADP	333.33	15,000	$45.00	AUD	$41.67
General Motors	227.27	15,000	$66.00	GM	$36.36
Wal-Mart	357.14	17,500	$49.00	WMT	$42.86
Anheuser-Busch	164.47	12,500	$76.00	BUD	$33.22
Procter & Gamble	272.73	15,000	$55.00	PG	$38.64
Mallinckrodt	517.24	15,000	$29.00	MKG	$50.86
Pfizer	333.33	18,333	$55.00	PFE	$41.67
J.P. Morgan	97.09	10,000	$103.00	JPM	$29.85
AIG	340.91	15,000	$44.00	AIG	$42.05
Microsoft	157.89	15,000	$95.00	MSFT	$32.89
Cisco	131.58	20,000	$152.00	CSCO	$31.58
Intel	204.08	20,000	$98.00	INTL	$35.20
Global Crossing	363.64	20,000	$55.00	GBLX	$43.18
Sprint PCS	101.01	20,000	$198.00	PCS	$30.05
Ameren UE	217.39	10,000	$46.00	AEE	$35.87
Enron	189.87	15,000	$79.00	ENE	$34.49
Mid-Cap SPDRs	365.85	30,000	$82.00	MDY	$43.29
AOL	327.99	32,143	$98.00	AOL	$41.40
Unisys	554.19	32,143	$58.00	UIS	$52.71
PeopleSoft	892.86	32,143	$36.00	PSFT	$69.64
Oracle	306.12	32,143	$105.00	ORCL	$40.31
QUALCOMM	80.76	32,143	$398.00	QCOM	$29.04
Applied Materials	361.16	32,143	$89.00	AMAT	$43.06
Comcast	297.62	32,143	$108.00	CMCSK	$39.88
					$1,677

SUPPLEMENTALS	Shares	$	Price	Ticker	Tckt
Ashland Oil		10,000		ASH	
International Paper	151.52	10,000	$66.00	IP	$32.58
Southwest Airlines	285.71	10,000	$35.00	LUV	$39.29
Times Mirror	187.50	15,000	$80.00	TMC	$34.38
Sysco	333.33	15,000	$45.00	SYY	$41.67
Amgen	72.46	5,000	$69.00	AMGN	$28.62
Charles Schwab	178.57	15,000	$84.00	SCH	$33.93
Dell	132.01	13,333	$101.00	DELL	$31.60
MCI WorldCom	80.81	13,333	$165.00	WCOM	$29.04
Peoples Energy		15,000		PGL	

DYNAMICS	Shares	$	Price	Ticker	Tckt
Uniphase	153.85	10,000	$65.00	JDSU	$32.69
Nextlink	454.55	10,000	$22.00	NXLK	$47.73
Broadcom	72.99	10,000	$137.00	BRCM	$28.65
Level 3	285.71	10,000	$35.00	LVLT	$39.29
Cree Research	454.55	10,000	$22.00	CREE	$47.73
Texas Instruments	131.58	10,000	$76.00	TXN	$31.58
C-Cube	333.33	10,000	$30.00	CUBE	$41.67

MUTUAL FUNDS	Shares	$	Price	Ticker	CUSIP	Ratio	Cost	Ticket
							$1,454	$50
Lord Abbott Dev Grth	2,446.98	30,000	$12.26	LAGWX	544006109	0.98%	$294	$25
SSgA Emerging Mkts	4,553.73	50,000	$10.98	SSEMX	784924789	1.25%	$625	$25
Hotchkis & Wiley Intl	2,253.27	50,000	$22.19	HWINX	441346400	0.89%	$445	$25
NE Investors	0.00		$11.12	NTHEX	664210101	0.61%	$0	$0

TABLE D.4 Valuations

	Current	VALUATION	Weights > 4 Fair Value Price	4 % Diff	2 STAR Stock	2 Sector	1 Fndmntl Score	Weights > Ticker	3 Stocstcs	1.5 MACD	0.5 RS	0.5 CCI	Tech Score
1		ADP						AUD		0			0.0
2		AIG						AIG		0			0.0
3		Ameren UE						AEE		0			0.0
4		Amgen						AMGN		0			0.0
5	77.00	**Anheuser-Busch**	81.50	6%	4	3.0	13.20	**BUD**	1	1	6	1	-1	6.0
6		AOL						AOL		0			0.0
7		Applied Materials						AMAT		0			0.0
8	39.25	**Ashland Oil**	35.50	11%	1	2.0	-0.23	**ASH**	-1	1	-2	1	1	-0.5
9		Broadcom						BRCM		0			0.0
10		C-Cube						CUBE		0			0.0
11		Charles Schwab						SCH		0			0.0
12		Cisco						CSCO		0			0.0
13		Comcast						CMCSK		0			0.0
14		Cree Research						CREE		0			0.0
15		Dell						DELL		0			0.0
16		Enron						ENE		0			0.0
17		Exxon						XON		0			0.0
18		General Electric						GE		0			0.0
19		General Motors						GM		0			0.0
20		Global Crossing						GBLX		0			0.0
21		Intel						INTL		0			0.0
22		International Paper						IP		0			0.0
23		J.P. Morgan						JPM		0			0.0
24		Level 3						LVLT		0			0.0
25		Mallinckrodt						MKG		0			0.0
26		MCI WorldCom						WCOM		0			0.0
27		Microsoft						MSFT		0			0.0
28		Mid-Cap SPDRs						MDY		0			0.0
29		Nextlink						NXLK		0			0.0
30		Oracle						ORCL		0			0.0
32		PeopleSoft						PSFT		0			0.0
33		Pfizer						PFE		0			0.0
34		Phelps Dodge						PD		0			0.0
35		Procter & Gamble						PG		0			0.0
36	360.00	**QUALCOMM**	195.00	85%	5	5.0	-18.85	**QCOM**	-1	-1	-5	-1	-1	-5.5
37		Schlumberger						SLB		0			0.0
38		Southwest Airlines						LUV		0			0.0
39		Sprint PCS						PCS		0			0.0
40		Sysco						SYY		0			0.0
41		Texas Instruments						TXN		0			0.0
42		Times Mirror						TMC		0			0
43		Union Carbide						UK		0			0
44		Uniphase						JDSU		0			0
45		Unisys						UIS		0			0
46		Wal-Mart						WMT		0			0

−1, corresponding to, "Yes, buy the stock" (1) or "No, wait" (−1). There can be no "Maybe."

In our sample, note that Anheuser-Busch is undervalued by 6% (current price of $77 is less than S & P's Fair Value rating of $81.50) with a STAR rating of four (out of five) and a total fundamental score of 13.21, a result of weighted assignments to each of the three scored categories: Fair Value difference (4 weight), STAR rating of the stock (2 weight), and STAR rating of the sector in which the stock resides (1 weight). The technical elements of BUD also look favorable. The stochastics (3 weight), the MACD (1.5 weight), and the relative strength index (0.5 weight) are all flashing +1s, or "Yes, buy." The commodity channel index (0.5 weight) is the only naysayer here, with a –1. With an overall score of +6, we would enter this position immediately.

On the other hand, QUALCOMM is 85% overvalued, although S & P assigns a five-star rating to both the company and the sector, resulting in a –18.85 rating. As well, QCOM's technicals appear almost as dangerous, showing negatives across the four readings, ending in a –5.5 total technical score. We'd wait on this one.

Ashland Oil falls squarely between BUD and QCOM. Its total fundamental and technical scores are almost neutral at –0.23 and –0.5, respectively. We would enter this one also.

Although somewhat busy, this site can be also be demonstrated to the client.

Profile

Table D.5 is a printout for the client. It shows the sectors and subsectors of each stock, as well as percentage and dollar holdings and snapshots of distribution, positions, annual income, and performance.

Tactical

Table D.6 is where we track our tactical moves. When we enter a position, we input the date, shares, and cost. Upon selling, we do the same, in addition to entering the round-trip ticket charge. This site calculates the net and gross returns on each equity. It tells us how many days we were in and what the annualized return would be.

It also delivers the total performance of the tactical strategy and brings in all totals from the Options location (which we'll review next) and combines them to show a combined tactical performance. As well, it shows the total return after taxes.

It also presents the profit weight of stocks and the profit weight of options in our tactical management. In this sample, 83% of our tactical profit was generated by stocks and 17% by options.

And finally, it shows us the absolute number of positions on which we lost money. In this example, we lost in Solutia and

TABLE D.5 Profile

S & P SECTORS		STOCKS	%	$
Energy	Equipment & Service	Schlumberger	1.5%	$15,000
	Oil & Gas/Refining	Ashland Oil	1.0%	$10,000
	Oil & Gas/Integrated	Exxon	1.5%	$15,000
Materials	Chemicals	Union Carbide	1.5%	$15,000
	Paper & Forest	International Paper	1.0%	$10,000
	Metals & Mining	Phelps Dodge	1.0%	$10,000
Industrials	Capital Goods	General Electric	1.5%	$15,000
	Transportation	Southwest Airlines	1.0%	$10,000
	Commercial Services	ADP	1.5%	$15,000
Consumer Disc	Autos & Components	General Motors	1.5%	$15,000
	Media	Times Mirror	1.5%	$15,000
	Retailing	Wal-Mart	1.8%	$17,500
Consumer Stpls	Beverages (Alcohol)	Anheuser-Busch	1.3%	$12,500
	Food	Sysco	1.5%	$15,000
	Household Products	Procter & Gamble	1.5%	$15,000
Health Care	Equipment & Service	Mallinckrodt	1.5%	$15,000
	BioTechnology	Amgen	0.5%	$5,000
	Pharmaceuticals	Pfizer	1.8%	$18,333
Financials	Banks	J.P. Morgan	1.0%	$10,000
	Investments	Charles Schwab	1.5%	$15,000
	Diversified	AIG	1.5%	$15,000
Information Tech	Software/System	Microsoft	1.5%	$15,000
	Hardware	Dell	1.3%	$13,333
	Networking	Cisco	2.0%	$20,000
	Semiconductors	Intel	2.0%	$20,000
Telecom Service	Alternative Carriers	MCI WorldCom	1.3%	$13,333
	Integrated	Global Crossing	2.0%	$20,000
	Wireless	Sprint PCS	2.0%	$20,000
Utilities	Electricity	Peoples Energy	1.5%	$15,000
	Gas	Ameren UE	1.0%	$10,000
	Multi-	Enron	1.5%	$15,000
Mid-Cap	S & P Dpstry Rcpts	Mid-Cap SPDRs	3.0%	$30,000
Information Tech	Internet Software	AOL	3.2%	$32,143
Information Tech	Consulting & Service	Unisys	3.2%	$32,143
Information Tech	Software/Application	PeopleSoft	3.2%	$32,143
Information Tech	Software/System	Oracle	3.2%	$32,143
Information Tech	Telecom Equipment	QUALCOMM	3.2%	$32,143
Information Tech	Semicndctrs-Equip	Applied Materials	3.2%	$32,143
Consumer Disc	Broadcast & TV	Comcast	3.2%	$32,143
Information Tech	Telecom Equipment	Uniphase	1.0%	$10,000
Information Tech	Internet Soft & Serv	Nextlink	1.0%	$10,000
Information Tech	Network Equip	Broadcom	1.0%	$10,000
Information Tech	Internet Soft & Serv	Level 3	1.0%	$10,000
Information Tech	Semicndctrs-Equip	Cree Research	1.0%	$10,000
Information Tech	Semiconductors	Texas Instruments	1.0%	$10,000
Information Tech	Electronic Equip	C-Cube	1.0%	$10,000

ASSET CLASSES	MUTUAL FUNDS	%	$
Small-Cap Growth	Lord Abbott Dev Grth	3.0%	$30,000
Emerging Markets	SSgA Emerging Mkts	5.0%	$50,000
International	Hotchkis & Wiley Int'l	5.0%	$50,000

BONDS	%	$
NE Investors		
Government	5.0%	$50,000
Corporate (High Grd)	2.5%	$25,000
MONEY MARKET	2.5%	$25,000

Distribution	
Core	35.3%
Volatile	22.5%
Disruptive	7.0%
Supplmntls	12.2%
Tactical	0.0%
Bonds & MM	10.0%
Mutual Funds	13.0%
TOTAL	100%
	$1,000,000

Positions	
Strategic	39
Tactical	0
Bonds & MM	23
Mutual Funds	3
TOTAL	65

Annual Income	
Stocks	$3,964
Bonds	$0
MM	$1,453
Mutual Funds	$1,255
TOTAL	$6,672
Yield	0.67%

Annual Performance	
1997	31.6%
1998	39.9%
YTD 1999	20.4%
Tax Savings	$ 5,268.20

Performance Cannot be Guaranteed

Table D.6 Tactical

TACTICAL

TODAY
15-Dec

NetTax
25.0%
22,276

		ENTRY					EXIT										
		Date	Shrs	Paid	Total	Total	Date	Sold	$$	Gross	%		Ticket	Net	%	Days	Annlzd
S	America West	24-Feb-99	100	18.50	1,850	1,850	22-Apr-99	20.78	2,078	228	12.3%		30	198	10.7%	57	68.6%
T	**Solutia**	**25-Feb-98**	**100**	**28.56**	**2,856**	**2,856**	**22-Apr-99**	**23.46**	**2,346**	**-510**	**-17.9%**		**30**	**-540**	**-18.9%**	**421**	**-16.4%**
O	Fremont General	1-Mar-99	100	16.96	1,696								30				
C	Zebra Technologies	2-Mar-99	100	26.68	2,668	2,668	22-Apr-99	30.46	3,046	378	14.2%		30	348	13.0%	51	93.4%
K	Callaway Nursery	10-May-99	750	1.38	1,031	1,031	9-Jun-99	1.97	1,477	445	43.2%		30	415	40.3%	30	490.2%
S	Frontier/GBLX	28-Jun-99	205	29.27	6,000	6,000	13-Dec-99	51.00	10,455	4,455	74.3%		30	4,425	73.8%	168	160.2%
	Daimler-Chrysler	8-Jul-99	100	90.50	9,050		9-Jun-99						30				
	Data Race	22-Jul-99	500	3.31	1,656		9-Jun-99						30				
	Global Crossing	22-Jul-99	200	41.88	8,375	8,375	13-Dec-99	51.00	10,200	1,825	21.8%		30	1,795	21.4%	144	54.3%
	Global Crossing	4-Aug-99	200	33.13	6,625	6,625	13-Dec-99	51.00	10,200	3,575	54.0%		30	3,545	53.5%	131	149.1%
	Frontier/GBLX	4-Aug-99	205	22.26	4,563	4,563	13-Dec-99	51.00	10,455	5,893	129.2%		30	5,863	128.5%	131	358.0%
	Red Hat	11-Aug-99	50	46.56	2,328	2,328	16-Aug-99	83.06	4,153	1,825	78.4%		30	1,795	77.1%	5	5628.7%
	Red Hat	11-Aug-99	50	46.56	2,328	2,328	17-Aug-99	65.00	3,250	922	39.6%		30	892	38.3%	6	2330.8%
	JDS Uniphase	29-Oct-99	25	160.50	4,013	4,013	15-Nov-99	197.50	4,938	925	23.1%		30	895	22.3%	17	479.0%
	NAVI	29-Oct-99	100	48.75	4,875	4,875	15-Nov-99	82.00	8,200	3,325	68.2%		30	3,295	67.6%	17	1451.2%
	Harmonic	2-Nov-99	100	56.41	5,641	5,641	15-Nov-99	68.44	6,844	1,203	21.3%		30	1,173	20.8%	13	584.1%
	MetroMedia	2-Nov-99	100	34.88	3,488	3,488	15-Nov-99	40.29	4,029	542	15.5%		30	512	14.7%	13	411.9%
	Stock Profit Wght >	**83%**			69,042	56,640		STOCKS	81,670	25,031	44.2%	3		24,612	43.5%	295	53.8%
	Options Profit Wght >	**17%**			15,063	10,525		OPTIONS	16,483	5,958	56.6%	4		5,089	48.4%	272	65.0%
	YTD Positions >	14			**84,104**	**67,165**		**TOTAL**	**98,153**	**30,988**	**46.3%**	**7**		**29,701**	**44.3%**		**55.7%**
	Loss Positions >	1															
	% of Loss Positions >	7%															

gained in the other 14 we liquidated, or we lost in 7% of the positions we've opened and closed.

Options

Much like the Tactical location, the Options site (Table D.7) monitors and records our performance with puts and calls. When the financial advisor takes a derivative position, the expiration month, strike price, symbol (for checking price quickly), date, number of contracts, and price are entered. Upon exiting, the date and total proceeds are recorded.

This sheet separates our put performance and call performance and then combines them for an overall derivative performance. As with the Tactical site, it also shows us the number of positions in which we took losses relative to those in which we held gains; in this case, 33% were loss positions.

Retirement Distribution

This site allows us to determine the parameters of distributing our managed assets upon our client's retirement, even if it is the day the client commences working with us. Data needed: retirement age, withdrawal age, whether the funds are qualified or not, withdrawal amount, income tax rate, withdrawal increase, performance adjuster, and diminished return adjuster.

We do not need to input the capital gains tax rate, because when we choose the income tax rate, the capital gains rate automatically changes: At a 28% income tax rate capital gain is 20%, and at a 14% income tax rate it switches to 10%.

The performance adjuster is a delicate and subjective tool. It allows us to dampen the return on our portfolios, with the understanding that any excessive performance in any previous three years might not occur in the future. We can assign a percentage of degradation to the average portfolio return. In this case we have presumed that the dynamic portfolio's historical three-year average return of 30.6% will be 50% less in future years, or 15.3%. All calculations of growth are now based on 15.3%. Better to be conservative and safe than to promise a rose garden and deliver weeds. This adjuster is used primarily on the aggressive,

TABLE D.7 Options

Summary boxes: **15-Dec** | % of Loss Positions > **33%** | **6** < Closed Loss Positions | **7,400** | **65.0%**

CALLS

	Exp	SP	Symbol	ENTRY Date	##	Cost	Cost	EXIT Date	Total	Gross	%	Tkt	Net	%	Held	Annlzd
TOTALS >				15,063		10,525			16,483	5,958	56.6%	0	5,089	48.4%	272	65.0%
Qwest	Oct	40	QWA JH	14-Jun	1	425	425	19-Oct	0	-425	-100.0%	30	-455	-107.0%	127	-308%
Global Crossing	Oct	60		18-Jun	1	338	338	19-Oct	579	242	71.6%	30	212	62.7%	123	186%
Xerox	Oct	50		27-Jul	1	413	413	15-Sep	181	-231	-56.1%	60	-291	-70.6%	50	-515%
Unum (Provident)	Nov	40		4-Aug	2	350	350	25-Oct	1,800	1,450	414.3%	30	1,420	405.7%	40	3702%
Wght >			**17%**			1,525	1,525		2,560	1,035	67.9%	0	886	58.1%	185	114.8%

(Calls net box: **1,751**)

PUTS

	Exp	SP	Symbol	ENTRY Date	##	Cost	Cost	EXIT Date	Total	Gross	%	Tkt	Net	%	Held	Annlzd
Wal-Mart	Jan	45		19-Mar	1	838	838	26-May	1,270	433	51.7%	60	373	44.5%	68	239%
Best Buy	Jan	45	BBY-MI	22-Mar	1	800						60				
Telefonos de Mexico	Jan	60	TMX-ML	22-Mar	1	713						60				
Merck	Sep	70		22-Mar	1	788	788	26-Apr	1,336	548	69.6%	60	489	62.0%	35	647%
Minnesota Mining	Jul	70		20-Apr	5	594	594	19-Jul	987	393	66.2%	30	363	61.2%	90	248%
Phelps Dodge	Sep	55		28-Apr	3	694	694	25-May	1,405	711	102.5%	60	651	93.9%	33	1038%
Alcoa	Oct	55		28-Apr	1	450	450	15-Sep	985	535	118.9%	60	475	105.6%	170	227%
Mueller Industries	Oct	35		13-Jul	1	269	269	16-Aug	413	144	53.5%	60	84	31.2%	34	335%
Zebra Technologies	Nov	35		13-Jul	1	244	244	19-Nov	0	-244	-100.0%	60	-304	-124.6%	129	-352%
Lucent Technology	Oct	70		14-Jul	1	438	438	26-Jul	259	-179	-40.8%	60	-238	-54.5%	12	-1657%
Bristol-Myers	Dec	75		14-Jul	1	525	525	23-Jul	725	200	38.1%	60	140	26.7%	9	1082%
Intel	Oct	65		14-Jul	1	450	450	19-Oct	0	-450	-100.0%	30	-480	-106.7%	97	-401%
Sony	Oct	115		14-Jul	1	488	488	19-Oct	205	-283	-57.9%	30	-312	-64.1%	97	-241%
Imgran Micro	Sep	35		27-Jul	1	525	525	30-Jul	688	163	31.0%	60	103	19.5%	3	2378%
HI / FN	Sep	95		3-Aug	1	1,050	1,050	13-Sep	3,500	2,450	233.3%	30	2,420	230.5%	41	2052%
Pier 1 Imports	Sep	10		5-Aug	4	1,650	1,650	13-Sep	2,150	500	30.3%	60	440	26.7%	39	250%
Dow (2000 @ 10,809)	Dec	110	LDK XF	3-Nov	2	2,275										
QQQ	Jan	145	QUE MO	17-Nov	1	750										
YTD Closed Positions > **18**			**Wght > 83%**			13,538	9,000		13,922	4,922	54.7%	4	4,204	46.7%	272	62.8%

(Puts net box: **5,649**)

222

dynamic, and moderate portfolios. The other two, being less aggressive, display less standard deviation and can be expected to perform more steadily over time.

The program handles the distribution differently for qualified money and nonqualified money—for obvious reasons. Qualified distributions are taxed as income. Some portion of a nonqualified distribution is taxed as capital gain, with the remaining portion taxed as income, depending on tax basis and income needs.

In the example in Table D.8, in order to demonstrate the effects of our variables on qualified and nonqualified distribution patterns, "Both" was input in the "Qualified" cell in our $1 million dynamic portfolio. The client retires at age 58 and wants $200,000 per year in today's dollars, starting at the age of 65. By then, at 2.50% inflation, the figure is at $237,737.

A Few Notes

The program we build should include required minimum distributions (RMDs) from qualified portfolios starting when our client reaches age 70½. The after-tax proceeds are then reinvested in a nonqualified portfolio under our continued management.

Capital gain comes out of our nonqualified portfolio only to supplement the dividend income generated, so the two equal the withdrawal amount needed plus the inflation factor we choose.

During our fictitious client's first seven years of retirement, it's assumed he has income sources elsewhere and doesn't need to tap our portfolio until age 65, at which time we've grown the balance to $3,074,155. At this point our client needs to start tapping our future value funds at $237,737 per year. It might be prudent to reduce the risk in the portfolio by moving gradually into our moderate portfolio. In the qualified account, this is simple. On the nonqualified account, tax consequences must be examined. Take a look at Table D.9.

We change the amount under management to our new figure and choose the moderate portfolio, which administers a higher yield. We've also changed the return adjuster from 50% to 33%. We change the retirement age to match the withdrawal age and the numbers play out.

TABLE D.8 Retirement Distribution

Parameters		Portfolio
Retirement Age	58	$1,000,000 Portfolio Value
Withdrawal Age	65	1.31% Portfolio Yield
Qualified?	Both	30.6% Historic Growth Rate
Pretax Income Needed PV	$200,000	15.3% Adjusted Growth Rate
Withdrawal Increase	2.5%	
Growth Rate Adjuster	50.0%	

DYNAMIC

The following columns are grouped as: NONQUALIFIED (Net, Growth, Balance; Capital Gains $$ / Tax; Income $$ / Tax; Rnvstd) and QUALIFIED (Net, Growth, Balance; Income Withdrwl / Taxes; RMDs; Reinvested Balance; RMD Taxes; Rnvstd Grwth; Altrnt Wthdrwl), plus Combined Balance.

Age	NQ Net	NQ Growth	NQ Balance	CapGains $$	CapGains Tax	Income $$	Income Tax	Rnvstd	Q Net	Q Growth	Q Balance	Income Withdrwl	Income Taxes	RMDs	Reinvested Balance	RMD Taxes	Rnvstd Grwth	Altrnt Wthdrwl	Combined Balance
58	1,000,000	153,092	1,153,092		0	15,122	2,722	15,122	1,000,000	153,092	1,153,092								1,153,092
59	1,150,370	176,112	1,326,482		0	17,396	3,131	17,396	1,153,092	176,529	1,329,620								1,329,620
60	1,323,350	202,594	1,525,944		0	20,012	3,602	20,012	1,329,620	203,554	1,533,174								1,533,174
61	1,522,342	233,058	1,755,400		0	23,021	4,144	23,021	1,533,174	234,716	1,767,890								1,767,890
62	1,751,256	268,103	2,019,359		0	26,483	4,767	26,483	1,767,890	270,649	2,038,540								2,038,540
63	2,014,592	308,417	2,323,009		0	30,465	5,484	30,465	2,038,540	312,083	2,350,623								2,350,623
64	2,317,525	354,794	2,672,319		0	35,047	6,308	35,047	2,350,623	359,861	2,710,484								2,710,484
65	2,666,011	408,144	3,074,155	197,421	39,484	40,317	7,257	0	2,710,484	414,953	3,125,436	237,737	66,566						3,125,436
66	2,789,676	427,076	3,216,752	201,494	40,299	42,187	11,812	0	2,821,133	431,892	3,253,025	243,681	68,231						3,253,025
67	2,920,961	447,175	3,368,136	205,601	41,120	44,172	12,368	0	2,941,114	450,260	3,391,374	249,773	69,936						3,391,374
68	3,064,875	469,207	3,534,082	209,669	41,934	46,348	12,978	0	3,071,665	470,246	3,541,911	256,017	71,685						3,541,911
69	3,223,153	493,438	3,716,591	213,675	42,735	48,742	13,648	0	3,214,209	492,069	3,706,278	262,417	73,477						3,706,278
70	3,397,791	520,174	3,917,965	217,595	43,519	51,383	14,387	0	3,370,384	515,978	3,886,362	268,978	75,314	255,271					3,886,362
71	3,591,081	549,765	4,140,845	221,396	44,279	54,306	15,206	0	3,542,070	542,261	4,084,331	275,702	77,197	261,983	255,271	71,476	39,080		4,339,602
72	3,805,658	582,615	4,388,273	225,044	45,009	57,551	16,114	0	3,476,162	532,171	4,008,333	282,595	79,127	267,314	484,857	73,355	74,228		4,493,191
73	4,044,555	619,188	4,663,743	228,496	45,699	61,163	17,126	0	3,384,629	518,159	3,902,788	289,660	81,105	270,828	753,044	74,848	115,285		4,655,832
74	4,311,258	660,018	4,971,276	231,705	46,341	65,197	18,255	0	3,264,709	499,800	3,764,509	296,901	83,132	271,173	1,064,309	75,832	162,937		4,828,818
75	4,609,778	705,719	5,315,497	234,613	46,923	69,711	19,519	0	3,113,648	476,674	3,590,321	304,324	85,211	270,173	1,423,408	76,158	217,912		5,013,729
76	4,944,732	756,997	5,701,729	237,155	47,431	74,776	20,937	0	2,928,793	448,374	3,377,167	311,932	87,341	262,374	1,835,335	75,649	280,974		5,212,501
77	5,321,429	814,666	6,136,095	239,257	47,851	80,473	22,532	0	2,707,721	414,529	3,122,250	319,730	89,524	252,303	2,303,035	73,465	352,575		5,425,285
78	5,745,981	879,662	6,625,643	240,830	48,166	86,893	24,330	0	2,450,622	375,170	2,825,792	327,723	91,763	234,317	2,834,448	70,645	433,930		5,660,240
79	6,225,424	953,061	7,178,484	241,773	48,355	94,143	26,360	0	2,154,003	329,760	2,483,763	335,916	94,057	209,802	3,432,051	65,609	525,418		5,915,814
80	6,767,853	1,036,102	7,803,955	241,968	48,394	102,346	28,657	0	1,819,473	278,546	2,098,019	344,314	96,408	175,694	4,101,662	58,745	627,930		6,199,681
81	7,382,590	1,130,213	8,512,804	241,280	48,256	111,643	31,260	0	1,447,495	221,599	1,669,094	352,922	98,818	134,958	4,846,542	49,194	741,965		6,515,636
82	8,080,366	1,237,037	9,317,402	239,551	47,910	122,195	34,214	0	1,041,660	159,469	1,201,129	361,745	101,289	82,794	5,674,271	37,788	868,684		6,875,400
83	8,873,532	1,358,464	10,231,996	236,600	47,320	134,189	37,573	0	603,137	92,335	695,472	370,789	103,821	20,153	6,587,961	23,182	1,008,562		7,283,433
84	9,776,315	1,496,672	11,272,987	232,217	46,443	147,841	41,396	0	138,068	21,137	159,205	380,059	106,416		7,593,493	5,643	1,162,501		7,752,698
85	10,805,089	1,654,169	12,459,258	226,161	45,232	163,399	45,752	0							8,750,351		1,339,606	389,560	8,750,351
86	11,978,715	1,833,841	13,812,556	218,152	43,630	181,147	50,721	0							9,700,397		1,485,050	399,299	9,700,397
87	13,318,905	2,039,013	15,357,919	207,867	41,573	201,414	56,396	0							10,786,148		1,651,269	409,281	10,786,148
88	14,850,668	2,273,513	17,124,181	194,936	38,987	224,578	62,882	0							12,028,136		1,841,407	419,514	12,028,136
89	16,602,799	2,541,750	19,144,549	178,927	35,785	251,074	70,301	0							13,450,029		2,059,087	430,001	13,450,029
90	18,608,461	2,848,800	21,457,262	159,347	31,869	281,405	78,793	0							15,079,115		2,308,487	440,751	15,079,115
91	20,905,848	3,200,511	24,106,359	135,623	27,125	316,147	88,521	0							16,946,851		2,594,422	451,770	16,946,851
92	23,538,943	3,603,616	27,142,559	107,099	21,420	355,966	99,670	0							19,089,503		2,922,444	463,064	19,089,503
93	26,558,404	4,065,870	30,624,275	73,014	14,603	401,627	112,456	0							21,548,882		3,298,954	474,641	21,548,882

TABLE D.9 Retirement Distribution

Retirement Age	65		Portfolio Value	$3,074,155
Withdrawal Age	65		Portfolio Yield	2.64%
Qualified?	Both		Historic Growth Rate	18.7%
Pretax Income Needed PV	$200,000		Adjusted Growth Rate	12.5%
Withdrawal Increase	2.5%			
Growth Rate Adjuster	33.0%			

MODERATE

NONQUALIFIED

Age	Net	Growth	Balance	Capital Gains $$	Capital Gains Tax	Income $$	Income Tax	Rnvstd
65	3,074,155	385,230	3,459,385	108,693	21,739	91,307	25,566	0
66	3,212,080	402,513	3,614,593	109,596	21,919	95,404	26,713	0
67	3,360,961	421,170	3,782,131	110,299	22,060	99,826	27,951	0
68	3,521,995	441,349	3,963,344	110,770	22,154	104,608	29,290	0
69	3,696,522	463,220	4,159,741	110,970	22,194	109,792	30,742	0
70	3,886,043	486,969	4,373,012	110,860	22,172	115,421	32,318	0
71	4,092,240	512,808	4,605,049	110,393	22,079	121,546	34,033	0
72	4,316,999	540,973	4,857,972	109,516	21,903	128,221	35,902	0
73	4,562,429	571,729	5,134,158	108,170	21,634	135,511	37,943	0
74	4,830,901	605,371	5,436,272	106,288	21,258	143,485	40,176	0
75	5,125,066	642,234	5,767,300	103,795	20,759	152,222	42,622	0
76	5,447,902	682,689	6,130,591	100,607	20,121	161,811	45,307	0
77	5,802,746	727,156	6,529,901	96,628	19,326	172,350	48,258	0
78	6,193,340	776,102	6,969,442	91,751	18,350	183,951	51,506	0
79	6,623,883	830,054	7,453,937	85,856	17,171	196,739	55,087	0
80	7,099,084	889,603	7,988,687	78,806	15,761	210,853	59,039	0
81	7,624,227	955,410	8,579,637	70,450	14,090	226,451	63,406	0
82	8,205,240	1,028,218	9,233,457	60,616	12,123	243,708	68,238	0
83	8,848,772	1,108,860	9,957,633	49,110	9,822	262,822	73,590	0
84	9,562,289	1,198,273	10,760,562	35,716	7,143	284,014	79,524	0
85	10,354,164	1,297,505	11,651,669	20,189	4,038	307,534	86,110	0
86	11,233,798	1,407,733	12,641,532	2,256	451	333,661	93,425	0
87	12,211,079	1,530,282	13,742,021			362,707	101,558	18,393
88	13,296,149	1,666,171	14,962,320			394,915	110,576	41,993
89	14,498,822	1,816,881	16,315,703			430,637	120,578	68,891
90	15,833,379	1,984,118	17,817,497			470,275	131,677	99,486
91	17,315,031	2,169,787	19,484,818			514,282	143,999	134,224
92	18,960,761	2,376,017	21,336,778			563,163	157,686	173,603
93	20,789,532	2,605,185	23,394,717			617,480	172,894	218,181
94	22,822,524	2,859,944	25,682,467			677,863	189,802	268,581
95	25,083,384	3,143,257	28,226,642			745,014	208,604	325,500
96	27,598,524	3,458,435	31,056,960			819,717	229,521	389,716
97	30,397,438	3,809,174	34,206,612			902,849	252,798	462,098
98	33,513,062	4,199,600	37,712,663			995,388	278,709	543,618
99	36,982,184	4,634,324	41,616,508			1,098,426	307,559	635,361
100	40,845,884	5,118,493	45,964,377			1,213,183	339,691	738,542

QUALIFIED

Age	Net	Growth	Balance	Income Wthdrwl	Income Taxes	RMDs	Reinvested Balance	RMD Taxes	Rnvstd Grwth	Altrnt Wthdrwl	Combined Balance
65	3,074,155	385,230	3,459,385	200,000	56,000	0	0	0	0		3,459,385
66	3,203,385	401,424	3,604,808	205,000	57,400	0	0	0	0		3,604,808
67	3,342,408	418,845	3,761,253	210,125	58,835	0	0	0	0		3,761,253
68	3,492,293	437,627	3,929,920	215,378	60,306	0	0	0	0		3,929,920
69	3,654,236	457,921	4,112,157	220,763	61,814	0	0	0	0		4,112,157
70	3,829,581	479,894	4,309,475	226,282	63,359	0	0	0	0		4,309,475
71	4,019,835	503,735	4,523,569	231,939	64,943	282,723	282,723	79,162	35,429		4,806,292
72	3,943,965	494,227	4,438,192	237,737	66,566	290,078	529,067	81,222	66,299		4,967,259
73	3,843,811	481,677	4,325,488	243,681	68,231	296,266	810,410	82,955	101,554		5,135,898
74	3,717,310	465,825	4,183,135	249,773	69,936	300,945	1,129,955	84,265	141,597		5,313,090
75	3,562,481	446,423	4,008,904	256,017	71,685	303,705	1,490,993	85,037	186,840		5,499,897
76	3,377,497	423,242	3,800,740	262,417	73,477	304,059	1,896,854	85,137	237,699		5,697,594
77	3,160,786	396,085	3,556,872	268,978	75,314	298,897	2,348,314	83,691	294,273		5,905,186
78	2,913,683	365,120	3,278,804	275,702	77,197	292,750	2,851,646	81,970	357,346		6,130,450
79	2,633,155	329,967	2,963,121	282,595	79,127	279,540	3,406,562	78,271	426,884		6,369,683
80	2,321,860	290,958	2,612,818	289,660	81,105	261,282	4,016,457	73,159	503,312		6,629,275
81	1,980,772	248,215	2,228,987	296,901	83,132	234,630	4,681,240	65,696	586,617		6,910,227
82	1,614,323	202,295	1,816,618	304,324	85,211	204,114	5,406,274	57,152	677,473		7,222,893
83	1,222,969	153,235	1,376,223	311,932	87,341	153,836	6,190,431	45,874	775,737		7,566,654
84	813,114	101,893	915,007	319,730	89,524	115,824	7,036,118	32,431	881,712		7,951,126
85	389,929	48,863	438,792	327,723	91,763	59,296	7,944,696	16,603	995,568		8,383,488
86				335,916		0	8,923,662	0	1,118,245	335,916	8,923,662
87				344,314		0	9,705,990	0	1,216,280	344,314	9,705,990
88				352,922		0	10,577,956	0	1,325,548	352,922	10,577,956
89				361,745		0	11,550,583	0	1,447,430	361,745	11,550,583
90				370,789		0	12,636,268	0	1,583,480	370,789	12,636,268
91				380,059		0	13,848,959	0	1,735,445	380,059	13,848,959
92				389,560		0	15,204,346	0	1,905,292	389,560	15,204,346
93				399,299		0	16,720,078	0	2,095,232	399,299	16,720,078
94				409,281		0	18,416,011	0	2,307,753	409,281	18,416,011
95				419,514		0	20,314,483	0	2,545,655	419,514	20,314,483
96				430,001		0	22,440,625	0	2,812,087	430,001	22,440,625
97				440,751		0	24,822,711	0	3,110,592	440,751	24,822,711
98				451,770		0	27,492,551	0	3,445,156	451,770	27,492,551
99				463,064		0	30,485,937	0	3,820,264	463,064	30,485,937
100				474,641		0	33,843,136	0	4,240,962	474,641	33,843,136

Capital Gains Analysis

This site calculates the average capital gains tax a client saves by not using a group of 10 mutual funds. Mutual funds throw off realized capital gains nearly every year. These taxes are unexpected by the client. They appear as a 1099 form in the mail every January. Take a look at Table D.10.

We have saved the previous moderate portfolio into which we transitioned our client during the discussion about retirement distribution. Distributions were made into mutual fund categories identical to the distribution of our moderate portfolio. A number of funds were researched to determine the average annual realized gains issued within each category. These gains were then applied to the allocation to determine each category's likely average realized gains.

They were summed and then multiplied by 20%, the capital gains rate. In this case our client saves $12,824 per year by not being in a mutual fund group similar to our moderate portfolio. No more agonizing surprises at the end of the year. This figure is transferred to the Positions site in the summary box so the client can immediately appreciate it.

A-Share Fees

Again, using the last client whose portfolio we changed from dynamic to moderate, we see that, according to the schedule we've employed, the first $1 million costs the client 1%, or

TABLE D.10 Capital Gains Analysis

MODERATE					
Category	Number of Funds Analyzed	Distribution	Average Rlzd Gains	Realized Gains	
Large Cap	421	$1,680,538	2.74%	$46,047	
Aggressive Grth	33	$107,595	2.74%	$2,948	
Mid Cap	204	$92,225	5.21%	$4,805	
Small Cap	158	$92,225	5.70%	$5,257	
Emerging Mkts	54	$40,989	4.85%	$1,988	
International	117	$153,708	2.00%	$3,074	
High Yield Bonds	0	$76,854		$64,119	< EQUIVALENT MUTUAL FUNDS GAINS
Bonds	0	$753,168			< TACTICAL RATE OF RETURN
Cash	0	$76,854			< TACTICALLY MANAGED ASSETS
		$3,074,155			< GAINS FROM TACTICAL MANAGEMENT
				$64,119	< NET GAINS
				20%	< CAPITAL GAINS RATE
				$12,824	< CAPITAL GAINS TAX

$10,000. Seventy-five basis points are applied against the balance, or $15,556. The mutual funds and Mid-Cap SPDR are creating $1,603 of fees. The net effect of the two is a 0.883% management fee.

An equivalent portfolio of A-share mutual funds would cost the client 1.364%, or $13,682 more per year. This is applying average breakpoints and amortizing the up-front load of $80,697 over 15 years before finalizing the fee percentage.

Table D.11 shows us the impact of using B or C shares.

Table D.12 shows that an equivalent portfolio of C mutual funds would cost the client 1.980%, or $33,703 more per year. A random selection of 12 mutual funds with parallel B and C shares was made. The average of these additional percentage increases was recorded and used to increase the base A-share expense ratio.

Note the combined savings on capital gains and fees of a $3,074,155 moderate portfolio:

	Cap Gains	*Fees*	*Total*
A shares	$12,824	$13,682	$26,506
B or C shares	$12,824	$33,703	$46,527

Complexity Factor

The structural complexity of each of the 10 sites is quite different. Of all 10 sites, Retirement Distribution (8) is the most complex to create. Fortunately for the builder, this spreadsheet, though massively important, is not crucial to the management of the assets in our selected portfolios. So passing on its inclusion will not diminish the quality of the rest of the sites, which are much more integrated. Retirement Distribution is critical but can be accomplished just as well with many software packages on the market.

The easiest are Tax Savings (9) and Fees (10). The first three—Distribution Assignments (1), Positions (2) and Shares to Purchase upon Market Entry (3)—are very closely interwoven. Distribution Assignments involves more data input and less formula construction. Building the Positions site is a matter of each

COMPARISON RESEARCH

MODERATE MANAGED PORTFOLIO

$3,074,155		
$1,000,000	$10,000	1.00%
$2,074,155	$15,556	0.75%
	$0	0.00%
$3,074,155	$25,556	0.831%

Mutual Fund Fees	$1,603	
Management Fees	$25,556	
TOTAL FEES	$27,159	
NET RATE	0.883%	

MUTUAL FUNDS PORTFOLIO

	C
	0.000%
Share Class	C
Load Percent	0.000%
Load Dollars	
Avg Expense Ratio	1.980%
FUND FEES	$60,863
NET RATE	1.980%

ANNUAL FEE SAVINGS	$33,703
ANNUAL TAX SAVINGS	$12,824
TOTAL SAVINGS	$46,527

COMPARATIVE PORTFOLIO WEIGHTED EXPENSE RATIOS

Cat	##	Dist	%%	Avg Ratio
Large Cap	421	53.5%	0.642%	1.20%
Aggressive Grth	33	3.5%	0.045%	1.28%
Mid Cap	204	3.0%	0.041%	1.35%
Small Cap	158	3.0%	0.049%	1.63%
Emerging Mkts	54	2.5%	0.052%	2.07%
International	117	5.0%	0.084%	1.68%
Bonds	178	27%	0.273%	1.01%
Cash	0	2.5%	0.000%	0%

A Shares	1.185%
B Shares	1.926%
C Shares	1.980%

RATIO INCREASE BY SHARE

B	C
0.75%	0.75%
0.72%	0.89%
0.88%	0.75%
0.74%	0.75%
0.69%	0.70%
0.72%	0.70%
0.75%	0.84%
0.74%	0.75%
0.54%	1.04%
0.75%	0.80%
0.79%	0.72%
0.83%	0.85%
0.742%	0.795%

TABLE D.12 Cost Analysis

COMPARISON RESEARCH

MODERATE MANAGED PORTFOLIO

$3,074,155		
$1,000,000	$10,000	1.00%
$2,074,155	$15,556	0.75%
	$0	0.00%
$3,074,155	$25,556	0.831%

Mutual Fund Fees	$1,603	
Management Fees	$25,556	
TOTAL FEES	**$27,159**	
NET RATE	**0.883%**	

MUTUAL FUNDS PORTFOLIO

3.625%	$100 th - $250 th
2.625%	$250 th - $500 th
2.125%	$500 th - $1 ml
0.000%	$1 ml & Up
$307	**BREAKPOINT (thous)**

A	**Share Class**
2.625%	Load Percent
$80,697	Load Dollars
1.185%	Avg Expense Ratio

$40,842	**FUND FEES**
1.364%	**NET RATE**

ANNUAL FEE SAVINGS	**$13,682**
ANNUAL TAX SAVINGS	**$12,824**
TOTAL SAVINGS	**$26,506**

RATIO INCREASE BY SHARE

B	C
0.75%	0.75%
0.72%	0.89%
0.88%	0.75%
0.74%	0.75%
0.69%	0.70%
0.72%	0.70%
0.75%	0.84%
0.74%	0.75%
0.54%	1.04%
0.75%	0.80%
0.79%	0.72%
0.83%	0.85%
0.742%	**0.795%**

COMPARATIVE PORTFOLIO WEIGHTED EXPENSE RATIOS

Cat	##	Dist	%%	Avg Ratio
Large Cap	421	53.5%	0.642%	1.20%
Aggressive Grth	33	3.5%	0.045%	1.28%
Mid Cap	204	3.0%	0.041%	1.35%
Small Cap	158	3.0%	0.049%	1.63%
Emerging Mkts	54	2.5%	0.052%	2.07%
International	117	5.0%	0.084%	1.68%
Bonds	178	27%	0.273%	1.01%
Cash	0	2.5%	0.000%	0%

A Shares	1.185%
B Shares	1.926%
C Shares	1.980%

cell retrieving the data from corresponding cells of the Distribution Assignment site and presenting it in a pleasant and orderly fashion. Shares to Purchase upon Market Entry is a simple generator of shares to be bought based on the distribution in the Positions location.

Profile (5) is a site that will produce a nice printout for the client. With the exception of the S & P sector and subsector identities (which have to be input by hand), it simply grabs cells from the Positions site and situates them in a presentable form.

Tactical (5) and Options (6) are simple profit-and-loss spreadsheets, involving starting position data relative to ending position data: when, how many shares, at what price. Profit or loss is then calculated and rates of return assigned, both absolute and annualized.

Finally, Valuation (4) is a very crucial element to our portfolio management. Once this location is developed, weights are assigned to each category. This is the preference of the financial advisor who is managing the portfolios.

Index

Absolute portion, ownership and, 183
Accountability, 2
Accounting firms, attorneys and, 89
Accounts, managed, 4
ADP (AUD), 104
Advent, 139
Advertising, 19
Advice, financial, 41, 73
ADV II, 158, 163
Advisor, 5
AdvisorInsight, 107, 109
AIG (AIG), 104, 200
AIM, 161
Alger, 161
Allocation percentages, 126
Ameren (AEE), 105, 134
American Skandia, 161
America Online (AOL), 105
Ameritas Life, 40, 161
Ameritrade, 33, 37, 40
Amgen (AMGN), 104, 200
Analysis, 138
    economic, 141
    portfolio, 135, 139
    quantitative, 24, 64, 103
    systematic, 109
    technical, 141–142
Analyst reports, 135, 141
Analysts, Wall Street, 109
Analyzer, 79

Anheuser-Busch (BUD), 104, 200, 217–218
Annuities, 58, 90, 157
    commissions on, 61, 64
    mortality and expense charges in, 51–52, 54–55
    no-commission, 4, 161, 164–165, 171, 190
    as only assets, 161
    proprietary, 169
    purchasing via Internet, 39–40
    salespersons, vs. asset managers, 65
    surrender charges on, 51–52, 54–55, 163
    variable, 96
Applied Materials (AMAT), 106
Archipelago, 47
A-shares, 166, 226–227. *See also* Mutual funds
Ashland Oil (ASH), 104, 134, 199, 218
Asset accumulation, 171
Asset allocation, 98–99
    model, 78, 99
Asset-based management fees, 51, 53–54, 57, 60, 62, 119
Asset information, gathering, 87
Asset management, 136
    fees on, 61, 162, 165, 181, 185 (*see also* Management fees)